Menzies Campbell: My Autobiography

Menzies Campbell:
My Autobiography

Menzies Campbell

HODDER &
STOUGHTON

First published in Great Britain in 2008 by Hodder & Stoughton
An Hachette Livre UK company

1

A CIP catalogue record for this title is available from the British Library

ISBN 978 0 340 89866 6

Typeset in Sabon by Hewer Text UK Ltd, Edinburgh
Printed and bound by Clays Ltd, St Ives plc

Hodder & Stoughton policy is to use papers that are natural, renewable
and recyclable products and made from wood grown in sustainable forests.
The logging and manufacturing processes are expected to conform
to the environmental regulations of the country of origin.

Hodder & Stoughton Ltd
338 Euston Road
London NW1 3BH

www.hodder.co.uk

To Elspeth

Contents

Author's Note

The idea for this book came after the general election of 2005 from the publishers themselves. I had never considered writing anything biographical. I did not keep a regular diary or a scrapbook.

I had settled comfortably into my role as deputy leader of the Liberal Democrats and principal spokesman on foreign affairs. I managed still to do a little legal work which I enjoyed. I expected this well-mapped-out existence to continue indefinitely. Certainly, I did not anticipate the events that led to Charles Kennedy's resignation, my election as leader of the party, nor my own resignation. This is a rather different book than was first envisaged.

I have tried faithfully and fairly to record my recollections. With the passage of time not only is there a sense of perspective but there is also an innocent determination to ensure that one's own version of events prevails. I count myself to have had a privileged life in which opportunity has always played a significant part. I see my life as one of experience and not of achievement. That it should interest others at all is a surprise.

In the preparation of this book I have been assisted by the recollections of relatives and friends. I wish to acknowledge the help I have received from my wife Elspeth, my sister Fiona Sinclair, my aunts Elma Hair and Marjorie Brown, Professor Sir Neil MacCormick, Donald MacCormick, Kenneth Munro,

Charles McKay, Professor Alan Alexander, Lynn Davies, John Wheatley, Alan Blair, David Steel, Jack Daniels, Anthony Garrett, Paddy Ashdown (for kind permission to reprint extracts from his published diaries), Archy Kirkwood, Carrie Henderson, Jane Bonham Carter, Mark Douglas-Home and Glasgow University Archive Services.

I should like to pay tribute to Rupert Lancaster of Hodder and Stoughton and Maggie Pearlstine, my agent, for their patience but also for their firm guidance when they thought I was exploiting that patience. AB of Hodder has assembled with the assistance of Rebecca Douglas-Home a collection of photographs which tells my story as eloquently as any text. The errors and infelicities are all mine – because, as those around me have often remarked, this is my book.

Menzies Campbell
January 2008

I

One of the fast crowd

Six a.m. Tuesday, 20 October 1964. Tokyo. In three and a half hours I'll be running in the Olympics against some of the world's best sprinters in a stadium packed with 80,000 spectators. I tiptoe out of bed trying not to wake my three room-mates. I wash, dress and walk to the dining hall. I eat a light breakfast: cereal, scrambled eggs, milk and tea. It's routine to me by now. I've been doing exactly the same for the last eight days preparing precisely for this moment.

A bus takes me to the training track thirty minutes away (I still remember the glare of the lights and the rain on the windows). I walk to the British team's dressing room under the Meiji Olympic Stadium. Now it's warm-up time. I need forty minutes. I'm on the practice track, behind the stadium. Where's my pass? So much security. This is Japan's welcome back into the world community of nations after Hiroshima. The guard stares officiously and nods me through. I jog for two laps under a gloomy grey sky. I'm warming up. I take off my blue track-suit top and jog for two more laps. Now exercises. Around me other athletes are also warming up for the 4 x 100 metre relay heats. They seem faster, bigger, stronger and more confident than me. There are eighty-four athletes in twenty-one teams competing for places in the final tomorrow. Will I be among them?

The other members of the Great Britain 4 x 100 metre relay team are on the training track. There's Peter Radford, a quiet, academic Englishman and bronze medal winner in the 100 metres in Rome four years earlier. He runs our first leg. Next is Ron Jones. He's Welsh, charismatic and prefers to warm up on his own. You could describe him as a cat who likes to walk by himself though we're all like that to some extent. I run third: an awkward, excited but apprehensive Scotsman. Last is Lynn Davies, a Welshman who has just won gold in the long jump, setting a new British record that will last thirty-four years. On paper this is a team that ought to have a chance of winning a medal but, thanks to the British selectors only deciding at the last minute to take a relay team to Tokyo, we're ill-prepared. We haven't had enough time to practise and we've never competed in that running order before.

The essence of winning a relay isn't the speed at which the athletes travel, but the speed at which the baton travels. This requires split-second transfers for the last three legs. On the training track we can see how much more practice other teams have had. We'll need all our strength, stamina, speed and nerve if we're to make it to the final. In the first heat at 9.30 in the morning we come third in 40.1 seconds. Italy comes first in 39.7; Poland second in 39.9. We're in the semi-finals but can we scrape through to the final the next day? If we can who knows what might happen? One of our competitors might drop a baton or be disqualified for putting a foot across a lane marking. Can we win a medal, a bronze perhaps? Who knows? In the semi-final we run 40.1 again and come fourth behind the USA on 39.5, equalling the Olympic record, France and Jamaica, both on 39.6. We're outrun but we make it to the final with the slowest qualifying time. We're exhilarated and astonished. Anything can happen, can't it? So we decide to gamble. 'Shit or bust' we call it inelegantly.

This is our plan. In the 4 x 100 metre relay the baton must pass from runner to runner within a 22-metre box. The runner receiving it is allowed to start his sprint 11 metres from the box. If he starts too early he risks having to slow down to let the incoming runner catch him before he exits the box. If he starts too late he'll be running too slowly when he takes the baton. Split-second timing is everything. The baton must always travel at maximum speed. Most relay runners, including me, make a mark on the cinder track behind them to help them time their runs. When the incoming runner passes the mark I'll take off. For the Olympic final we decide to place these check marks further back: in other words I'll start earlier. The danger is the incoming runner may not catch me within the 22-metre box.

To have any chance of a medal we must run faster than we have ever done before in our lives. We decide we have nothing to lose.

The day of the final dawns. Every relay runner's secret dread is dropping the baton. Today it is mine. Will I become 'The Man Who Dropped the Baton at the Olympic Final' in the newspapers tomorrow morning? We go to the warm-up area for one last practice. The thirty-two fastest men in the world are there, sprinting, stretching and passing batons. No one runs flat out in case he pulls a muscle. Everyone holds back just a little. As I glance around it seems to me I'm the only one who's apprehensive. Perhaps they're just better at disguising their feelings.

Forty minutes before the race we're taken to a waiting area in the Olympic Stadium. We sit, trying to keep warmed up, shaking our muscles. Everyone's doing it. The tension grows. I'm an unsophisticated twenty-three-year-old from Glasgow. Yet I've got this competitive spirit. I want to do well. I want to win. Then the moment comes. An official takes us to our starting stations. There's a pathway underneath the first row of the grandstand so we walk out of sight of the huge crowd now buzzing with anticipation for the relay final. Since I'm running the third leg I walk the furthest, three-quarters of the way round the stadium. I and my seven rivals stride in silence, everyone in his own capsule of thoughts. Radford stops at the first running station. Then Jones. Then me. Davies takes a different route: he walks down the straight to his starting position for the last leg.

The final is seeded. Because we're the slowest of the eight qualifying teams we'll be in one of the two worst lanes: the inside or outside. The Americans, the fastest qualifiers, are in one of the two best lanes, three or four. We draw inside. It's better than drawing outside but it has two drawbacks. The cinder track on the inside is broken up and rough from previous races and the bend is tighter than in other lanes. I'm running the bend. I go back down the track from my starting zone to make my check mark. A Japanese official stops me although I have done the same in the previous two rounds. I still make a mark of sorts – I put some grass on the cinders.

I go back to my starting position and stay standing as the race begins. I see Radford running the first leg. He passes the baton safely to Jones. I take up position on the inside of my lane. I get down, crouch, lean on my left arm and look under my right shoulder watching for Jones to hit my mark. The crowd's shouting. My heart's pounding. Jones hits the check mark and I take off. Later I'll see a film of the race and I'll realise my start was slow. But, at the time, it feels good. Jones catches me in the 22-metre transfer box. Halfway through the box I put my right arm back and lock it so it's a steady platform. My hand's open waiting for the baton. It's a hollow grey metal tube. I feel it and close my fingers tight around it. Thank God, I've got it. A huge sense of relief.

Now I'm pounding down my lane. White plastic tape marks its right-hand edge. One step across it and I'm disqualified. Now for the bend. Bend running and straight running are very different. I'm good at bends. On a bend you have to use the right side of your body more. That's why I hold the baton in my right hand. I think I'm fourth or fifth when I hand over to Lynn Davies but I can't be sure. We have a good baton change. 'Go on, go on, go on,' I scream after him as he sprints down the track against the seven fastest men in the world. Can he lift himself again after expending so much effort winning the long jump gold medal in the wind and rain puddles seven days ago? Does he have reserves left?

Davies runs a good leg but we know we're not in the medals. We collect our track suits and sit in the stand. We're disappointed. Our Olympics are over. We drink Coke and receive congratulations from the other British team members. We still don't know where we've come. America wins in 39 seconds dead, a new world record. Our time is 39.6, a tiny fraction slower but an unbridgeable gulf on the athletics track. We are eighth and last, but we break the UK record. We feel vindicated. In the *Scotsman* newspaper the next day, Harold Abrahams reports: 'Although much maligned, the men's sprint relay team set up the best time ever by a UK team – 39.6 sec, only 6/10ths sec worse than the winners – yet they finished last.'

I leave Tokyo with a sense of pride and relief. We've been here four weeks. It's too long, the longest I've ever been away from home. But for those four weeks I competed at the very peak of my sport. I worked for it, dreamed of it and finally achieved it. For less than 40 seconds on a damp October day in Tokyo I was among the thirty-two fastest men in the world, a competitor.

I remember it as vividly as if it were yesterday.

2

Childhood

For the first days of my life I was called one name by my father and another by my mother. He would peer into my crib and call me Walter. Then my mother would tuck me in and call me Menzies. 'I'm not having him called Walter,' she would say. 'He'll get Walter, Walter, Wallflower when he gets to school. I'm not having it. He's going to be Menzies. I won't have a son of mine with the initials W.C.'

This battle of wills went on for weeks. My mother's family watched it agog, wondering which parent would win. Both names came from my father's side of the family: Walter was traditionally given to the eldest son of alternate generations. My father was George; his father was Walter, his George, his Walter and so on. Now it was my turn to be Walter. My mother prevailed. I was christened Walter Menzies Campbell but she decreed nobody would ever know me by my first name. Thereafter, I was called Menzies, pronounced 'Mingus'.

Later in their marriage their disagreements would lose the humour of this crib-side tussle of wills. My father was a drinker. His moods were unpredictable. When he had been drinking an atmosphere of tension and uncertainty entered our home. He was argumentative with my mother and, later, when I was a teenager, with me. There would be no resolution to my parents' disputes until he retired at sixty-five and moved with my mother to Argyll. Only then did they achieve the companionable harmony that eluded them for much of their marriage.

It is impossible to write an account of my childhood and adolescence without making mention of his drinking since it had a profound effect upon me. It dictated the atmosphere at home, leaving its mark.

In the course of writing this book I discovered my sister Fiona and I have the same strong aversion to whisky. I cannot drink it. I don't like the smell of it. If someone gives me a bottle of whisky as a present it remains unopened. I have a cupboard full of whisky at home, all presents for speaking at this or that dinner or event, all untouched. Ask my sister about it and she will tell you with revulsion, 'I can't stand the stuff. I can't stand it.' It's visceral for both of us.

Although my sister's retrospective of my father is different in emphasis to mine – she remembers with the greatest clarity his generosity and warmth; I his temper – each of us was imprinted in adolescence with this life-long distaste for whisky. It's a smell we associate vividly with our father and, certainly in my case, with the arguments and tensions it ushered into our home. One benefit I derived from my father's drinking was a greater understanding of why people did it. When, much later in life, I had to confront Charles Kennedy, when he was leader of the Liberal Democrats, about his drinking it made me sympathetic to him because drink is often a refuge for those suffering from intolerable stress. I am sure it was for my father.

Despite the tension his drinking brought to my childhood, I remember him with affection. He was a good father but, for some reason, when I was on the cusp of moving from adolescence to adulthood he found me a provocation for his anger. My sister had a much less troubled relationship with him. As a teenager I was apprehensive of him; she did not appear to be. Whereas I was an obedient son who didn't answer back, she would sometimes go toe to toe with him. Perhaps her character was better designed for dealing with him than mine. I understand her warm memory of him because I recognise all the virtues in him that she describes.

I was born in the early morning of 22 May 1941. My parents had spent every night of the previous two weeks in an air-raid shelter a few minutes' walk from their home, a small ground-floor flat in Park Road, near Kelvin Bridge in Glasgow. A doctor friend arrived before the nightly blitz blackout, put a bottle of whisky on the table and said, 'Whatever happens tonight, we're not going anywhere.' I arrived at 1.40 a.m. before the blackout was lifted. The bombers stayed away from Glasgow and the Clyde that night. The *Glasgow Herald* reported on the day of my birth the intense battle for control of Crete and that fuel rationing might cause further cuts to Glasgow's municipal bus services.

One of my aunts remembers me as a very long-limbed baby. I was certainly big, weighing 9lb 4oz at birth. My memories of my first years are few and far between. My mother, Elizabeth, but always known as Betty, wrote in a 'Baby' book: 'From the moment you were born, Menzies, you never gave me one moment's trouble. You sleep all night and seldom cry. At one year old you are crashing about the house still as good as gold but you certainly have a mind of your own.' I have an indistinct memory of being alone for long periods with my mother when I was very young. My father, known within the family as Alistair, was often away. He was in charge of bomb damage control in several London boroughs. Because of the importance of his wartime role, we had a telephone in our home, which was unusual for the period. The telephone number was Western 6072. When my father was in London and living in a hostel he used to ring home in the evenings. I remember my mother telling me later he often had to break off because a Doodlebug flying bomb was overhead. My mother could sometimes hear their familiar but terrifying droning down the phone line as he was speaking to her. I also have a recollection of gunfire, probably the air defences along the Clyde.

There was a family tension in my parents' marriage from the very beginning. My maternal grandmother had taken a strong dislike to my father and banned him from her house. She relented only when she was seventy, some twenty years after my mother and father married. Reaching three score years and ten seemed to bring with it a spirit of forgiveness in her. My grandmother was a strong woman who had firm ideas about proper and polite behaviour. My father's habit of swearing (mildly by the standards of today) and his swagger offended her soon after she met him. A pre-marriage encounter on the phone wrecked any chance of reconciliation. My father had phoned to speak to my mother but my grandmother answered. She berated him for what she regarded a dreadful misdemeanour: 'No gentleman keeps a girl out until 10.30 on the Sabbath night,' she said. He told her to go to hell three times in ten seconds, according to family legend. In pre-war, respectable, God-fearing, middle-class Scotland it wasn't behaviour designed to win over a prospective mother-in-law.

My mother's and father's arguments early in their marriage often revolved around my grandmother. My father referred to her with mocking sarcasm as 'the Duchess'. My mother, who was extremely close to my grandmother and physically very like her, found herself caught uncomfortably in the clash between them. The consequences were distressing for her. When she visited my grandmother she had to do so without her husband. Although my mother was quieter than my father, she was intelligent, strong-willed, well-read and capable of standing up for herself. It was an inflammatory blend of personalities.

My parents had met in, of all unlikely places, a General Post Office in the Possilpark area of Glasgow. My mother, a civil servant, worked in the post office. My father lived nearby. He was a joiner by trade but had set up his own contractor's business: joinery, repairs and construction work. He employed four or five men and seemed to be prosperous. He'd worked hard for it. His brother went dancing four nights a week when they were young men while my father went to night school to better himself. Prosperity suited him. He had a car and lots of girlfriends. He was generous and he was funny. His bonhomie made a party go with a swing.

The good times were not to last. The war clouds gathering over Europe brought his business almost to its knees. As the likelihood of peace diminished so did his customers. Who could afford to buy new windows or doors with war and financial uncertainty looming? Around the time my parents married he had to close the business before it collapsed. My grandmother used to say that he had gone bankrupt but it wasn't so. For two terrible nights in March 1941, two months before I was born, German bombers blitzed Clydebank. If he had been able to keep his business going a bit longer he might have made a lot of money repairing the damage as others did. Instead he went to London to oversee bomb damage repair for the Ministry of Labour.

I can see why my mother was attracted to my father. He was raffish, always smartly dressed in hand-made suits and a black Anthony Eden-style Homburg hat. He was a strong, decisive personality, good company, and persistent in his pursuit of her. I imagine she was flattered by his attention. They split up once before their engagement but I don't know why. My twin aunts, leaning over the banisters as ten- or eleven-year-olds, overheard a conversation between my mother and her stepfather. Apparently, after their split, my father waited every day for her as she went to work. She took two buses and he was always sitting in his car as she got off one bus to catch the other. 'If you don't want to get into his car you don't have to,' my mother's stepfather said. It seems my father's pursuit of her had tipped temporarily into something more worrying than flattery, at least from my grandmother's and my step-grandfather's perspective.

At this distance it is impossible to guess what went on between them and what exactly drove my grandmother to say, 'You marry that man and he'll never darken my doorstep and I'll never darken yours.' But the consequences for my mother were severe. She was as strong-willed as her own mother and married my father on 2 August 1940, in Possilpark, his home territory. It was her twenty-fifth birthday; my father was six years older. On the marriage certificate she described herself as a Post Office sorting clerk and telegraphist; he as a building contractor.

She must have loved him very much to marry him in the face of such strong family opposition. None of my mother's family attended the wedding. Her twin half-sisters, my aunts, were not even allowed to be bridesmaids. My grandmother's only contribution to the day was to buy my mother a black suit trimmed with fox fur which I'm told she wore for the ceremony. My mother had chosen it with economy in mind: she could wear it again after the wedding. I was born nine months later, presumably a honeymoon baby though in the prurience and uncertainty of adolescence I used to wonder whether I was premature or they were premature!

Did my mother regret her decision to marry my father at such a personal cost to herself? She was far too proud to let anyone think so, though there are some clues that suggest the price she paid was a high one. There was, of course, my grandmother's implacable opposition to my father and the rows it generated between my parents. My mother's group of long-standing girlfriends also seemed gradually to disappear. She was very close to them, criss-crossing Scotland on hill-walking expeditions with them. She was a founder member of the Scottish Youth Hostels Association. After her marriage she and her friends had less and less contact. Did they too come to disapprove of my father or did they simply drift away as they married and had their own families?

Perhaps of more significance was a noticeable change in my mother's character. Before she was married she was calm, with a quick sense of humour, according to one of my aunts. Afterwards she became more nervous, edgy, though she could still be funny (for example, she called a particularly slow cleaning lady 'flash').

One of my earliest memories is of my sister being born. I was ten days short of my third birthday. I don't think I was expecting her to arrive, nor do I have any recollection of my mother's pregnancy. Suddenly one day I was given a baby to hold and told: 'This is your sister.' I was surprised by this baby. I didn't feel challenged by her or displaced by her although I do have a memory of her being pretty, bright-eyed and quick-witted.

I have no other strong memories of childhood until I went to school at the age of five. I attended Willowbank Primary School, about ten minutes' walk from our home in Park Road, a short street leading to Kelvingrove Park to the west of Glasgow city centre. I have a class photograph of my time there. The children all look well fed and cared for despite the receding war. A rather severe-looking woman called Miss Telfer stands in one corner of the photograph. I remember her as a good teacher, one of a number of women of her generation who never married and who dedicated their lives to teaching in primary schools. The absence of so many young men at two world wars possibly influenced their decision.

My time at Willowbank School was happy but my parents were less settled on it than me. My mother was determined I should move to a better school. She was driven by educational rather than social aspiration, though the schools she investigated also happened to be further up Glasgow's postwar social pecking order. I remember my parents taking me to Glasgow Academy, Glasgow High School and Hillhead High School to determine whether I was capable of passing their entrance examinations. Glasgow Academy, founded in 1845, was, and still is, a private school with a record of academic achievement. Glasgow High School and Hillhead High School were at that time more akin to good English grammar schools. They were local authority schools (although the High School is now independent) which charged modest fees. My mother must have badgered the headmaster of Hillhead's primary department because, without warning, aged seven, I was uprooted from Willowbank and sent to Hillhead.

The differences were immediately apparent. At Hillhead there was compulsory uniform. Caps had to be worn. It was a school filled with high expectations as well as the sons and daughters of doctors, solicitors and managers. Teaching was traditional and rigorous. We learned our tables by rote and we were drilled in English grammar, in my case by a Miss Brydon, who was built like a battleship and clad in swathes of black bombazine held together over her substantial and straining bosom by a cameo brooch. Every Friday she would write a sentence on the blackboard and the class was required to parse it. Failure to do so correctly was often accompanied by a sharp blow to the knuckles with a ruler.

I enjoyed this regime despite the looming Qualifying Examination known by generations of Scottish children as the 'Quali'. Its consequences were all-pervasive. Pass it and you moved seamlessly into Hillhead's secondary department and virtually a guarantee of middle-class prosperity. Fail it and suddenly your childhood certainties were destroyed. What school would I go to? What prospects would I have afterwards? Failure was not contemplated.

The first part of the examination consisted of an essay lasting one and a half hours. Shortly after it Mr Davidson, my form teacher, took me aside and told me I had received 20 out of 20 and that this augured well for the rest of my exam. I felt the pressure easing a little. The rest of the exam was marked out of 130. My mark was 125. I passed with the designation 'S1' which not only guaranteed my place in the secondary department but also put me in the top stream. This meant I would receive tuition in two languages. My parents' response to my success was muted. After all, I had only matched their expectations.

For me, the most traumatic part of the year was the Qualifying Dance. We were instructed, red in face with embarrassment, how to do such old-fashioned dances as the Canadian Barn Dance. My toes still curl at my awkwardness at having to hold, if only with the lightest touch, the waist of a reluctant twelve-year-old schoolgirl as we danced round the school gymnasium trying not to step on each other's toes. For a child who disliked parties and could often be found at them reading a book in a corner, the Qualifying Dance held more terrors for me than the exam itself.

I left primary school with a growing passion for sport, particularly rugby and running. (By now I knew I could run faster than most of my contemporaries, but certainly not all of them. At Sports Day I was usually in the final of whatever event was ordained for my age group, but I wouldn't necessarily win it.)

I also left primary school with a slowly dawning realisation that my father was drinking. I knew, too, of the hostility and arguments between him and my mother. His habit was to go drinking after work. He never drank at home. At weekends he would be sober, in deference to family life. I didn't know why his drinking fell into that pattern although I can guess at it now. He was an ambitious man working in an intensely political environment. He had become deputy general manager of Glasgow Corporation's Housing and Works Department and wanted badly to become general manager. The job was essentially in the gift of the Labour chairman of the housing committee, who was always on the lookout for a drinking companion.

As I grew older, his drinking had an increasing impact on me. In my teens, there was a collision between us. My maturity combined with my emerging opinions seemed to anger him. He wanted the best for me and yet he didn't want to lose me. He wanted me to stay within his sphere of influence. I was clearly an object of pride for him within Glasgow where he was becoming a powerful figure. Later on, he would refer to me as his son, 'the Olympic runner'. My sister thinks he tried to live the lost opportunities of his own life through me.

The clash between us took me by surprise. As a small boy, I had been devoted to him. I was in awe of him and wanted to please him. If anything, I was too obedient. I have two strong memories of my father when I was a young child. One is of him leaving for work – he first went to work for Glasgow Corporation's Housing Department in 1947. The other is of him taking me on day trips. My mother would accompany us sometimes but mostly it would be me and my father. We went to Kelvingrove Art Gallery and Museum, the staple bolthole for Glasgow parents on wet west of Scotland weekends. We went to the zoo at Calderpark which opened in 1947 but has closed since. Sometimes we went trout fishing outside Glasgow. We must have gone by bus because he didn't have a car then. At one stage he had a thing about boats and we went to look at all the boats moored on the White Cart and Black Cart Waters which flow into the Clyde to the south and west of Glasgow. We returned home via Glasgow Airport where we had tea. There was no friction between us on these trips. He was good company and we got on well. It was a postwar father and son combination with happy memories; and I have them.

But even then he knew what he expected of me. Aged six, I was asked, as all children are asked, what I wanted to be when I grew up. My father's response was immediate: 'You're going to be a lawyer.' And that is what I became. I don't think I did so as an act of obedience to my father, certainly not consciously. By the time I went to Glasgow University in 1959, I wanted to be a lawyer. Whether this was because the idea had been planted in me and took root when I was young I have no way of telling, though I'm told my father never deviated from his career choice for me. First I was to be a lawyer; then I was to be a judge. He would frequently make reference when I was older to my becoming 'Lord Campbell of the Court of Session'. (As it turned out he was not being over-ambitious. I could have become a judge in 1996 but turned down the opportunity in favour of continuing a political career.) He may have been unusual in having such a single-minded view of my future career, although I imagine he was typical of his time. He believed strongly in education and in bettering yourself by hard work. In this, though not always in other areas of his life, he did as he preached. He started his working life as a joiner and ended it, as he had wanted, as general manager of what was then Glasgow Corporation's Building Department which employed 5,700 people. By any standards he made a success of his working life.

My mother's attitude to education and work was the same as his, although she was open to more career possibilities for me. Like many mothers then, and now, she wanted me to do whatever would make me happy. I wonder now whether this reflected a concern about the effect unhappiness at home was having on me. Pride and the climate of the times stopped her from discussing it with her own family. She never did so with my aunts, her two half-sisters. I was solitary by nature and bookish by habit. My sister, who was a more ebullient, resilient character, has recently described me as 'an only child who wasn't only'. It's not a description that I recognise but I can see how others might have come to that view of me. I was self-contained but I was contented.

My recollection of childhood until the end of primary school is for the most part a happy one. We did what other families did. We went on bucket and spade holidays, not every summer but most summers, to St Andrews, St Monans and other Scottish seaside towns and villages. I remember a holiday on the Island of Mull and a fishing holiday beside Loch Etive in the West Highlands. One summer, when we didn't go on holiday, possibly for financial reasons, my father used his old joinery skills to make a bagatelle board. On another occasion he made me a set of cricket stumps which gave me considerable social cachet in the neighbourhood. I was the boy with a complete set of cricket stumps. Even in football-mad Glasgow that counted for something.

We lived according to a routine that was both commonplace and comfortable by the standards of the time. Despite postwar rationing of a shilling a week for meat (tuppence of which had to be spent on corned beef) we didn't want for food. My mother was inventive and practical in the kitchen. She bought sheep's head, tongue, tripe, kidneys and liver. She made soup three or four times a week. The food was wholesome and always home-cooked. She was determined that we would be well fed and grow up strong to protect us from the risk of tuberculosis (TB) which had killed her father when she was three. It was an obsession in those days and one that she shared. Family meals were always at the kitchen table.

Home was a two-bedroomed, groundfloor tenement flat with a shared garden at the back and near a busy junction leading west out of Glasgow. My parents moved there when they were married, renting it initially for six months. My mother's pregnancy with me made them extend their tenancy but, when I was on the threshold of secondary school, I didn't question why they were still renting a flat with too few rooms for their adolescent children to have a bedroom each. Like some of my contemporaries, I slept on a sofa-bed in the sitting room. I thought nothing of it as a teenager even though my father was becoming increasingly successful in his career. By now he had a reasonable salary, he had his own car and his children were pupils at a fee-paying school attended by Glasgow's respectable, aspirational middle classes.

Hillhead Secondary was on a different campus to the primary; it was in Oakfield Avenue, ten minutes' walk from my home in Park Road. It was a 1930s red-brick building with corridors open to the wind and rain. (I gather they have since been walled up.) It was well equipped with science laboratories, art rooms and a gymnasium for both boys and girls. In the 1950s it was a Glasgow west end institution. Its fees and selection procedures inevitably made it a contributor to social division, but it provided a sound education for those who passed through it, including the comedian Stanley Baxter who preceded me among a generous supply of doctors, lawyers, teachers, professors and accountants. There were between 700 and 800 boys and girls. My age, raging hormones, acne and the presence of so many girls growing into young women made an uncomfortable, embarrassing mixture for me. I took my refuge in sport: athletics and cricket in summer and rugby in winter. (In rugby, my speed dictated that I played on the wing which led to my nickname Ming. I was 'Ming on the wing'. The name stuck, although my sister and aunts always call me Menzies.) I became a tearaway fast bowler and an equally tearaway fast batsman on the cricket pitch. My running was getting better: I won the overall school sports championship in my age group at junior, intermediate and senior level. On the rugby pitch my team was more or less unbeaten for three years.

My sporting success came at the price of academic performance. I fell into the bad habit of doing just enough work to get through, until one traumatic year when I did too little work to pass a maths exam. My teacher was well intentioned but difficult to follow. At least he was for me. The end-of-term maths exam was so hard that six marks were automatically added to everyone's score to compensate. Even with this helping hand I didn't make the pass mark of fifty. My failure caused difficulties at home and led to me giving up maths. I was fifteen at the time, the age when decisions had to be made about which Highers (the Scottish equivalent of A levels) I would take. Maths and science were eliminated. I specialised instead in Latin, Greek, English and History (which I failed).

I don't believe my school work suffered because of my parents' rows or my father's drinking even though I remember one frightful flare-up when he threatened to leave my mother. I must have been thirteen or fourteen. He never did leave. Nor did he change his habits until he retired. If my mother had married him twenty years later I'm sure she'd have divorced him. She belonged to a generation that disapproved of divorce and which tried to make the best of a bad situation for the sake of the children.

My teenage home life took on a routine that kept me out of my father's way. I'd come back from school at 4 p.m., have high tea at 6 p.m. and then catch a bus or tram to the nearby Mitchell Library to do my homework. I'd return home at 10 p.m. I did this every school term night, apart from Fridays, for four years. On Friday nights I'd go to the local cinema. The programme started at 7.30 p.m. and I would return home at 10.30.

At the weekends, sport was a bond between me and my father. He'd drive me to rugby matches or athletics meetings on Saturdays and would be generous and good-humoured. In the evening we would gather together to listen to the big Bush radio in the sitting room. *Top of the Form*, a general knowledge contest between schools, was a particular favourite. Many years later, when I appeared on *Desert Island Discs*, the first piece of music I chose was Wagner's 'Ride of the Valkyries' because it took me back to one of those evenings listening to *Top of the Form*. I remember hearing this extraordinary music and a girl contestant, about the same age as me, identifying it correctly. I was astonished she knew so much. When friends dropped by at the weekends, as they often did, my parents and they would discuss politics, a constant topic of conversation at home.

At school I was scraping by in the classroom but succeeding everywhere else. In time I became captain of the athletics team, secretary of the cricket club, joint chairman of the literary and debating society and a prefect in fifth form. I did, though, have two serious setbacks, one of which threatened my continued participation in athletics and sport.

By the time I was fifteen, I was six feet two inches tall, the same height as I am now, and I weighed twelve and a half stone. Also I was fast. Few could catch me on the rugby pitch. Consequently, I was promoted to play in an age group above my own. One wet afternoon we were playing seven-a-side in preparation for a schools tournament. I was running with the ball and dummied a pass which sent the opposing players the wrong way. I carried on running and then fell flat on my back for no obvious reason. I thought I had pulled a muscle but it was astonishingly sore. Two of my team-mates helped me home. I was unable to move and a consultant orthopaedic surgeon had to be brought from Glasgow Royal Infirmary to examine me.

He diagnosed a slipped epiphysis, an uncommon condition of the hip joint. In adolescence, muscles can develop quickly but bone structures take longer to strengthen and firm. My muscles had become so strong that the ball of the thigh bone had slipped backwards. (I have since read a layman's description of this condition: it's like a scoop of ice cream slipping off the top of a cone.) The consultant's prognosis was good but it meant I had to spend six weeks in bed. I worried that my sporting career had come to an end, and it was a difficult and uncomfortable time for me. My only consolation was the number of pretty girls who visited me offering black grapes and comfort.

The other setback was less alarming in its potential long-term consequences although it so infuriated my father that he considered moving me to another school. At Hillhead it was established convention for the first-choice fifth-form prefect to become school captain the following year. I was the first choice and the rugby captain. A pupil called Derek McKinnon was second choice. When we returned to school for the start of sixth year I assumed I would become school captain. I was wrong. Derek McKinnon did. My father took the insult personally. He threatened to remove me from Hillhead and investigated sending me to Glasgow High School instead. The storm blew over as quickly as it had come. When his hurt pride had subsided, it was realised that moving me might be counterproductive for my university prospects. So I became school vice-captain without ever receiving an explanation for it.

My non-academic achievements could hardly have been higher. I was in the rugby, cricket and athletics teams. The previous summer I had run for the Scottish schools in an international against England and Wales. In the sixth form I and a pupil called Mark Cantley, who arrived at Hillhead by way of Portora Royal School in Northern Ireland, teamed up for debating competitions. We won the English Speaking Union West of Scotland Schools' Debating Trophy and an inter-city school debating contest between Glasgow and Edinburgh. (By a curious coincidence Mark Cantley is the father-in-law of Tim Farron, Liberal Democrat MP for Westmorland and Lonsdale.)

In the classroom, however, I was surviving day by day but only just. I didn't know it then but I was jeopardising my chances of going to university. Although neither of my parents had gone to university, they assumed without question that I would. Hillhead High also made the same assumption. So halfway through sixth form I was dispatched along with a group of other pupils to meet the studies adviser at Glasgow University's Faculty of Arts. Before the meeting I had prepared an application form on which I had written with great certainty that I wished to take an MA followed by an LLB. In the space marked profession, I wrote with equal sureness one word: Advocate.

The meeting with the studies adviser was perfunctory, lasting no more than fifteen minutes. He asked me what examinations I had passed and what examinations I was sitting. When I told him he responded by saying something that I heard as 'polly con' but which was really 'Pol.Econ', the abbreviation for political economy, the traditional Glasgow way of referring to economics. So I found myself committed to a subject about which I knew nothing. The adviser also talked to us briefly about being a student at Glasgow. He said we would drink a lot of sherry and learn not to spill cups of tea on young ladies. I did neither.

The next stage of my life beckoned but I made it to Glasgow University only by the skin of my teeth. At least one of my contemporaries at school failed university entrance with better exam grades than mine. For those who do not know Glasgow, my move to university didn't bring with it a widening of my geographical boundaries. My parents' flat in Park Road was approximately ten minutes from Hillhead High School as well as ten minutes from Glasgow University. The consequence was that from birth, childhood, school to university I was destined to live and work in a triangle the longest leg of which was a ten-minute walk. It was an existence that could only be described as provincial.

3

University friends

For my first day at university in September 1959 I wore my old school blazer with the braid removed. It was what you did in those days: everyone made do and mend no matter how well off they were. Glasgow University drew its students predominantly from the city surrounding it, and particularly from those schools against which I had played rugby and cricket for the past six years. Many of the eighteen-year-old freshers walking that day towards the university tower, loftily peering across the River Kelvin and Glasgow from Gilmorehill, were dressed like me. We lived in an era of formality. Students routinely wore jacket and tie. Three years later, when I started my LLB, I and my fellow law students would wear suits, stiff collars and bowler hats.

As I joined the long queue at the matriculation hall behind the Hunterian Museum, I remember distinctly an exhilarating sense of life changing in spite of the routine familiarity of my surroundings. (I had, after all, grown up to the chime of the university's clock and the urgent but fainter 'Hurry Bell' which rang immediately after the hour to hurry students to their next lecture.)

I handed over my matriculation fee and received a card upon which were two Latin words, *Natio Glottiana*, taken from the name given to the Clyde by Tacitus. It meant I was born in the county of Lanark. Outside was the annual freshers' fair, a bustle of stalls, milling students and university club evangelists all

vying to sign up new members. I remember a Kelvinside
Academy old boy (he was wearing the tie) saying nicely,
'How about joining the Liberals?', and me paying the half-
crown membership fee. I have since said my affiliation to the
Liberals was 'my first act of rebellion' because both my parents
voted Labour. In truth, it was neither rebellion nor the apparently thoughtless whim I've described. From the age of fifteen, as
I became politically aware in a household that reverberated to
political discussion, I had grown to admire Jo Grimond, the
Liberal leader. His brand of urbane, charismatic but principled
politics attracted me much more than the unreconstructed,
industry-led socialism of the Scottish Labour Party. In particular, I felt Grimond spoke for me when, soon after becoming
leader in 1956, he attacked Anthony Eden's imperialistic and
disastrous dispatch of troops to the Suez Canal. So, emotionally,
I belonged to the Liberals long before I strolled through the stalls
at the freshers' fair. My intellectual underpinning in liberalism
followed a year later when I read John Stuart Mill's *On Liberty*
as part of my moral philosophy course.

On my way to the Union building to pay the two guinea
membership fee, I met Neil MacCormick, a fellow first-year
student and son of one of the most political families in Glasgow.
In 1934 his father John had engineered the merger of the
National Party of Scotland and the Scottish Party to form the
Scottish National Party (SNP). His brother Iain, later SNP MP
for Argyll from 1974 to 1979, ran the Nationalist Association at
Glasgow University, a mantle that Neil would inherit on his way
to becoming professor of public law at Edinburgh University
and SNP member of the European parliament from 1999 to 2004.
He was knighted in the Queen's Birthday Honours in 2001. I had
known Neil since the age of fifteen though more as rival than
friend. We had been schoolboy debaters: he for Glasgow High
School; me for Hillhead High. We had also been on opposite
sides in schoolboy rugby matches. He was the High School first

XV's pack leader and he recollects deciding to 'fix' me, as he put it, because I was, in his view, a 'menace'. On this meeting though, he was full of warm good humour. 'Come and meet my cousin,' he said and we carried on into the Union. His cousin was Donald MacCormick, the secretary of the Labour Club who later became a celebrated broadcaster and presenter of *Newsnight*. The Labour Club chairman was then a West Highlander called John Smith and the treasurer was a gangly, bespectacled student by the name of Donald Dewar.

And so I fell effortlessly into a group of young men drawn together by the pull and camaraderie of the Union, coffee room discussions, the excitement of formal political debating and, of course, late night drinking and boisterous post-debate parties. Why one generation of Glasgow University students should have produced a Labour leader, a Liberal Democrat leader, a Lord Chancellor as well as a Secretary of State for Scotland who became the first of Scotland's post-devolution First Ministers is a question I'm often asked.

There are a few possible explanations, the most compelling of which is that Glasgow University's political debating tradition coincidentally became strongest during the 1950s and early 1960s just as Conservatism (and, perhaps more importantly in Glasgow, Unionism) passed a historic high-water mark in Scotland. John Smith, Derry Irvine and Donald Dewar were the most celebrated of a group of intelligent, articulate students who were brought eventually to prominence in the consequent realignment of political power. All three, like me, graduated MA and LLB. But Derry was different in one significant respect. He was an infrequent visitor to the Labour benches in Union debates. His focus was the law not Glasgow University Union politics, despite his close friendship with John Smith. We knew him as a prodigiously intelligent, focused and hard-working student who was clearly destined to be an eminent legal figure. He inhabited the fringes of the political crowd. From Glasgow, he went to Christ's College, Cambridge, to study English Law.

The impression sometimes given in contemporary references to this period is that these emerging personal relationships were forged among a small band of people. In fact, the opposite was the case. There was a large and shifting circle of close as well as distant acquaintances probably typical of any campus. Many of these have also gone on to be well known in their chosen fields: for example Jimmy Gordon, now Lord Gordon of Strathblane, who became a media tycoon with Radio Clyde and latterly Scottish Radio Holdings; and Meta Ramsay, now a baroness, who became a foreign policy adviser to John Smith after a long and now publicly recognised career in intelligence. New people joined the circle; regulars dropped out after graduation or when exams loomed on the horizon. At any one time there were perhaps 400 students actively involved in the gossip, politics or organisation of the men's Union, the women's Union, the Students' Representative Council and the political clubs.

Those of us who lived within walking distance of the university were more likely to congregate there by night and to be active in its corporate life. The coffee room was a favourite and informal meeting place. The Union's beer bar which closed at 10 p.m. was another popular hangout. From 9 p.m. there would usually be a group of students from the political clubs there. Famously, the basement of Donald Dewar's home, or, more accurately, the basement of his parents' stylish house on the southern edge of Kelvingrove Park a few minutes' walk from the university, was a regular night-time haunt. The Dewars were haute bourgeoisie compared to the rest of us but kindly and indulgent to Donald's student friends.

From memory, the basement had a sitting room, two bedrooms, one of which was Donald's, and a separate entrance from the street. Quite regularly Donald would entertain anything up to sixty students (as long as they brought their own drink). There was music (I remember Robin Hall and Jimmy McGregor records on the gramophone), singing and conversation until the early hours of the morning. At some stage during the evening a delegation of party-goers would climb the stairs to meet Donald's parents. I was invariably a member of this group because my athletics training meant I didn't drink. I was one of the few students downstairs who could be relied upon not to be sick on Dr and Mrs Dewar's carpets as we marvelled at their collection of Scottish Colourist paintings. Donald later admitted to an interviewer he was always glad to see me in his basement throng because he knew when he sent me upstairs his parents would feel reassured the party down below was not as wild as it sounded.

The curious thing about these parties was that Donald seemed in his element, enjoying the role of host. Yet, paradoxically, he did little to make himself popular beyond his basement. Donald, whom I grew to like enormously in adulthood, was an acerbic figure at university. He could be unsympathetic, with a sharp tongue that he sometimes used to great effect.

I remember one example of this particularly. In 1964 I became president of the University Union. By tradition, the Union held a formal ball on the Friday before Christmas as a gift to the president. I wore white tie, the men black tie and the women long dresses. Guests from other university Unions had also been invited. It was usual practice for a toast to be made to the president at the dinner beforehand and I asked Donald if he would do it for me. He agreed, but on the night he was in a dreadful mood, and he proceeded to rip into me for five minutes before proposing the toast. Among other insults, he said my debating style left no cliché unturned (probably true!).

Donald MacCormick has since revealed that Donald Dewar told him he modelled himself at this time on a character in short stories by Saki, the pen name of H.H. Munro. The character, called Clovis, was a young man who was very cutting, sarcastic and liked to be studiedly rude.

When we weren't gathering in Donald's basement we were in the large and welcoming flat belonging to Neil MacCormick's parents which was perched on the hill across the River Kelvin from the university. Or else we were at post-debate parties in the Union which usually started late and went on until very early.

The first one of these parties I attended followed a debate on home rule for Scotland and Wales and the reunification of Ireland. It was in November 1959, the second debate of the year, and I made my maiden speech from the Liberal benches in support of home rule. A report of the debate described the standard of first contributions as 'fair' though the Maiden Speakers' Prize was 'withheld'. Nevertheless my reward came in the guise of the president of the Liberal Club, a student called Alistair McKinlay. He slipped me a coveted ticket for the party afterwards in the Reading Room, nicknamed the 'Squeezy' on dance nights because it was kept dark and promising for student romance. The home rule debate was when I first became aware of John Smith. He concluded for Labour with what I remember as a coruscating and fluent speech. My clear recollection is that he spoke in favour of the motion backing self-government for Scotland and Wales and the reunification of Ireland proposed by the nationalists. However Neil MacCormick remembers the opposite. The contemporary report of the proceedings sheds no light on this but does record mysteriously that John Smith 'marred an otherwise fine contribution by lapsing astonishingly (in the circumstances) though hardly unpredictably into religious bigotry of the most expendable variety'. As I discovered later he was not just a good performer in debates, he was the life and soul of the parties afterwards. There would be a barrel of beer, an urn of coffee, sandwiches and singing: a mixture of folk, Gaelic, Protestant and Catholic songs. Nowadays singing songs like 'The Sash My Father Wore' is rightly regarded as sectarian. We were incredibly naïve: we thought they were just good songs. Singing them certainly didn't seem sectarian to us at the time even though Glasgow was, by any definition, a sectarian city. Catholic children went to Catholic schools; Protestant children went to non-denominational schools. Religious discrimination was commonplace. The test was the apparently innocent enquiry: 'Which school did you go to?'

For many of us, university was the first experience of a community of mixed religions. This was before the Troubles in Northern Ireland erupted in the late 1960s. So, for us, the songs had little active political charge in them, or none of which we were really conscious. The Protestants among us would happily sing the Catholic songs; and the Catholics the Protestant songs. John Smith was one of the most enthusiastic singers, one of the reasons he was regarded as having 'Orange' leanings. John would always be the person shouting 'one more song' at the end of every party. Incidentally, John was also a good Gaelic singer. Another post-debate entertainment was playing tournaments: one student was a horse, another student a rider and together they would try to unseat the student rider on an opposing horse. John enjoyed it hugely, as did Derry Irvine on his rare appearances at debates. Derry excelled at being the horse because he was large and difficult to knock over. I can still see John astride Derry charging towards their luckless opponents surrounded by a motley crowd of jeering students.

With all the distractions of the Union and athletics, more of which later, I allowed my studies in first year to slip, not learning from the close call of my university entrance. Most of my fellow students were taking an MA with honours in four years. But at home it was felt, with justification, that I should take an ordinary MA in three years because I intended to follow it immediately with a law degree, an LLB. Paying for six years at university was a considerable financial commitment for my family. Because of my father's income, I didn't qualify for a maintenance grant.

In first year I took English, Greek and Political Economy. Greek lectures lasted from 9 a.m. until 10 a.m., after which Neil

MacCormick and I would repair to the Union's coffee room for an hour before English started at 11 a.m. Our professor, an eminent Shakespearean, would regale us with his encyclopaedic knowledge of Anne Hathaway's Cottage but, unfortunately for me, seldom deviated into textual analysis. It caused my first, though not my last, academic shock. Before the end-of-term English exam I revised my extensive notes on the cottage but the questions were entirely on the texts. I scraped through but only because the pass mark was 30 per cent.

A worse shock was to come. At the end of first year I took three examinations and passed only one, Greek. I failed English and Political Economy at which I had floundered all year. At home the news was treated like a death in the family.

My academic ignominy was compounded by over-ambition on the running track. When the athletics season began in April 1960 I set myself the target of winning a Blue in first year. In pursuit of this ambition, I spent too much time on the running track, too little revising for my exams. Even so, I failed to win my Blue which had to wait until the following year. I was now so gloomy about my prospects that I remember vaguely considering whether I should join the Hong Kong police. Other students in a similar position had already done so. The salary was good and, I think, tax-free. My father was more practical. He told me I must spend the summer working hard for my resits in September, instead of taking up a summer job to give me pocket money for the winter term. It was with considerable relief that I opened my resits results. I passed them both. I had learned a painful lesson.

Only in the political arena had my first year ended according to plan. I was elected unopposed as treasurer of the Liberal Club, a position that guaranteed me an official speaking role at every Union debate. I had stepped on to the rising escalator of student politics. I could now expect to be secretary of the Liberal Club in 1961–2 and president in 1962–3, the same year that Donald Dewar would become president of the Union.

Debates at the Union mirrored the traditions of the House of Commons but with modifications. There were six political clubs (Tory, Labour, Liberal, Independent Socialist, Scottish Nationalist and a party called Distributist which followed the agrarian dreams of G.K. Chesterton). Each political club took it in turns to form the 'government' and to propose motions or resolutions. The leader of the 'government' party was called 'prime minister'. There was a 'leader of the opposition' and a 'speaker'. In the gallery sat 'distinguished strangers'.

Perhaps, on reflection, it's no wonder so many graduates of the Glasgow Union found their way to Westminster. It was second nature to them. Debates followed an established routine. They started at 1.15 p.m. when the secretaries of the political clubs set out their opening positions. Pity the club secretary speaking at 1.45 p.m. when the audience moved en masse to the door for the start of afternoon lectures at 2 p.m. Novices spoke in the afternoon; the more experienced speakers in the early evening. The club treasurers rose to address the House at about 7.30. Question time, a rowdy and amusing interlude of sketches, stunts and jokes, started at 10 p.m. Then it was the turn of the club presidents or, in Labour's case, the chairman to speak. The debates were scheduled to end at midnight but often carried on until 1 or 2 a.m.

Glasgow University Magazine routinely carried commentaries on the speeches. For example, in December 1960 it described me as 'the great white hope' of the Liberal Club but added that I had 'found nothing to say' after delivering some good quips in a debate about raising the rate of income tax and capital gains tax to 50 per cent. (Incidentally, the motion was proposed by John Smith.) In the same debate Donald Dewar was described as 'still lean and hungry-looking, in spite of dinner'. The following year, in a debate on nationalising land, steel, road haulage and tenanted houses, and (for good measure) abolishing hereditary titles, the magazine said I emerged a giant from the 'motley midst of semi-experienced speakers' with little to say though I said it 'loudly'.

After my first year exam scare, I completed the rest of my MA without further alarm. By year two I had acclimatised to university life, fulfilling my academic commitments as well as extra-curricular activities in the Union and on the running track. I was awarded a Blue after qualifying for the British Universities Team at the World Student Games in Bulgaria in 1961. I graduated in 1962.

When I embarked on the first year of my LLB in October 1962, I did so with a sense of excited anticipation. I was president of the Liberal Club and the rectorial election campaign was about to begin in fury. (The rector in the medieval Scottish universities is the one position that the students control by direct election.) It was to be the term's dramatic highlight.

The political context of the time was Conservative dominance. At the 1955 general election the Tories won 50.09 per cent of the popular vote in Scotland. Contrast that with the 2005 general election when they polled 15.8 per cent. By the early 1960s the Tory Party was beginning its long decline though Glasgow University Conservative Club was still the biggest of the political clubs. Indeed, the Conservative vote on campus had secured the rectorship at the two previous elections. Rab Butler was victorious in 1956 and Lord Hailsham in 1959. The Conservative candidate in 1962 was Edward Heath, described in his election adverts as 'one of the youngest and most talented members of the cabinet'. The Labour and Liberal clubs joined forces to stop a third Conservative victory. Our problem was the lack of a credible candidate. I remember discussions eddying backwards and forwards about the type of candidate we should nominate. Should it be someone who could be a working rector, properly representing the interests of the students and chairing the university court? Or should it be a symbolic figure, a statement of 'student idealism' as Kenneth Munro, chairman of the Labour Club who has remained a good friend, described it recently?

Donald Dewar suggested Albert Luthuli, Africa's first Nobel Peace Prize winner and president of the African National Congress (ANC) until his death in 1967. There was no prospect of Luthuli ever becoming anything more than a symbolic rector because the South African government had confined him to his home in Stanger, Natal, for his part in organising the non-violence campaign against apartheid in the bloody aftermath of the 1960 Sharpeville Massacre. Would Luthuli beat Heath? We decided to put it to the test, but first, according to the election rules, we needed a letter from Chief Luthuli agreeing to stand.

It seemed to take for ever. Then one day the letter arrived and with a mixture of relief and excitement we launched our candidate on campus. Luthuli's candidacy also caused a stir off campus. It had the backing of, among others, Harold Wilson, who sent 'a small contribution' by cheque, and Barbara Castle, who sent £1. Bertrand Russell sent a message of support praising Luthuli for his 'distinction in the service of mankind'. It was becoming a big media story. The *Daily Express* accused us of not having a letter of authority from Luthuli and I paid three guineas from my own pocket to hire a room for a rebuttal press conference in the Central Hotel, Glasgow. We flourished Luthuli's letter defiantly before the assembled reporters, who included George Reid, later Presiding Officer of the Scottish parliament.

The Heath campaign had different troubles to contend with. Dissident Tories and Liberals who could not bring themselves to support either Heath or Luthuli had found another candidate, the Earl of Rosebery, who was backed by Beaverbrook's *Express*. The Scottish Nationalists fielded Dr Robert McIntyre, president of the Scottish National Party. The growing rivalry between, in particular, the Luthuli and Rosebery camps led to all kinds of skulduggery. Mark Stuart in his biography of John Smith, published in 2005, relates one of these stories. One night the Rosebery campaign committee was holding a party in its headquarters when Donald appeared outside accompanied by about thirty Luthuli supporters. Stink bombs were thrown and the police arrived.

Worse was to follow. A student called Charles McKay, a Rosebery supporter, defected to the Luthuli campaign carrying with him an invoice from Grants of St James's, the wine and spirits merchants, for £117 13s 5d. It was the Rosebery campaign's drinks bill. We published it in one of our campaign leaflets. The more controversial and still unresolved question is whether McKay also defected with keys to the Rosebery campaign headquarters. According to Stuart's book, either that night or some night later John Smith, Donald Dewar and McKay, who was secretary of the Liberal Club, coincidentally acquired a quantity of whisky and gin. Stuart reveals what happened next. Kenneth Munro, who was the European Commission's representative in Scotland from 1988 to 1998, found John Smith and Donald Dewar on his doorstep in the early hours one morning. They announced: 'We've got a taxi, can we bring in some things?' The 'things' turned out to be several cases of whisky and gin which they stuffed under Ken's bed where they remained until the Luthuli celebration party after the election. Was the whisky and gin stolen from the Rosebery campaign? Or did the drink come from somewhere else altogether? As Stuart rightly concludes, more than forty years later the answer is still murky.

Luthuli was elected rector on 21 October 1962, with 1,291 votes, 447 more than his nearest rival Robert McIntyre, the nationalist candidate. Rosebery and Heath polled 832 and 733 respectively. We had succeeded in ending the Tory succession.

I had another prize in my sights during my year as Liberal president: the debating trophy for best political club. I set about it with assiduous planning and conscientious application. Marks were awarded for speeches, for the number of interventions –

points of information in Union language – in debates, for stunts at question time and so on. There were even points for the number of people sitting on your benches during debates. So I made sure we gathered in as many points as we could. It was all done with orchestrated deliberation, but I was proud when we won the trophy. It was a valuable lesson at playing and winning long-game politics, an experience that stood me in good stead when I became a Liberal member of parliament twenty years later and party leader almost twenty years after that.

I ended my term as Liberal Club president in 1963, the same year my family decided to move home to a terraced house in Verona Avenue in the respectable western Glasgow suburb of Scotstoun. The house was a street or two away from my grandmother as well as from one of my aunts. The move meant the end of my grandmother's twenty-three-year-long frost over my mother's marriage.

I transferred my political ambitions to climbing the Union hierarchy. I became Debates Committee Convener in May 1963 and then Union secretary in October. In between the two, I had another academic hiccup. I had been trying to cram my LLB into two years instead of three. It meant taking five different subjects in first year, including Scots Law 1 and Scots Law 2, in other words all of Scots law in one academic year. It was over-ambitious and not surprisingly I failed both. I faced the prospect of resits in September but I was also expecting to be picked for the World Student Games in Brazil that summer. I couldn't go to Brazil and take resits at the same time – the timetable would not allow it.

I went to see my professor, David Walker, in trepidation. He had chaired a university Senate inquiry into our Luthuli campaign expenses, including the quantities of drink it mysteriously acquired. I knew he was a stickler for the rules but he was surprisingly generous to me. I told him about the prospect of going to Brazil with the British Universities Team.

He said, 'What do you think your chances are of going to Brazil if you don't go this summer?'

I said, 'Pretty remote.'

So we agreed amicably that I would go to Brazil, miss the resits and extend my degree by another year.

By now I was becoming better known on campus for athletics than student politics. My name was starting to appear on the back pages of newspapers. In May 1964 I became president of the Union and in October I went to the Olympic Games in Tokyo. The Union Board's minutes record in clipped sentences my unfolding success in athletics. After my return from the Olympics, the Union gave me a silver salver with interlinking Olympic rings engraved on it and the words 'Tokyo 1964'. My thanks are recorded in the Union's minutes of 7 December 1964. Then this rather too flattering valediction was minuted on 23 February 1965: 'The board thanked Mr Campbell for his work throughout his term of office and it was agreed that he was one of the only Presidents who had brought more prestige to the Union than the Union had brought to him.'

It was a reference to my growing fame as a sprinter. This was my other life, the one that was my passion, my driving force, and the one that very few of my university friends could share or even understand. Winning at international level became my obsession. Power and speed are the vital ingredients of success but perseverance provided a helpful following wind for a raw-boned, inelegant Scotsman.

4

The flying Scotsman

On a hot summer's day when I was seven years old, my mother called me inside from the communal garden at the back of our flat to listen to the radio. I sat down beside her and for the next fortnight seldom moved away. I was mesmerised by the BBC's crackling commentary of the 1948 Olympic Games, staged on a temporary track at Wembley Stadium in London. After the grey deprivations of the postwar years, the commentators seemed to be describing an occasion of unbelievable colour, excitement and romance.

A new cast of heroes, or rather heroines, entered my childhood. I remember their names as if they were running yesterday. There was Fanny Blankers-Koen, a thirty-year-old mother of two from the Netherlands, who won gold medals in the 100 and 200 metre dashes, the 80 metre hurdles and the women's 4 x 100 metre relay. Her main rival in the 80 metre hurdles was a British ballet teacher called Maureen Gardner. They were so well matched that Gardner won the silver medal by recording exactly the same time as Blankers-Koen, the 'flying housewife'. Then there was Shirley Strickland, an Australian sprinter and hurdler, who took up running seriously only a year before the Olympics. She won one silver and two bronze medals, the beginning of a remarkable career which led to an Olympic gold medal in 1952 and two in 1956.

My strongest memories are of these three women athletes. I must have listened to the radio commentary through my mother's ears and to the rise and fall of her interest because a seven-year-old boy would never normally choose a trio of women as his Olympic heroes. By the time of the Olympics closing ceremony on 14 August 1948, the world of international athletics was fixed in my mind as impossibly glamorous. More than a decade later, when I flew abroad for the first time to an athletics meeting in Communist Bulgaria, I realised how misguided my childish awe had been.

When I began to run competitively, athletics was full of plucky amateurism and Corinthian spirit. It was like a real-life *Chariots of Fire*. We ran on grass, in spiked shoes that were like boats; in shorts that were long and billowing, and with track suits that were anything but stylish or sleek. We looked just like the extras in David Puttnam's film, but the similarities extended beyond superficiality. *Chariots of Fire* still captures the anxieties and fears of the dedicated amateur athlete better than any other film I've seen, any book I've read, or any radio programme I've heard.

Towards the end of my running career I experienced all too briefly, in America, a different kind of athletics, one a world away from windswept, rain-soaked training tracks and self-regarding administrators so commonly found in Britain. In the warm sun of California, I discovered the absolute joy of running fast indoors and outdoors with facilities (and weather) that few athletes in Britain then enjoyed. It was there, running quicker than I had ever done before or since, that I beat a startling young athlete called O.J. Simpson, and broke the British 100 metres record to become the fastest man in Britain. It was a record that would not be broken again for seven years.

The long journey from wet grass and baggy shorts to running exuberantly in California began for me at Garscube Harriers, one of a number of running clubs in and around Glasgow. Many of them had 'Harriers' in their names because their members were interested in running long distances in cross-country or road races. Like Garscube Harriers itself, many of these clubs were founded in the late nineteenth century and enjoyed a boom in popularity just when Scotland was declining into the gloom of depression in the 1930s. Young men with no jobs and no money found that for the cost of a pair of running shorts, a vest and a pair of sandshoes they could have both recreation and a social life. In that at least, little had changed when I joined Garscube Harriers in the mid-1950s as a teenager. The club was refreshingly egalitarian in membership and spirit.

When, later, I became a solicitor's apprentice as part of my law degree at Glasgow University, I used to go straight to Garscube Harriers from my office in suit, stiff white collar and bowler hat, the regulation dress for a lawyer in the 1960s. In the club dressing room, my bowler would hang on a peg beside the overalls of a riveter who had come straight from work at one of the great Clyde shipyards. Our training track, if it could be called that, was a cluster of Glasgow University-owned playing fields at Garscadden, north-west Glasgow, in the middle of one of the hard-edged housing estates that still characterise so much of the city. In those days it was a cold, bleak place neither conducive to training nor good performances in competition.

Despite membership of Garscube Harriers, where I came under the immensely practical coaching influence of Donald McDonald (known as 'Donnie'), university was the launch pad of my senior athletics career. On reflection, launch pad is a misleading description since it suggests that I progressed along a fast and uninterrupted trajectory. How I wish that I had.

In 1960, my first summer season at Glasgow University, and in 1962, when I was excluded from membership of the Scottish team to the Commonwealth Games in Perth, Australia, I had setbacks, disappointments and injuries like most athletes. In that first year I must have seemed unbearably over-confident, so determined was I to win a Blue. I spent the winter circuit-training indoors in preparation for outdoor training to begin in

April. When it did, my form deserted me: I had recorded better times in my last year at school. Then Glasgow University had a match against St Andrews University. It was on a track I still see every time I go to St Andrews in my Fife constituency. I won the 440 yards in a time that was then a new ground record. For a few weeks, my running was everything I hoped it would be: fast and comfortable. It gave me an exhilarating sense of sheer physical power. My form did not last.

At the end of the university athletics season the four so-called 'ancient' Scottish universities – St Andrews, Glasgow, Edinburgh and Aberdeen – met for the annual Scottish University Championships. That year, by coincidence, it was also in St Andrews. Again I was in the 440 yards, but the outcome was very different. The starter called the athletes to their marks but took up a position from which he could not see all the runners. He fired the gun before a number of us (including me) were ready. I started the race several yards behind and was comfortably beaten by an Edinburgh medical student called Bob Hay, who was fast over both hurdles and flat.

The experience dented my confidence. A bad race can do that. Confidence drains away just as quickly as it surges. Instead of risking myself in open competition at the Scottish Athletics Championships a few weeks later, I chose shame-facedly to run as a junior in the 17–19 age group for which I was only just qualified by a few days. I won the 440 yards, but in place of the thrill of victory I felt embarrassment. To make matters worse, I was not awarded a Blue by Glasgow University. My athletics career was to become full of ups and downs but my competitive instinct would gnaw away at me; I would work harder and harder until I forced myself back into contention, physically and mentally.

The university unwittingly assisted my return to form. Its grass running track at Westerlands in Glasgow was replaced with a new cinder track for the start of the 1961 season. At last there was a good surface for outdoor sprint training, although a long way from the all-weather surfaces of today. The track opening in May was marked by an athletics contest between the Achilles Club, of Oxford and Cambridge students past and present, and the Atalanta Club, the Scottish equivalent from Aberdeen, St Andrews, Edinburgh and Glasgow universities. I was in poor form because of a hang-over injury from winter rugby – ironically, given the rival team, it was an Achilles tendon injury. I learned a valuable lesson: if I was going to succeed at athletics I would have to stop playing rugby.

My injuries healed and with the new cinder track my training improved. At the university's internal competition, with a cross-wind assisting me on the bend, I ran the 220 yards in 21.7 seconds, half a second faster than ever before. More significantly, it was within the qualifying time for the British Universities Team going to Bulgaria that summer to compete in the World Student Games. (Nowadays I would probably be given a drug test for such a dramatic improvement in form.)

Would I be selected? I wanted desperately to be, but lost hope when the Scottish representative on the selection committee pressed my case only for it to be dismissed by the metropolitan-minded selectors based in London, who queried whether there were any reliable time-keepers in Scotland. None of them had ever heard of Walter Menzies Campbell 350 miles to the north in Glasgow. A late cancellation a fortnight before the team was due to leave for Sofia forced the selectors to think again. My name was added to the team sheet. I was elated. My ambition to compete at the highest level was beginning to propel me beyond my experience. I had neither been abroad, flown in an aeroplane, nor taken part in international competition until then.

Before travelling to the games in Sofia, I ran in the Edinburgh Highland Games, the grand (and inaccurate) name for a meeting organised by Edinburgh Corporation every August before the city's famous international arts festival. The contest was held at

Murrayfield, home of the Scottish Rugby Union, on a grass running track of irregular dimensions. There were five laps to the mile instead of the customary four. Some of the events were also over unorthodox distances. I was invited to run in the 300 yards because of my recent 220 yards performance and my selection for the British Universities Team. The winner of the race broke the tape in 30.8 seconds. I finished third in 30.9, my best performance. The importance of the time was lost on me and the crowd until the announcer said I had just broken a fifty-three-year-old Scottish record. The previous best time by a Scot over 300 yards had been set in 1908 by a Lieutenant Wyndham Halswell, an Olympic gold medal winner and an officer in the Highland Light Infantry who died in the First World War.

My father, who had driven me to Edinburgh, was so over-whelmed by my record-breaking run he did something so out of character that I find it hard to believe even today. He climbed the fence and ran over the lush Murrayfield turf to congratulate me. When he reached me he shook my hand awkwardly and said simply, 'Well done.' It was an extraordinary gesture at a time when public reserve was not just the fashion but the rule.

Soon afterwards the British Universities Team assembled in London. The night before we flew out, I slept in the spare room of the secretary of the British University Sports Federation who had a flat in Kensington. One of my team-mates enjoyed a broken night's sleep on the sofa. So much for the glamour of international sport. The following morning we made our way to Gatwick Airport and boarded the plane, a Vicker's Viking, to Bulgaria. Those of us with seats at the front were not allowed to board until those sitting further back had done so. Otherwise, the plane might have tipped forward on its nose with an expensive and impressive crunch. We refuelled in Munich and landed in Sofia, making a small bit of aviation history in the process. Our flight was the first British civilian aircraft to land there since 1945.

If the journey was a culture shock for me, it was nothing to arriving in Bulgaria, then a hard-bitten and colourless Communist country. My memories of Sofia are of desperate poverty, grim faces and atrocious food. Our accommodation was in student halls of residence; each room had three beds, a cupboard and a strong smell of distemper. Its impact on me was so profound that I was never tempted to have romantic notions about state Communism, unlike many students of the 1960s and 1970s.

At the games, I ran in the qualifying heat of the 400 metres, took off much too fast, led into the home straight, then 'tied up' and was easily run out of the final. My hopes for a medal now rested on the 4 x 400 metre relay in which I was running the third leg. We came third. For this achievement I received, in a cardboard case, a rather undistinguished bronze medal, which I still have, complete with its nylon ribbon. I ended the 1961 season with my first international medal and a Blue from Glasgow University.

At the World Student Games one of the team managers was the bursar of St Catherine's, Oxford. He wrote to me soon after our return to Britain suggesting I should switch universities. 'Come to Oxford and get a Blue. It would do you a lot of good,' he said. Of course, I was flattered and wanted desperately to go. My father dismissed it out of hand. 'What's wrong with Glasgow?' he asked. The next time I had the chance of a university place outside Glasgow I would take it, despite my father's opposition.

At the start of the 1962 athletics season, I had hopes of being selected for the Scottish team at the British Empire and Commonwealth Games in Perth, Australia, in November. In early season competition, I equalled the Scottish 100 yards record and broke the previous Scottish 220 yards record. Normally, this would have meant certain selection for Perth but there was a snag. I came second in both races to one of the most gifted athletes Scotland has ever produced: Mike Hildrey from Balfron, outside Glasgow, who was inevitably nicknamed the 'Balfron Bullet'. He was a most elegant athlete with an easy, graceful stride. My running owed much to sheer muscle and effort. Competing against Hildrey, I felt a carthorse by comparison.

When the twelve-strong athletics team was announced my name was missing. I was bewildered by my exclusion. There was a cartoon in the student magazine showing me with my travel bag and the name Perth crossed out. Some years later I was told the inside story of the selection committee's deliberations. The names of the first five athletes were chosen quickly because of their outstanding form in competition. Then I was nominated for sixth place. Another athlete was nominated against me. There was a vote and I lost. I was never nominated again; not for seventh, eighth, ninth, tenth, eleventh or twelfth place. If my performances were good enough to contend for sixth place why was I not nominated for any of the lower places? I was disappointed. My only consolations were becoming Scottish 440 yard champion and an invitation to run for Edinburgh against its twin city, Munich, in Germany. It was an enjoyable trip but no substitute for Perth.

The following year, 1963, turned into a watershed year: winning my first international gold medal and a clean sweep of Scottish sprint titles, the 100, 220 and 440 yards. The last person to win all three had been Eric Liddell nearly forty years before. It involved seven races in less than twenty-four hours. At the end of the last event – the 440 yards – I rather melodramatically collapsed and had to be supported, to the consternation of several members of my family.

The big event of the summer was the World Student Games in Brazil. I was desperate to go. My early training went badly, mainly due to niggling injuries. Imagine my huge relief when I was selected for the British Universities Team and then my absolute dismay when I feared I would not be able to go to Brazil after all. As I recounted in the previous chapter, I failed two Scots Law exams in the first year of my LLB. If I went to the games that summer I could not take the resits in September. The alternative was to extend my LLB by a year. My professor and I agreed on this course. My relief was greater than I can describe. I was going to Brazil.

Nowadays Porto Alegre, 400 miles south of Rio de Janeiro, is better known for hosting the World Social Forum, a large and chaotic annual anti-globalisation summit. In 1963 it staged a relaxed, chaotic but ultimately enjoyable student games. The Brazilian authorities had a comical attitude to bureaucratic regulation. There was then an international protocol stating that accommodation for women athletes had to be surrounded by a fence at least twelve feet high. The Brazilian response was to erect poles twelve feet high around the women's quarters. The poles were connected by a single strand of wire at the top so that anyone could (and did) walk underneath it. Sometimes, though, the Brazilian attitude was less comedy, more chaos. Track events took place at approximately the time they were scheduled; and the track itself was atrocious. By the end of a day's competition the inside lane was so churned up it looked like horses had used it, not humans.

I ran in the heats of the 400 metres, but did not make the final. My only other event was the 4 x 400 metre relay. On the morning of the final our anchor man, Adrian Metcalfe, one of Britain's best ever 400 metres runners, leaped out of his bed with such enthusiasm that he stubbed his toe painfully on the bedroom door. Such was the damage it looked as if he might not be able to put on his running shoes, never mind compete. We saw our medal hopes slipping away. But grimacing all the way, he managed to hobble to his starting mark on the track. Then adrenaline took over and, baton in hand, he breasted the winning tape in first place. The gold medals were ours. Standing on the winners' podium to the sound of Gaudeamus Igitur, the student hymn, was a moment of sheer pleasure.

Back in Glasgow, in the autumn of 1963, I suffered something of a sporting and personal crisis. I had too many commitments. My academic work was suffering. Something had to give. I had started a part-time apprenticeship with a firm of solicitors to run concurrently with the final year of my degree. I attended lectures at the university in the morning and late afternoon and went to the office in between. I was active in the Union, and hoped to be president the following year. After the emotional high of Brazil, training in the rain seemed such a drudge despite the beckoning Olympic Games in 1964. I said publicly that I intended to retire from competition. My heart was no longer in it but nor could I let it go. It was like losing faith but still feeling you had to attend church. I began to frequent the Glasgow University gym where one of the physical education staff, Jim Donnachie, prescribed a course of weight-training, then in its infancy for athletes. I became stronger. Sprinting requires strength: the sprinter and the shot putter have more in common than the long-distance runner. Gradually over the winter, my enthusiasm returned. My so-called 'retirement' was forgotten and by the summer of 1964 I harboured what I thought were forlorn hopes of selection for the British team for Tokyo.

Luck and my winter weight-training did the rest. Each year there was a match between a Scottish Amateur Athletic Association select and the Atalanta Club. The meeting was due to be held at Pitreavie, near Dunfermline, on one of the better cinder tracks in Scotland. The day before the meeting, I received a letter inviting me, very surprisingly, to take part in the Women's Amateur Athletic Association Championships in London. In those days the women's AAA found it difficult to attract television coverage of its championships without staging men's invitation events as well. So I was asked to run in two of these events, the 100 metres and the 200 metres, at White City in London (now the site of BBC

Television Centre). Should I go to London or to Pitreavie? I booked a flight from Glasgow to London for the morning of the championships and told the organisers of the Pitreavie meeting that I would not be representing the Scottish universities the following day. My decision was not popular. 'It's rather short notice,' said a clipped Edinburgh accent, communicating volumes of disapproval over the phone. As I made my way to London, I knew I had blotted my copybook. Events made it hard for me to regret my choice, however.

The first race on track at the White City was the men's 100 metres. I ran 10.6 (equal to 9.7 for the 100 yards), my fastest ever. Better was to come in the 200 metres. Producing form that I had never shown before, I won the race in 20.9 seconds, comfortably inside the Olympic qualifying time. The result caused consternation among better-known British athletes who expected to represent Great Britain at the Olympic Games, and interest among those journalists who had been enthusiastic enough to attend the rather sparsely populated women's championships. A round of applause greeted the announcement of my times at the Pitreavie meeting. Somehow I doubt the possessor of that clipped Edinburgh accent joined in.

The following week was the AAA men's championships, also at White City. I ran in the 100 yards and 220 yards (championships were still imperial; invitation events had become metric). I ran 9.7 in the 100 yards and qualified easily for the final of the 220 yards which I won, equalling the championship best performance of 21.1 seconds. My reward was even more media interest and an invitation to the champions' dinner in the House of Commons. I still have some of the press cuttings reporting my AAA victory. They were filled with references to 'the flying Scot' and other predictable journalistic flourishes. All kinds of invitations for television appearances and interviews followed. I was selected to run for Britain against Finland, an event I remember for a reason other than running. I was in Helsinki when Donald Dewar married Alison McNair, a board member of the women's Union at Glasgow University. She had been in my sister's class at school and I had played rugby with her brother. The marriage was dissolved in 1973. Later, she married another of my student acquaintances, Derry Irvine. Scotland is a very small place.

Even now I think of the summer of 1964 as a golden time in my life: I became president of Glasgow University Union in May; I passed my examinations and I was on the brink of selection for Britain's Olympic team. One morning a letter in a plain white envelope arrived for me at my parents' home in Verona Avenue, Scotstoun. It was from the British selectors offering me a place in the athletics squad. Although they asked me to keep it confidential until the team announcement to the press, I told my parents and my sister. The following day when the announcement was made I was besieged in my solicitors' office by phone calls and press men. One photographer wanted to take a picture of me jumping for joy. Shyly, I agreed instead to a photograph of me, in full lawyer's attire, with my briefcase under my arm. I loosened up sufficiently later to model the British team's 'walking out' uniforms holding hands with soon-to-be golden girl Mary Rand. They called me the 'James Bond of British athletics' afterwards.

Until then my family had greeted my sporting successes with reserve, but Olympic selection was an exception. They arranged a party on the eve of my departure. My mother cooked for the guests, while my father made sure there was plenty of beer, whisky and bonhomie. Studiously sober because of my training regime, my memory of the evening is that my father's friends were considerably more badly behaved than mine.

In races before I flew to Tokyo I found it difficult to reproduce my winning White City form. I accepted too many invitations to run at athletics meetings around the country and spent too little time training to build my fitness and strength.

In Glasgow, there was no particular ceremony when I set off on my Olympic adventure. My parents were not given to shows of emotion, to children or to each other, in public or in private. My mother said something like: 'Make sure you change your socks.' My father shook me by the hand. I could just as easily have been going off for a camping holiday in the Highlands.

I was excited and nervous as usual, only more so because I was about to run in the Olympic Stadium in Tokyo in front of 80,000 people. In big black headlines the *Daily Record* in Scotland boasted of Britain's medal prospects. I was one of few Scots in the team so, inevitably, my name kept appearing in print. Even in those days the media cranked up the pressure. On the eve of our departure for Tokyo a journalist approached me at a TV studio where I was taking part in a discussion programme and said, 'We'll give you £5,000 to spill the dirt on the Olympics when you come back.' Although I said no, this encounter and the other media interest both flattered and unsettled me. I had never had such attention before. I felt the burden of expectation when I climbed the stairs into the Comet 4 jet which was to fly the team from London to Tokyo. Mid-flight, the aircraft developed engine trouble and so we spent several unscheduled hours at Karachi Airport. From start to touchdown in Tokyo the journey took thirty-two hours, hardly the best preparation for the Olympics. Fortunately, there was time to recover. We were to spend a month in Tokyo, the longest I had ever been away from home. But, as it proved, there was also time for boredom. With little to do apart from train, eat or watch films, I found the atmosphere oppressive. Our accommodation was cramped. We were in houses purpose-built for the postwar American army of occupation. They were designed for families of three or four but we were packed in four to a room, twelve or fourteen to a house. There was a perpetual queue for the bathroom. It was uncomfortable and, until the games began, monotonous.

I had three room-mates. They were Robbie Brightwell, British team captain and Olympic silver medallist; John Cooper, double Olympic silver medallist, who died in the 1974 Paris air crash; and John Sherwood who came third in that famous race in Mexico City in 1968 when David Coleman, the BBC sports commentator, said, 'It's Hemery. Hemery takes gold, Hennige the silver. Who cares who's third?' Well, Sherwood cared. He was third. Brightwell and Cooper were tough, experienced athletes and I felt like a boy in their company even though I was twenty-three. I remember feeling apprehensive and slightly wondering why I was in Tokyo at all.

Early in the competition Mary Rand won the long jump with a new world record, becoming Britain's first female Olympic gold medallist. That evening she arrived in the cafeteria where the British team were eating, put her gold medal on the table and said, 'There you are. I've done it, now you can go and do it.' I remember the surge of confidence it gave us. A few days later her room-mate Anne Packer won gold in the 800 metres. Then Lynn Davies won the men's long jump and Kenneth Matthews the 20 kilometre walk. Britain ended third in the athletics medals table behind America and the Soviet Union.

My first heat in the 200 metres was at 9.30 a.m. on Friday, 16 October. My strict training routine since arriving in Tokyo of waking at 6 a.m., eating breakfast, taking the bus to the Olympic stadium and spending forty minutes on the practice track paid off. I won the heat comfortably in 21.3 seconds. My elation was short-lived, however. Later that day, in the second round, I drew the difficult outside lane and felt heavy and leaden. I finished sixth in 21.7 seconds. Only the first four went through. I was hugely depressed, inconsolable. My last chance of Olympic success was the 4 x 100 metres four days later.

As I described in Chapter One, the GB team, with me running the third leg, reached the finals. But despite setting a new British record of 39.6 seconds, we came in eighth and last. I will always treasure the memory and the satisfaction that comes from competing against the world's greatest athletes. Did I enjoy it? If I was being honest I would have to say it wasn't a particularly happy experience. When I look back at the Olympic Games, I remember the long periods of boredom, the temptation to over-eat and the difficulty of training with little supervision. I had reached the very peak of my sport. I had worked for it, strived for it, dreamed of it and finally I had achieved it. But it was not an enjoyable time, even if it is still one that will be forever vivid in my mind. For any sportsman, competing in the Olympic Games is an enormous but daunting honour. Running is a solitary activity. You can train with others, receive help, encouragement, advice and inspiration from them, but on the track you're on your own and you alone take responsibility for victory or defeat. The pressure can eat away at you. It did at me in Tokyo. There is a post-Olympics picture of me walking down the steps of the plane at London Airport. I am wearing a cowboy hat given to me by a black American 400 metre runner and a grin of relief to be back home.

I may have left the Olympics without a medal, but there were other accolades. I still have the certificate acknowledging our record-breaking relay run, bearing the signature of Prince Philip, honorary president of what was then the British Amateur Athletic Board. There was a reception for the returning team at Buckingham Palace. The following year there was also the sweet satisfaction of revenge. The British sprint relay team, me included, beat the Poles who won silver in Tokyo. The BBC occasionally plays the flickering black and white film of the race.

My Olympic exposure had the effect of propelling me into a different kind of public life. In 1965, aged twenty-four, I was appointed to the UK Sports Council by the legendary Willie Ross, one of Scotland's greatest Secretaries of State. I sat alongside Walter Winterbottom, the renowned England football manager, Roger Bannister, the first man to run a sub-four-minute mile in recorded history, Lord Porchester, the Queen's racing manager, and T. Dan Smith, whose name became synonymous with the Poulson scandal in the 1970s. I captained the UK athletics team against Germany, the last international match of the season, and then, in 1966, unusually, became team captain for the year. The sport's administrators thought I was a quiet Scotsman but I didn't live up to their expectations. My captaincy coincided with a growing mood of rebellion among athletes intolerant of the patronising administrators who ran the sport. My year reverberated to arguments about the quality of food for athletes at international events. The experiment of appointing a captain for a full year was discontinued when I left. It was done to stop the athletes having such a strong voice again. They said my year-long captaincy had affected my track performances. There was some truth in what they said, although I would put the blame on a niggling series of injuries which disrupted my training.

My complaints about the sports administrators in Britain soon paled into insignificance when I flew with the Scottish team to Kingston, Jamaica, for the 1966 Empire and Commonwealth Games. (Henceforth the word Empire would be abandoned.) Our accommodation at the University of the West Indies was rudimentary. We had no hot water for the duration of the games. The heats of the 100 yards were on Friday, 5 August. The *Glasgow Herald* reported the following day that they were held in an almost deserted stadium. A special correspondent wrote: 'Eight heats sifted out the dross, the first four in each heat going into tomorrow's second round, and if anyone were looking for surprises there were none. W.M. Campbell (Scotland) was in what might be called an easy heat and went over the line together with J. Owiti (Kenya) and O. Adekunle (Nigeria). All were given 10 sec, the Scot taking second place but little weight should be placed on the times because of a wind that came and went every half minute.' I was eliminated in the next round.

A freak accident affected my performance and risked my entry in the 220 yards three days later. Training before the second 100 yards heat, I ran on to the grass in the centre of the National Stadium without noticing a sprinkler head poking out. I hit it with my left foot. A spasm of pain shot through my small toe which became very swollen. By Monday it must have subsided again because the *Glasgow Herald* reported the heats of the 220 yards in a gusting headwind: 'The 21.4 sec by W.M. Campbell (Scotland) in winning his heat proved to be the second fastest of the morning and he had obviously recovered from a toe-stubbing at the end of last week. From the outside lane he was well into his stride and some of his old majesty appeared to have returned.'

Then he continued, in my view unkindly: 'At the same time, let us not be fooled into thinking of his chances in terms of a medal.'

As it turned out my critic was right. I came second in the second round but only fifth in the semi-finals with a time of 21.2 seconds. My games were over but my semi-final run won the admiration of Christopher Brasher in the *Scotsman*. He wrote: 'Ming Campbell ran magnificently, his neck muscles like wire cords, but the competition is just too hot. Never have I seen such sprinting and Campbell did extremely well to reach the semi-finals.'

The following day Brasher chose a different theme for his *Scotsman* report. There was, he wrote, 'an air of despondency in the Scottish team's quarters'. Indeed, there was. The corrosive effect of a series of poor performances was taking its toll.

By the halfway stage Scotland had won only one silver and three bronze medals, compared to England's haul of 18 gold, 13 silver and 12 bronze. The sense of failure was all the more acute because Scotland had just won the contest to stage the 1970 games. Worse was to follow when two Scottish boxers were sent home in disgrace. They had got drunk, bought thunderflashes and wandered along the verandah outside our bedrooms lobbing them in. The explosions rocked the camp. I remember a burly hammer thrower, Lawrie Bryce, telling the two boxers to stop it or he would knock their heads off. His threat carried some weight – he was the Scottish Universities Heavyweight Boxing Champion. The two miscreants did as he said and they were sent home on the next flight. Scotland's embarrassment was partially counterbalanced by Jim Alder winning gold in the marathon.

My return to Scotland was brief. I captained the British team at the European Championships in Budapest at the end of August. Then, thirty-six hours after returning from Budapest, I crossed the Atlantic to begin a year-long post-graduate scholarship in the sun of California.

I had my father to thank for it. Two of his friends, one a timber merchant, the other a glass merchant, were members of Glasgow Rotary Club, which awarded annually a post-graduate scholarship to study anywhere in the world. My father's two friends, archetypal Glasgow merchants with three-piece suits, watch chains and a bit of dash, suggested I should apply for it. The scholarship was an ambassadorial appointment involving speaking tours of Rotary Clubs. By this time I was an Olympic athlete with two degrees (I finished my LLB at Glasgow in 1965 and was carrying on my legal apprenticeship) and with ambassadorial experience on the Sports Council and as captain of the UK athletics team. When I heard I'd won it, I applied to Yale but was turned down because my law grades at Glasgow were not good enough. Then I tried Cornell in New York State and also Stanford, near San Francisco Bay in California. Both accepted me to study international law. I chose Stanford because it was out west and because the weather would be wonderful for running.

Everything was arranged and then, suddenly and bewilderingly, my father turned against it. I don't think he wanted me to leave his sphere of influence. My sister's engagement added to the pressure on me not to go. Her wedding was in November. I would miss it if I took up my place at Stanford. I dug in my heels, probably emboldened by losing a similar battle with my father over Oxford five years before.

I went to Stanford in September 1966 and immediately felt homesick. I rented a room in a professor's house off campus. The other students cycled or drove to lectures but I had to walk for twenty-five minutes. I had no car and could not bicycle because it would build the wrong muscles in my sprinter's legs.

If I was irked by the inconvenience of my domestic arrangements, the opposite was the case in athletics. I joined the Athens Club in Oakland, a track club with mostly black athletes. I ran at indoor meetings, something I had never done in Britain. I trained in the sunshine in the long Californian running season, and discovered very quickly why America turned out such wonderful athletes.

Word soon spread that I was a former Olympic athlete. I ran at the Maple Leaf Centennial indoor meeting in Toronto. I ran in San Diego. My sprinting responded to the new conditions. When the outdoor season began I ran faster than I had ever done before. At Mount San Antonio on 29 April 1967, I won the 100 metres. *Athletics Weekly* reported: 'Ming Campbell achieved the most notable British sprint victory since Peter Radford's heyday when he defeated a strong field in the 100m. His time of 10.2, equivalent of 9.3/9.4 for the 100y, was wind-assisted but the quality of the opposition testifies to the brilliant form that the 25 year old Scot is currently enjoying.' On 13 May at Fresno I beat an eighteen- or nineteen-year-old talent called O.J. Simpson, who later abandoned athletics for the big money of American football. *Athletics Weekly* again reported the race: 'The Flying Scotsman, "Ming" Campbell, added another gem to his collection of sprint times when he was clocked at 9.5 for the 100y, a personal best. He was narrowly beaten by Jerry Bright (9.5) but he in turn finished ahead of O.J. Simpson (9.6), Bernie Rivers

(9.6) and Larry Dunn (9.6).' But for a half-pulled muscle in the last 10 to 15 yards, I would have run 9.4, a new British record. A week later, on 20 May, I travelled to San Jose and ran at the meeting where Tommie Smith broke the world records for the 440 yards and the 400 metres. In 1968 his black-gloved, Black Power salute on the gold medal rostrum would become the media image of the Mexico Olympics. On the same San Jose track, on a brilliant blue Saturday afternoon, I ran 10.2 in the 100 metres, breaking the British record. The following Saturday, on 27 May, at Modesto, I ran 10.2 again, equalling my own record. I had reached the absolute peak of my running career.

California seduced me. I loved the weather and the lifestyle. Did I really want to go back to Scotland, to the rain and to live with my parents again? Late at night, talking to other law students, I toyed with the idea of taking the California Bar exam and becoming an American citizen. The idea lost its attraction when I realised it would make me eligible for the draft and for fighting in Vietnam. I remember a conversation with two law students, who were trying to avoid the draft, about us opening a legal practice in Vancouver, across the border in British Columbia, Canada. Nothing came of it. It was just student talk. My year in the Californian sun ended. I flew back to London and, jet-lagged, went straight to the AAA championships at White City. I won the 220 yards, becoming champion for the second time.

As I travelled north to Scotland, to complete the last twelve weeks of my legal apprenticeship, I knew my running career was almost at an end. Training in the rain had little appeal after the heat and sunshine of Stanford. Also, I needed a job. A friend arranged interviews with two firms of Glasgow solicitors. One offered me £1,750 in my first year; the other £1,250. My father suggested instead that I go to the Bar, becoming an advocate. He said he would support me for twelve more months and then I must fend for myself. Should I go to the Bar or should I become a solicitor? I rang my sister Fiona for her advice. 'Don't be a bloody fool,' she said. 'Take the money.' One of Scotland's senior judges, Lord Milligan, finally persuaded me. He had been Lord Advocate, Scotland's senior law officer, in the Macmillan government and was, more pertinently for me, honorary president of the Scottish Amateur Athletic Association. Before I went to Stanford he took an interest in my career. 'You must go to the Bar,' he exhorted me. On my return from America I wrote to him for advice on becoming an advocate. He wrote back saying I should consider 'devilling' for a highly regarded junior counsel by the name of H.D.B. Morton. He added: 'P.S. I understand his politics are a bit leftish.'

And so my athletics career ended and my legal career began.

5

Elspeth

On the first working day after New Year's Day in 1968 I became a 'devil'. I sat at a desk with an inconveniently sloping top in the corridor of the Advocates' Library in Parliament House, Edinburgh, home of the Supreme Courts of Scotland and, as its name suggests, of Scotland's former parliament until the Act of Union in 1707. The devils sat together and often ate together. Sometimes we went to the nearby Traverse Theatre café where lunch cost three shillings and sixpence and talked earnestly (as befitted serious young lawyers) about the personalities we encountered at work, the cost of second-hand wigs and our career prospects. There were about half a dozen of us: Hazel Aronson, who became Scotland's first female Supreme Court judge; Colin McEachran, now a QC; Donald Booker-Milburn and Andrew Lothian, now both sheriffs; and Bobby Younger, who too became a sheriff. He was brother of George, who was both Scottish and Defence secretaries in Margaret Thatcher's governments. We did our devil-masters' bidding, or as near to it as we could manage in those early days. I managed barely at all.

H.D.B., or Hugh Drennan Baird, Morton was a shy and busy son of the manse. His known Labour Party affiliation brought him a thriving practice of personal injury cases, typically trades unions claiming damages for their injured members. The result was that he could give me little of his time. For the first month or so contact between us was slight and, for me, awkward. He would ask me to prepare a case in draft, I would do it and then he would put a red pen through it. After work I would walk from Parliament House, past St Giles Cathedral, the 'High Kirk' of the Church of Scotland, and down the hill to Waverley Station to catch the train back to Glasgow, wondering how this would resolve itself. It transpired that he had been wondering the same thing. One day he said, 'This won't do,' and suggested I spend Mondays working with him at his chambers. As was, and still is, the practice, Scottish advocates had their chambers at home. So, every Monday, I went to his house in a crescent in Edinburgh's Georgian New Town and learned the business of becoming an advocate. I would arrive at 11 a.m., work for two hours, have lunch with Hugh and his wife Muriel, work for two more hours, then commute back to Glasgow. His shyness and my novice's incompetence soon wore off, though I think the former did so more quickly than the latter.

During the next eight months I must have drafted as many as ninety personal injury cases. I sat in on Hugh's client consultations and prepared draft opinions. I learned the style in which he liked drafts to be prepared (and later used them as templates when I set up practice on my own). Over time, as we became friends, I grew to admire him, his knowledge, his brevity in court and his unerring sense of principle. As Lord Morton of Shuna, he became Labour's Scottish legal affairs spokesman in the Lords and three years later, in 1988, a Scottish Supreme Court judge. He died from cancer in 1995, aged sixty-five. His obituary in *The Times* described him as 'a judge in the finest tradition of the Scottish law. Modest, pragmatic, direct and, in an age of long-winded judgements, sparse and to the point, he brought to the Bench a strong sense of the place that the law should occupy in Society.' I could not have had a better teacher, nor have been taught by a better man.

November 1, 1968 is lodged in my memory for ever. It was the day I was called to the Bar, my pupillage over, the day I would set up practice on my own and the day my father ended his financial commitment to me. It was the deal we had struck. He would support me while I trained to be an advocate, then I would be on my own. I could hardly complain. I was twenty-seven. It cost £500 for my entry to the Faculty of Advocates, the self-regulating representative body for Scottish advocates, and for my petition, as it is called, to the court for admission. It was, I think, also a proud day for him and my mother. They came to the admission ceremonies at Parliament House, my father as ever in a smart suit and bowler hat, my mother wearing her fur coat.

First, I was admitted to the Faculty of Advocates in the reading room. Hugh Morton proposed me and Brian Gill, an old friend from Glasgow University and now Scotland's second senior judge, seconded me. George Emslie, Dean of the Faculty, then asked the assembled advocates whether it was their will I should be admitted to their number. Their assent was indicated by a muted and traditional tapping of feet. There were three other 'intrants', as we were called. Afterwards the Dean of the Faculty walked purposefully out to the main corridor followed by the four intrants wearing evening tail coats, white ties and black waistcoats but, at this stage, neither gowns nor wigs. The crowds of advocates, passing jurors and court officials parted as the procession headed for Lord Thomson's court for us to be sworn in and to sign the roll of court. By tradition, the case interrupted by this ceremony was an undefended divorce. Finally, a Faculty officer presented me with my first gown and wig. I bowed to the judge and he bowed back. I was now entitled to put up a brass plate on the front door of my home (not that I had one in Edinburgh) with the words 'Mr Campbell, Advocate' on it.

More importantly, I could also begin to earn some money. Doing so as a devil had been forbidden. How much I would earn and how quickly played on my mind as my parents took Hugh and Muriel, Brian and me to lunch at the North British Hotel on Princes Street, five minutes' walk from the courts. My worldly wealth amounted to an overdraft of £50 in my account at the Royal Bank of Scotland. This was Friday. On Monday, I would need to start earning. After lunch I walked back up to Parliament House with Hugh. Along the broad main corridor of the building is a row of wooden boxes, each bearing an advocate's name. These were where advocates received court papers and instructions. One box now bore my name. Inside it was my diary, put there by my clerk, who received a commission on any fees I earned, and to my surprise a set of papers for a case due to be heard in Edinburgh Sheriff Court on Monday. The fee was written on it: seven guineas. My career as an advocate had begun.

It was an inglorious start. I defended a woman charged with careless driving. The case was scheduled for 10 a.m. but, as usual on a Monday, the business of the day was delayed by the procession of drunks and petty criminals appearing from custody after the weekend's nocturnal rowdiness. My client and I hung around until late in the afternoon wondering if the case would ever be called. By this time I was much more nervous than her, even though she knew I was a beginner. Eventually, we were called into court. I cannot remember exactly what I said to the sheriff, and nor do I wish to since it was so hesitant. She was found guilty. I have retained two vague impressions of the case. The first is that she was very nice to me afterwards, surprisingly so, and the second is that I left the court building feeling I had not acquitted myself well. Still, I had earned seven guineas.

In those days, young advocates aimed to have receipts of £1,000 in their first year, out of which they paid their dues to the Faculty of Advocates, their travelling costs to courts around Scotland and, if they subscribed to it, the bill for the so-called 'bag service' which delivered court papers and instructions to advocates at home in their New Town chambers. Generally, these expenses amounted to between 20 and 25 per cent of receipts. So an advocate kept at least £750 before tax from receipts of £1,000. This was a good first income in 1968. John Smith's receipts in his first year were £1,100. Could I make the same? I thought I could for my first few weeks. Every day there were papers waiting for me in my box at Parliament House. Then my fragile practice faltered. My work dried up. It was a difficult and lonely time. By now I had moved out of my parents' home in Glasgow and was sharing a flat with two Glasgow university friends, John Cowan and John Newman, in Edinburgh. I knew few people in my newly adopted city and no matter how diligently I attended court, as a new junior counsel is expected to do, paid work proved hard to find. I use the expression 'paid work' deliberately because inexperienced advocates like me were required to do considerable amounts of unpaid work for more senior advocates.

We stood in the corridors ready for our clerks to put us into court at short notice to do procedural chores of case work for our seniors. We appeared before the judge taking the 10 a.m. Motion Roll to fix adjournment dates or the dates for hearings to begin. We picked up the pieces of divorces, arguing for interim aliment (alimony in England) of, say, £1.50 for a child. Often we were handed cases at the door of the court with no time to prepare. We read the papers hurriedly as we walked to our seats in front of the judge. But none of it earned us a penny. Our seniors received the fees. On one occasion I did four undefended divorces for an advocate who was also a part-time sheriff. His box was next door to mine in the court corridor. Some weeks later I was standing at mine when he stood beside me opening the letter containing the cheque for my work. He turned and walked away carrying my earnings with him. It was exploitation but for a purpose. It gave young advocates a means of advertising themselves. The theory was that if you worked competently at short notice and without charge for a solicitor then he might send you paid instructions thereafter. Sometimes, the theory held true.

The system of paying fees also worked against young advocates like me with no savings and less than nothing in the bank. Nowadays the Faculty of Advocates runs a central fees collection office. Then, there was no system for chasing fees. Advocates were at the mercy of solicitors. Although the fee for every case was marked on the case papers, receiving it could take months. Some solicitors were conscientious, others not. One big firm used to boast that it paid for its Christmas party out of the interest it earned from its advocates' fees account. Advocates never liked to complain to solicitors about slow payment out of fear that their instructions would go to another, more compliant advocate.

To begin with, my life as an advocate was precarious. My practice grew in fits and starts. Undefended divorces were my staple. I added some crime. Then I found a source of regular income acting as junior counsel to the advocate-depute, the crown prosecutor in Scotland's High Court. (In Scotland, the High Court hears serious criminal cases; in England, it is the principal civil court.) I was paid ten guineas a day for appearing in court at his side and £4 10s subsistence for travelling to the High Court sitting outside Edinburgh. For £4 10s I could stay in the Station Hotel in Aberdeen or Perth, eat a good dinner and still have ten shillings left over. I enjoyed the money and the work but there was a danger in it. If I spent too much time away from Edinburgh word would spread I wasn't serious about building up a practice. Nothing was further from the truth. Bit by bit my income grew until I managed, like John Smith, to have receipts of £1,100 in my first year. I had achieved my first legal milestone.

In my second year, my receipts rose to £4,300 and I began to attract some bigger cases. I remember in 1969 appearing before Lord Wheatley at the High Court in Dumfries, losing the case narrowly by a majority verdict and the judge calling me to his room afterwards to compliment me on my defence. I also have a memory of appearing as the junior counsel to George Carmichael QC, a most civilised and urbane man, in two murder cases in Glasgow. My recollection is not of the trials but of my discomfort sitting in court with severely grazed knees after playing rugby for Edinburgh Wanderers in the final of the Middlesex Sevens at Twickenham the previous Saturday. At the lunch break I had to search Glasgow for plasters to stop my knees rubbing against the hard cloth of my lawyer's trousers.

My law career was taking off but my social life wasn't. I decided to move out of the flat I shared with my Glasgow friends to have a better opportunity of meeting more people in Edinburgh. A young advocate called John Wheatley, the son of the judge who had praised me in Dumfries, asked me if I would like to rent a room in a Georgian flat in Edinburgh's New Town. I said I would but shrank from telling my Glasgow friends. When I did, they were disappointed with me. I think they thought my move to the more fashionable New Town was motivated by snobbishness, though really it was driven by loneliness. I was spending weekdays at Parliament House and nights briefing myself on work for the following morning. I travelled to Glasgow on Saturdays to be the in-house lawyer for the *Sunday Mail* newspaper (I succeeded John Smith in the role) where I earned eight guineas for my legal advice on the stories they planned to publish. I slept at my parents' home in Scotstoun on Saturday nights and took the train back to Edinburgh on Sundays. Moving in with John Wheatley and his flatmate Peter Rodger, an apprentice solicitor, would give me the opportunity to build a network of new friends in Edinburgh. Their flat in Scotland Street was also within a few minutes' walk of the other Georgian streets where most of the Faculty of Advocates' members lived.

One acquaintance I had already made was a flamboyant and talented lawyer by the name of Nicholas Fairbairn, who became

Conservative MP for Kinross and West Perthshire and Solicitor General for Scotland until, typically, verbal indiscretion forced his resignation in 1982. I met him first with Hugh Morton in the robing room at Glasgow Sheriff Court in 1968. Even at that stage he attracted scorn and admiration in equal measure for his flamboyance and brilliance in front of a jury. Later, sadly, alcoholism and right-wing theatricalism combined to render his public image more tragi-comic. The Nicky Fairbairn I met was a courteous, charming and witty man. He said he'd heard a lot about me, more a reference to my exploits on the running track than in the courtroom, I imagined. He was immensely nice to me that day and remained so thereafter. Nicky and I worked for the same stable of advocates run by a clerk called Gilbert McWhannell whose speciality was criminal cases. Nicky had the pick of murders because he was so good in court. Sometimes I assisted Nicky as his junior, as did Michael Ancram, later an MP and deputy leader of the Conservative Party. One Monday, as we appeared together in a murder trial in Glasgow, Nicky said, 'What are you doing on Friday night?'

'Nothing,' I replied.

'Well, bring your black tie. We're going dancing.'

Nicky knew I had no car so offered to give me a lift from the High Court in Glasgow to his home, Fordell Castle, a sixteenth-century tower house just north of Dalgety Bay, Fife. Nicky and his first wife, Elizabeth, had bought it and restored it after their marriage in 1962. They lived with their three daughters in a comfort and style I had seldom seen before. My background was one of tenement flats and terraced houses in Glasgow. I wasn't used to a large house in lovely grounds within which was even a chapel dedicated to a saint called Therotus. We arrived in time for tea, me with my suitcase containing my dinner jacket and black tie. Nicky led me up the stone stairs to the first-floor drawing room. Standing in front of the large open fireplace was a glamorous thirty-year-old woman with swept-back dark hair.

We were introduced. I caught her first name, Elspeth, and gathered that she must know the Fairbairns well since she was godmother to their daughter Anna. After tea we went off to change for supper at Fordell and then dancing, at the Black and White Ball at the Assembly Rooms, Edinburgh, in aid of the Traverse Theatre of which Nicky was chairman. Elspeth re-emerged prettily in a pink dress with a grey bodice which she had bought for judging a Miss Scotland competition. I didn't know then that Nicky had been her divorce lawyer, nor that he had rung her to tell her about me being one of the guests. Elspeth remembers him saying, 'This terrific athlete who is my junior in a case in Glasgow is coming as well. He's called Menzies Campbell.' Journalistic shorthand over the years has turned our meeting into a blind date arranged by Nicky.

At the risk of spoiling a good story, it wasn't quite like that. We were two people in a large party, others of whom were single. After supper we drove in a number of cars over the Forth Road Bridge to Edinburgh for the dance. I and my suitcase, now containing my work clothes, caught a lift with Nicky and Elizabeth. The other passenger was Elspeth. At the ball we danced two or three times, but Elspeth's memory is that we danced together all night. The Fairbairns dropped me off at my flat in Edinburgh on their way back home to Fife. As I climbed the stone stairs to my door I remember thinking, Gosh, that's a pretty girl. By then I knew that her full name was Lady Grant-Suttie, that she lived in Killearn, a village under the Campsie Fells north of Glasgow, that she was divorced and had a four-year-old son called James.

More importantly, I also had her phone number. I rang her the following day, then the next and the next. Either there was no reply or Elspeth's au pair would answer in a strong French accent: 'Lady Grant-Suttie ees not ere.' I was beginning to feel embarrassed, wondering whether Elspeth was hiding behind the au pair to avoid my calls. I resolved to ring one last time. Elspeth answered. She agreed to go to the cinema with me at the weekend.

We met beforehand at the North British Hotel in Glasgow but talked so much we missed the film. Instead we went to Ferrari's, then Glasgow's best restaurant but long since closed. I ordered a bottle of white wine and Elspeth said, 'That's good. My father told me never to trust men who order half bottles.' Afterwards Elspeth gave me a lift in her blue Fiat 850 sports car, bought defiantly with her divorce settlement, to my parents' home before driving back to Killearn. My mother and father had not been expecting me, nor did they know of my fast-growing attachment to this titled, well-connected, divorced single mother. Any one of those descriptions would probably have caused them concern; the combination certainly so. The following Saturday, Elspeth came to my flat, accompanying me to the Scottish Television studio at the Gateway Theatre in Edinburgh where I took part in a discussion programme with, among others, Germaine Greer. We were becoming inseparable. The pace of our relationship was such that Elspeth suggested lunch with her parents at Easter the following week. The plan was that I would go to the *Sunday Mail* in Glasgow on Saturday night as usual, spend Easter Day at home with my parents and have lunch on Easter Monday with Elspeth's parents at their home, Gaidrew, near Drymen and Loch Lomond. Elspeth would pick me up on Easter Monday morning in Glasgow where I was taking evidence on commission from a witness who was too ill to attend court.

I concealed the arrangement from my father. He had given me a lift to the office in central Glasgow where I was meeting the witness. My father offered to wait and to take me to the station for the train to Edinburgh when my work was done. I told him not to bother. Instead I met Elspeth who drove me to lunch and my introduction to the Urquhart family.

Elspeth's background was as exotic as mine was ordinary. Even her birth was unusual, in a nursing home in New Delhi named after Lady Willington, wife of the Viceroy appointed in 1931. Lady Willington's favourite colour was mauve. So everything in the nursing home had to be mauve, including the loo paper. It was wartime. Elspeth's mother Pamela, aged twenty-two, and Elspeth were sent home by convoy around the Cape of Good Hope. During the six-week journey back to England their convoy came under frequent torpedo attack. Ships went down all around them but they arrived safely. Elspeth's father, Roy, was a rapidly rising army officer. From India he went to the Middle East, Italy and, famously, commanded the 1st Airborne Division in the Battle of Arnhem. In the film *A Bridge Too Far*, his role is played by Sean Connery. Postwar, while I was beginning to play rugby at Hillhead School, Elspeth was in Malaya where her father was trying to suppress the Communist insurgency. Major-General Urquhart's next posting was to Austria where the family lived in a mansion by a lake, had use of a flat in Vienna and a private train. Elspeth commuted at holiday time from a convent boarding school in Devon. The only similarity in our upbringing was that both our fathers denied us places at Oxford University. In Elspeth's case her father's reaction to Oxford's offer was to tell her that 'people don't like blue-stocking women'. Instead she went to a kind of finishing school called the House of Citizenship in Buckinghamshire.

Sometimes I wonder what would have happened if our fathers had made different decisions. We would have been at Oxford together. Would we have met? Instead Elspeth went to work for Conservative Central Office, finding both Iain Macleod and Rab Butler 'charismatic and interesting', then for the Royal Aero Club in London. She lived in a social whirl, falling for a handsome, Canadian-born baronet who had inherited an estate near North Berwick in Scotland when he was only seven. She married him in 1962. Sir Philip Grant-Suttie was, by Elspeth's account, 'dashing; never boring'. Their son James was born in

1965 but their marriage crumbled. Elspeth divorced him in 1969, going to live with her parents who by now had moved back to Scotland.

Gaidrew was a large, comfortable house surrounded by gardens and a tennis court. As I shook hands with Elspeth's parents it occurred to me I had never met a family with such a different history to my own. Then I discovered that Elspeth's father and I had one thing in common. Unknown to me until then he had run in the 440 yards final at the Scottish Athletics Championships in 1924 against Eric Liddell, coming fourth. He knew of me and my track exploits. At lunch I sat beside Elspeth's mother, who seemed to me to be a formidably strong woman, good-looking and self-assured. Conversation was polite but strained; at least it was for me. After lunch we went for a walk at Loch Ard and then, to my relief, Elspeth drove me away. She told me later her father's reaction to me.

She asked him, 'Well, what do you think?'

Her father apparently replied, 'Don't let him slip.'

I had not felt I was on trial at the lunch. Clearly, I had been wrong. Elspeth's father needn't have worried. Giving Elspeth the 'slip' was the last thing on my mind. That evening she gave me dinner at her two-bedroom cottage, which she rented from Sir John Wilson, the Queen's Philatelist. I remember what was on the menu: marinated kipper fillets and chicken pie. After dinner she was to take me to Milngavie for the train to Glasgow Queen Street Station and then on to Edinburgh. Somehow the time for the train passed. I spent the night with Elspeth.

Soon after, we began to talk about becoming engaged. We were so certain of it ourselves that we discussed it in front of friends. I remember a conversation in the galley kitchen of her cottage about announcing our engagement to coincide with a charity performance of *Fidelio* by Scottish Opera at the Theatre Royal, Glasgow, which Elspeth had organised to raise funds for Shelter. David Steel was Shelter Scotland's chairman. Someone suggested: 'Wouldn't Elspeth's engagement to an Olympic athlete be good publicity for the charity night?' It was said as a joke, but somehow the *Daily Express* got wind of it and decided to run the story. We begged them to delay so that we could tell our parents first. Mine still didn't even know of Elspeth's existence. The *Express* conceded but regretted its decision not to publish after what happened later.

I rang my mother, took a deep breath and told her about Elspeth. I said, 'I'm going to get engaged to someone who's got a title and a child.' I thought I would deliver all the bad news in one sentence. I could feel my mother's shock at the other end of the phone line. She had little time for the titled or 'toffs'. Elspeth was both, one by marriage, one by birth. I arranged to go home the following evening to speak to my parents. When I did my father failed to turn up. I returned to Edinburgh on the train without seeing him. The next day it was all over the *Evening Times* in Glasgow. I am certain my father leaked it to the paper's local government correspondent. The consequence was fury at the *Daily Express*, especially as Elspeth had previously but briefly sold some stories to its William Hickey gossip column to earn some money when in dispute with her ex-husband over maintenance payments. The *Express* felt it had been betrayed by one of its own.

A greater worry for me was the engagement ring. I couldn't afford big diamonds like Elspeth's first husband, Sir Philip Grant-Suttie. Elspeth, typically, said, 'Bugger diamonds.' We went to the only jeweller's shop I knew in Glasgow (it supplied the trophies and prizes for the annual Cowal Highland Games in Argyll where I used to run) and we found a ring for £100. Fifteen years later, the ring slipped from Elspeth's finger as she swam in the sea off a beach in Italy. We spent hours looking for it, hoping every morning it would be washed ashore. The beach boy Giorgio assured us it was lost for good. The seabed where it fell was rocky, he told us. The ring would have lodged there.

Twelve months later the ring was washed up on the shore. Giorgio found it and it was returned to its owner.

Wearing her ring, Elspeth and I went to meet my parents the next weekend. It was an awkward occasion. They had never met anyone like Elspeth and were not sure how to react to her, their future daughter-in-law. I remember my mother's concern that we should have something to eat before I went to my night lawyer's job at the *Sunday Mail*.

The next day we went together to Elspeth's parents. In the drawing room with the door closed Elspeth's father seemed pleased by our engagement. Much to her and my amusement he told me that Elspeth was 'no spring chicken' and asked me to be sure my engagement to her 'was not just physical infatuation'. Lastly, he said he would not pay for another wedding for Elspeth. I was spared his command to Philip Grant-Suttie at a similar point before Elspeth's first marriage. 'Don't be formal. Just call me General,' he told Philip. Its absence made no difference to me: calling him 'General' seemed the most appropriate form of address anyhow.

Elspeth went alone some days later to have lunch with my father in the North British Hotel in Glasgow. It was a stiff affair to begin with as it was bound to be but Elspeth left it feeling my father had goodwill towards her. He said to her how proud he was of me and how he hoped marriage would bring us happiness.

Elspeth told her son James about our wedding plans. 'And afterwards he'll be coming to live with us,' she said.

'What? All day AND all night?' said the puzzled four-year-old.

All that remained for Elspeth and me was to set the date. At first we were not in any hurry to marry. Then we changed our minds, partly because the Commonwealth Games were to be staged in Edinburgh that summer and I had agreed to write athletics reports and commentaries daily for the *Scotsman* newspaper. Why wait? Let's get married before the games begin, we said. On 12 June 1970, only three months after we met and on a beautiful summer's day, we were married at Buchanan Parish Church beside Loch Lomond. Elspeth wore a pink and white striped dress with a pink bodice, large white collar and matching pillbox hat. (Less noticeable was a missing contact lens. She had swallowed it by mistake and spent much of our short honeymoon trying to find it again!) We had sixty guests, few of them my friends. My allocation of invitations had been almost entirely used up by my mother instantly asking all their smartest friends from Glasgow. The reception was at Elspeth's parents' home, a few miles from the church. My father-in-law had relented partially over his refusal to subsidise Elspeth's second wedding. He paid for the food; I paid for the champagne which he insisted on tasting first before I bought it. (I got it from the Staff Club at Edinburgh University because I was a part-time law tutor there.) My flatmate John Wheatley was best man, who read out the telegrams. Nicky Fairbairn made an impromptu speech and, typically, caused a stir doing so. He made a reference to the Red Road high-rise council flats in Glasgow which at that time were controversial because they were so high – the tallest in Europe – and unpopular with tenants. (So much asbestos had been used in their construction that the building workers were called the 'white mice' by their families.) Nicky joked that Elspeth and I were unlikely to go house-hunting at Red Road. But it was a joke with a deliberate barb. My father was in charge of Glasgow Corporation's large building department, as Nicky knew. Elspeth remembers my father scowling, and my sister believes our father was hurt by the reference. Nicky's bad manners certainly caught my father off-guard. Contemporary references to our wedding occasionally report a guest describing us 'as Britain's fastest man marrying Britain's fastest woman'. If someone did say it I never heard it, though I would have laughed if I had.

We married on a Friday afternoon. I had to be back in court on Monday. Our honeymoon was two days in Ireland, or that was the intention. We drove from the reception to Glasgow Airport to discover the Aer Lingus flight to Dublin was fog-bound. In the airport concourse we bumped into a sheriff called Bill Henderson. 'What are you doing here?' he asked.

'We've just got married,' we replied, 'but now we're stuck. There's fog in Dublin.'

'Well,' he offered kindly, 'I've got a very nice spare room . . .'

We returned instead to the rendezvous for our first date, the North British Hotel in Glasgow. After dinner we bought a first edition of the *Daily Record* newspaper. There was a huge photograph of us on the front page. We scurried back to the hotel, only emerging again at breakfast-time when the head porter greeted us with: 'Good morning, Mr Campbell and Lady Grant-Suttie.' By now the fog had lifted and we flew to Dublin without further delay. We drove to Cork for our weekend honeymoon and flew back on Sunday evening.

I moved into Elspeth's cottage and immediately realised it would be impossible for me to run my legal practice successfully from there. One of the difficulties was my inability to drive. There was a reason for it. Seven years before, when I was still a student at Glasgow University, I witnessed an accident near my parents' flat in Park Road. I was walking towards the junction when I heard a screech of brakes. Looking up I saw a woman flying through the air like a large doll. I never knew whether the woman lived or died but the image of her flying so abnormally and the car that hit her, with Lansdowne Church in the background became lodged in my mind. It made me unconfident behind the wheel. I failed my test three times before I met Elspeth who persuaded me forcefully of the impracticality of living in Killearn without a driving licence. While I took another set of lessons, Elspeth drove me to Stirling Station for the morning commuter train to Edinburgh and collected me from the station in the evening. Killearn was far from an ideal base for an advocate's practice. Living outside Edinburgh's New Town signalled a dilettante attitude towards the law. If I was going to become a successful advocate we had to move.

It was the first crisis of our marriage. Elspeth, by her own admission, left her cottage in Killearn 'kicking and screaming'. We bought a second-floor Georgian flat in Edinburgh with what seemed at the time to be an imprudently large mortgage of £8,500. I put my brass plate 'Mr Campbell, Advocate' on the front door with pride. Elspeth made the dining room and hall an informal gallery for displaying Nicky Fairbairn's watercolour and oil landscapes. Occasionally one of our dinner guests would admire them and Elspeth would say: 'Well, they're for sale if you'd like one.'

By now the fragile beginnings of a political career were stirring in the background. At Elspeth's charity performance of *Fidelio* David Steel had said to her: 'We must get Ming to stand as a candidate'.

Before my wedding I took a phone call from Alan Blair, a Liberal councillor and solicitor in Greenock, who had over-lapped with me at Glasgow University. 'Can I bring some people to see you?' he said mysteriously. We met at the Liberal Club in Princes Street, Edinburgh (in a building now occupied by Debenhams!).

'We'd like you to be the Liberal candidate in Greenock,' they said.

I replied, 'Well, I'm about to get married and I don't think the timing makes much sense.' The election was on 18 June, six days after our wedding. (My memory is different to Alan Blair's who remembers ringing me and approaching me soon after the election.)

We had a drink and parted on good terms. I would hear from Greenock's Liberals again.

6

Fighting and losing

Marriage changed me. I recognise now how selfish I had become in my pursuit of ever faster performances on the running track. Although I had given up top-class athletics by the time I met Elspeth, its relentless demands and its narrow, unforgiving focus left their marks on me. Looking back now I can see how self-centred I had become. Perhaps that was why my previous relationships had disintegrated in the clumsy, insensitive ways they did. Meeting Elspeth made me more tolerant, even liberal, and introduced me to a different way of life. My parents had expected me to marry a doctor, a teacher or a nurse, certainly not a socially accomplished woman whose friends were rich, or landed or titled, and sometimes all three. I had 'married up' even though it sounds archaic to say so in these days of social mobility.

Marriage brought me a second family, Elspeth's parents, her two sisters and brother, and a five-year-old stepson, James, who spent a great deal of time with us. I felt myself being absorbed in the nicest way possible by the Urquharts. We visited them for Sunday lunch and at Christmas, and we holidayed with Elspeth's mother in the cottage she rented every summer at Shieldaig, a village in Wester Ross on the north-west coast of Scotland. James came with us too and we would fish for mackerel in the sea and explore the wild Applecross Peninsula. When James went to prep school, at Craigflower in Fife, we used to take him out for international rugby matches at Murrayfield and send him back again stuffed with food after tea in our flat. My relationship with James was always an easy one. I didn't try to impose myself on him as a stepfather and, probably as a consequence, I had a friendly relationship with James's father, Philip. Sometimes when Elspeth was away, I would go to East Lothian to have dinner with him and James. I was flattered when James asked me to do one of the readings at his father's funeral in 1997. I read the passage from John Bunyan's *Pilgrim's Progress* which includes the lines:

> When the day that he must go hence was come, many accompanied him to the riverside, into which as he went he said, 'Death where is thy sting?' and as he went down deeper, he said, 'Grave, where is thy victory?' So, he passed over, and all the trumpets sounded for him on the other side.

Afterwards Elspeth's mother, Pamela, said to me firmly, 'Very good reading. I want you to read that for me when I die.' (And I did. Her funeral was in May 2006.)

My life in Edinburgh also changed with marriage. It was more fun. Elspeth and I went out to drinks and dinner parties or to the theatre. We lived the enjoyable, easy, gregarious life of a metropolitan couple. If by night I became more social, by day my focus stayed on work. I was determined to make a success of my legal practice. A wife and a mortgage drove me all the harder. I used to work seven days a week. On Saturday mornings I would go to court and do three or four undefended divorces, have lunch with Elspeth in an Italian restaurant called Cosmo's and then go to Glasgow to cast my lawyer's eye over the stories appearing the following day in the *Sunday Mail*.

As I became busier, I thought no more of pursuing a political career and took little active interest in the Liberal Party. From memory, the last political event in which I'd been involved occurred a month or two before I met Elspeth in spring 1970. At David Steel's invitation, I had spoken at the Volunteer Hall, Galashiels, in the Scottish Borders, in opposition to a controversial Springbok rugby tour. The Springboks were scheduled to play in the town and David, the local MP, was in the awkward position of also being president of the Anti-Apartheid Movement which was part of the 'Stop the 70 Tour' protest campaign. Stopping the tour was an unpopular cause in the rugby-mad Borders and it threatened David's constituency majority. My reputation provided him with a credible sporting ally at a moment of acute need. At the following general election he held his seat by fewer than 600 votes. My friendship with David stems from that time, although I had met him before when I was active in the Glasgow University Liberal Club and he was similarly engaged at Edinburgh University. Why I decided to pick up politics again in autumn 1973 after three years of marriage is now a mystery to me. Perhaps it was simple opportunism. The convenience of a by-election in the constituency of Edinburgh North where I lived tempted me to try my hand at standing for parliament.

The by-election was precipitated by the elevation of the sitting Conservative MP, the Earl of Dalkeith, to the House of Lords on the death of his father, the Duke of Buccleuch. The seat was safely Conservative – Johnny Dalkeith had polled 52.8 per cent at the 1970 general election compared to 37 per cent for Labour and 10 per cent for the Liberals – but there was potential for growing the Liberal vote.

The political backdrop was also favourable. About three months earlier, on 26 July, the Liberals had won two stunning by-election victories: Clement Freud in Isle of Ely and David Austick in Ripon. Both were taken from the Tories. Could it happen again in Edinburgh North? I walked into the Scottish Liberal HQ in Edinburgh and said, 'I'd be interested in trying for the nomination.'

'Well, the selection committee meeting is tonight. Come along if you want to,' was the unexpected reply.

I walked home intrigued at the prospect of winning the nomination but increasingly aghast at my uncharacteristic impetuosity. How could I keep my legal practice and fight a by-election?

I went to the selection meeting with very mixed feelings and unprepared for the inquisition to come. There were two other prospective candidates waiting for interview: Ronnie Guild, who had been Tony Blair's housemaster at Fettes College, the public school in Edinburgh; and Lionel Daiches, an eminent and eloquent QC. Guild turned up with a portable file detailing every pothole in the constituency (or so it seemed to me). Daiches arrived with his mesmerising voice and wonderful vocabulary. I brought along my uncertain political ambition.

Not surprisingly, Guild won it. I helped in his campaign, speaking at a public meeting and driving voters to the polling stations on election day. The result was a disappointment for the Liberals. Guild was beaten into fourth place behind Labour and the Scottish Nationalists. The Tory candidate Alex Fletcher won it. Rather than killing off my political appetite the campaign whetted it, particularly when I heard the result of the Berwick-upon-Tweed by-election held the same day. Alan Beith stole it from the Conservatives with a wafer-thin Liberal majority of fifty-seven votes.

Twelve weeks later my phone rang. It was Alan Blair from Greenock again. 'You've been married almost four years and been active for the Liberals. Would you be our candidate now?' he said.

I drove to Greenock that Sunday to meet the local party executive over lunch in the unforgettably named Tontine Hotel. My candidacy was discussed with a sense of urgency. Ted Heath had called a snap general election for 28 February in his 'who governs Britain?' stand-off with the trades unions. The election was in three weeks. I drove back to Edinburgh to await a phone call confirming the Greenock Liberal Party's offer. When it came, I asked Elspeth for her opinion. 'It'll be good fun. Let's do it,' she said.

We arrived in Greenock two weeks and two days before polling day for my formal adoption meeting. The *Greenock Telegraph* reported my maiden speech in the constituency. Ming Campbell, it said, 'attacked everything he did not agree with – the Tories, the Socialists and particularly Messrs Heath and Wilson'. Elspeth and I spent the night in our temporary home for the election, a flat at the back of the house belonging to William and Elspeth Riddle. He was the former Liberal Provost of Greenock who had stood for the party in the 1970 general election and she became a Strathclyde Regional Councillor.

The first upset of the campaign was Elspeth's. She had bought an election wardrobe of purple and yellow after seeing the campaign colours of Liberal leader Jeremy Thorpe on television. On our first day in Greenock she realised her mistake. Red and yellow were the local campaign colours. It led to some hurried readjustments.

For a candidate so naïve, I was lucky to fight my first general election in a constituency with an experienced Liberal organisation and a long tradition of liberalism even though the seat was safely Labour. Dr J. Dickson Mabon, who would later defect to the Social Democratic Party, had held it for nineteen years. (He was a former president of the Glasgow Union like me and we had a lot in common. We became and remain good friends.) By February 1974 it had become safer still for Labour after a boundary change had added Port Glasgow to the old Greenock seat. Port Glasgow was dyed-in-the-wool Labour.

A big issue of the campaign was Labour's manifesto threat to nationalise shipbuilding. Scott Lithgow employed 7,500 men in the constituency, who were largely Labour voters and were in favour of nationalisation, thinking it would safeguard their jobs.

I remember rowdy dock gate meetings where the language from the workers was so bad that I shielded Elspeth by making her sit in the campaign car.

'Will Dr Mabon be allowed to vote according to his conscience when the time comes to vote on the nationalisation of the shipbuilding industry?' I asked. 'Dr Mabon's silence must be for one of two reasons. Either he is against nationalisation but feels unable to support the party line or he supports nationalisation and is afraid to lose votes by saying so.'

For two weeks we tried everything we could to attack Labour's vote. Alan Blair, my agent who went on to become leader of Inverclyde Council, and I leafleted the commuter trains to Glasgow. We would get on the train at Greenock West Station, hand out our leaflets, disembark at Greenock Central then do the same on the return journey. We even canvassed the workers at Thomas Auld, a well-known local bakery, at 5 a.m. as they made fresh morning rolls.

Despite adverts in the *Greenock Telegraph* asking voters to 'Swing to Ming' the result was a foregone conclusion: Dick Mabon won with an increased majority of 11,776; I came second.

Elspeth and I returned to Edinburgh, at once disappointed by the Greenock result and excited by the political prospects to come. Elspeth had been right: the election was fun. She had enjoyed it as much as I had. We did not have long to wait for the next one. The general election had ushered in Harold Wilson as Prime Minister at the head of a precarious minority government. He went back to the country in October 1974 and I went back to Greenock.

This time my campaign was more aggressive. I attacked the local bus monopoly, (again) opposed shipyard nationalisation and then, more controversially, took a swipe at Dickson Mabon personally. The Liberal-leaning *Greenock Telegraph* reported it under the splash heading: 'Why Has Mabon No House Here? –

Ming'. The sub-heading was: 'Liberal candidate slates Greenock MP's record'.

I stormed: 'Nineteen years is a bit long to find a house even in a constituency with housing problems as bad as ours. I believe that here and now Dr Mabon should tell us why he has failed to honour his pledge to find a house in Greenock.'

Mabon was incensed. He demanded to see the editor and wrung out of him a front page story two days later. 'Liberal Campaign Gutter Politics, Says Mabon' was the paper's front page headline. In the accompanying story, Mabon never referred to me by name once. Instead he described me with all the distaste of a man wiping something nasty off his shoe as 'the Liberal candidate'.

'The Liberal candidate,' he raged, 'knows he is not telling the truth.' Mabon said he had no intention of moving his seventy-four-year-old mother from his family home in Bishopbriggs, to the north of Glasgow, when he lived such a short distance from Greenock and Port Glasgow. He did not intend, he added, 'to get into the gutter with the Liberal candidate'.

The campaign also got rough on the street. I remember visiting a little parade of shops in a housing estate in Port Glasgow with the usual accompanying group of supporters handing out leaflets when a man suddenly appeared in front of us, drunk and cursing, with a knife in his hand. Jimmy Boyd, one of my supporters who had served in the navy during the war, shepherded us away. He disarmed the man, whose temper had erupted when an off-licence had refused to serve him. It was a disconcerting incident which was soon turned into a joke by my campaign helpers. Alan Blair remembers them deciding to mark 'doubtful' on my would-be attacker's canvass card.

There was less levity about the election result. Dick Mabon won with a small increase in his majority. The Scottish National Party, which was on a roll across Scotland, came second, forcing me ignominiously into third place ahead of the Tories. I retreated to Edinburgh.

Later that autumn, walking along Princes Street in Edinburgh, after lunch I met George (now Lord) Mackie, former chairman of the Scottish Liberals, and Robert Smith, the Scottish party chairman, emerging from the Liberal Club.

'What are you two up to?' I said.

'We've been discussing the party in Scotland and, in particular, we've been discussing you and why you mustn't go back to Greenock. You'll never win Greenock but if you went somewhere else and built it up you might win,' they said. I couldn't argue with their assessment. Despite my fondness for Greenock and its people, Mabon's majority was impregnable to a Liberal now that Port Glasgow was part of the seat.

The October 1974 election left a corrosive legacy in Scottish liberalism. The party had fielded candidates in almost all seventy-one Scottish constituencies but without the money to provide them with campaign resources. Stories were rife of candidates left without election leaflets, of exhausted volunteers hand-writing and sealing envelopes for dozens of constituencies. Many of the candidates were annoyed at being so publicly and humiliatingly exposed. Only three were elected MPs – Jo Grimond in Orkney and Shetland, Russell Johnston in Inverness and David Steel in the Borders – exactly the same number as in the two previous general elections.

The resentment simmered during the winter and boiled over at the party's 1975 spring conference in Ayr when I was proposed as a challenger to Robert Smith as party chairman. When the vote was counted we discovered the result was a tie. No one knew what to do next. A vote like that had never happened before in Scottish Liberal history.

Supporters of the two rival candidates met in huddles before the result was declared to the conference delegates. Should there be a second vote immediately? What would happen if it was another tie? I thought the simplest solution was for me to stand down to allow Robert Smith's re-election unopposed. Chairing a party now stained with the bad blood of my rivalry with Robert Smith had suddenly lost its attraction for me. I wanted to back out. My dismay at causing such a divisive split was exacerbated by news of the deteriorating state of the party's finances because of its over-ambitiousness in fielding so many candidates the previous October. The party was substantially in debt. The first job of the chairman would be to tackle its rapidly rising overdraft. When I told George Mackie I wanted to pull out he looked at me in horror. 'You can't. You mustn't,' he insisted.

After the tied result was announced to the delegates I expressed in public the doubts I had expressed in private. I said perhaps it would be best if I dropped out and Smith continued as chairman. I remember clearly David Steel's wife, Judy, letting out an agonised cry of 'Oh, no,' when she heard what I was saying. Now I was torn by letting down my supporters. The vote was re-run and I won it by two votes. John Lawrie, an Edinburgh councillor, but more importantly for the party's growing financial crisis, an actuary, was elected unopposed as treasurer.

Our first job was to stop the party going bust. The overdraft was £15,000 and the party's only asset was its headquarters, a flat in the west end of Edinburgh. In those days of lower property values it was not at all certain whether selling it would pay off our overdraft. Even if it did, the Scottish Liberals would be left without a headquarters. We had to find another way of raising money, and quickly. Russell Johnston, MP for Inverness and leader of the Scottish Liberals, had a friend, Bob Robertson, who was chairman of Dumbarton Football Club.

'How can we raise some money?' Russell asked him.

'Why not run your own pools?' the friend suggested, adding, 'I know a chap who can do it for you.'

The chap in question started working from a back room in party headquarters. The 'pools' were in reality more like an early version of the lottery. Each card bore random numbers.

The winning cards had numbers matching that week's football results. A team of agents distributed the tickets to shops in Edinburgh and soon, miraculously, the money began to flow in. The party's debt was in retreat. In time it would be eliminated. Even though our 'pools' salesman was single-handedly transforming the party's finances it did not exempt him from the poisonous atmosphere in the party executive following my narrow election as chairman. Executive meetings would last from 9 a.m. until 6.30 p.m. as those who had supported Robert Smith against me argued over every decision. I remember a three-hour debate about whether the car we had bought for our pools salesman should have a radio in it costing £26.

'This guy's the only thing that has stopped us going bankrupt and we spend hours arguing over this,' John Lawrie and I said in exasperation.

My profile in the party and beyond was growing now that I was chairman, partly because there were too few Liberal MPs to meet the demand for TV interviews and speakers at Liberal dinners. One night in 1975 I spoke at the annual dinner of East Fife Liberals in a hotel in the little village of Lower Largo on the Firth of Forth. Later, after appearing on a BBC Scotland equivalent of *Any Questions* called *Matter of Opinion* in Dundee, Elspeth and I drove south over the Tay Bridge to St Andrews to a meeting attended by half a dozen senior members of the East Fife party. It was held in the home of Jack Daniels, constituency party secretary and a member of the Scottish Liberal executive. They wanted to vet me as a potential parliamentary candidate. I answered their questions and Elspeth and I were asked to wait in the kitchen. Five minutes later we were called back.

'Would you do it?' they asked.

I had reservations and asked if I could think it over. My answer when it came was 'no'. I was reluctant to take on another time-consuming commitment when I was already party chairman and becoming increasingly busy in my legal practice. Fay Black, a member of the local party executive, must have reported my decision to her brother-in-law, David Steel. He rang me.

'Can I persuade you to change your mind?' he said.

He did and rather against my better judgement. I was formally adopted as the Liberal candidate for East Fife in January 1976. As winter turned to spring, the first rumours of a swirling crisis in the party at Westminster began to reach me. In my role as Scottish party chairman, I received increasing numbers of phone calls from Geoff Tordoff, Liberal Party chairman in England, David Steel and George Mackie, briefing me on the unfolding drama around the private life of Jeremy Thorpe, then our leader. Revelation followed revelation. Thorpe's unravelling had begun, unknown to us all at the time, the previous October on Exmoor when a former male model called Norman Scott, walking a friend's Great Dane, was confronted by Andrew Newton, a former airline pilot, with a gun. Newton shot Rinka the dog and then allegedly pointed the gun at Scott. Newton's trial and conviction in March 1976 gave Norman Scott the stage to claim a relationship with Thorpe, alleging that Thorpe had threatened to kill him if he spoke about the affair. Scott sold letters to the press which he said were from Thorpe. One of them included the now infamous line: 'Bunnies can and will go to France'.

Some time later, Thorpe came to stay with us in Edinburgh. We held a drinks party for him and drove him to his speaking engagement at the Edinburgh University Liberal Club annual dinner. The students delivered him back before midnight and we settled down for a drink before going to bed. The television was on in the background, but we had not realised what the programme was. Elspeth and I froze when we realised it was a play about homosexuality. Thorpe had tuned in to it too, and the next half an hour was rather uncomfortable.

On the day of Thorpe's resignation as leader on 9 May 1976, David Steel, who was chief whip, rang me as Scottish party chairman to warn me. He said, 'I think you ought to know – Thorpe is resigning in half an hour.' I was about to begin a contentious consultation with legal clients and foolishly rang Radio Forth, the local radio station in Edinburgh, to give an embargoed statement on Thorpe's departure to be broadcast once the news had broken. In my naïveté I hadn't realised that an embargo in such circumstances was worthless. I had given the radio station an exclusive which, fast as sound, travelled the airwaves of Britain. The chairman of the party in England, a dentist, was in his surgery grappling with a patient's teeth when he heard my voice on the radio telling the world about Thorpe's resignation. David Steel rang me later to deliver a mild reproof. I was expecting something fiercer.

It would be another three years before the party could consign the Thorpe affair to history. In 1977 Andrew Newton was released from prison and claimed he had been hired with a £5,000 contract to kill Norman Scott. Thorpe and three others were charged in 1978 with conspiracy to murder. The trial was scheduled to begin a week after the 1979 general election. Thorpe lost his seat. He and his co-accused were found not guilty after a thirty-one-day trial, every cough and splutter of which filled the newspapers. It was a dark period for the Liberal Party, relieved only by the election of David Steel as leader to replace Thorpe.

Two years before the Thorpe affair's courtroom dénouement I had resigned as Scottish party chairman to concentrate on building the Liberal base in East Fife and also on my legal career. Ironically, I left the party's finances in the black just at a time when mine were going fast into the red.

In 1977 I had virtually given up private legal practice to become a crown prosecutor or advocate-depute. It was a routine career move for any Scottish advocate aspiring to become a judge. It was expected of you, but the expectation came at a price. I became salaried for the first time in my career, and the salary was considerably less than I had been earning in private practice. We had already moved flats to release capital to finance a little farmhouse near Port of Menteith, in south-west Perthshire, close to where Elspeth's parents had moved. Now we had to downsize again to pay off my growing overdraft. We bought a small flat in Candlemaker Row, a street in Edinburgh's Old Town, five minutes' walk from the High Court.

What were my ambitions as my fortieth birthday approached? I wanted to become a judge, just as my father always wished, rather than an MP. I was a lawyer first, politician second. The general elections in 1979 and 1983 did little to dissuade me from this view even though I increased the Liberal vote in my new constituency substantially, reducing the Tory majority to around 2,000 by 1983.

East Fife, or North-East Fife as it became for the 1983 election, had a recent history of strong Tory allegiance and a distant, though celebrated, one of liberalism. It was the seat of the last Liberal Prime Minister, Herbert Henry Asquith, who held it from 1886 to 1918. Liberals continued to win it more often than not during the next forty years but then lost their grip on it. Sir John Gilmour, a Conservative, won it in a 1961 by-election (when the Labour candidate was a young Glasgow University student by the name of John Smith) and held it for the next eighteen years. John Gilmour's retirement from politics for the 1979 election gave the Liberals an opportunity to build up a sizeable vote again. The change in Conservative candidate coincided with the Scottish National Party falling out with the strong local candidate it fielded in 1974 and the backwash from the lost devolution referendum in Scotland on 1 March, two months before the general election. Could the Liberals come through the middle between a new (and weaker) Conservative and a new (and weaker) Nationalist? The *Dundee Courier* seemed to think so. 'A Conservative stronghold for many years, East Fife, with the retiral of Sir John Gilmour, might now be considered to be approaching the status of a marginal.'

For one mad moment (there always is one) in the campaign we thought we could win it. We couldn't. I came second, doubling the Liberal vote to 10,762. Barry Henderson, the Conservative, also increased the Tory vote on the back of Margaret Thatcher's first election triumph. His majority was 9,355.

Mad moments apart, I always thought it would take two elections. Now I knew it would. In my speech at the count I said, 'I intend to seek reselection as the prospective candidate,' committing myself to the constituency for the next five years.

We packed up our bags in the castle that had been our temporary home for the campaign and went back to Edinburgh. (The castle was owned by Angus Grossart, founder of the Scottish merchant bank Noble Grossart and a contemporary of mine at Glasgow University. Our grand lodgings had given rise to a campaign joke about 'the radicals living in the castle'.) Four years later, the next time we fought a general election, the political context would be substantially changed in my favour. Would it be changed enough?

The emergence of the Social Democratic Party on 26 March 1981 brought with it the thrilling possibility of a left of centre alliance challenging credibly for government. The SDP was formed by the defection of twelve MPs from Michael Foot's unhappy Labour Party. The defectors were led by the so-called 'Gang of Four', former cabinet ministers Roy Jenkins, David Owen, Shirley Williams and Bill Rodgers. (My old adversary Dickson Mabon from Greenock and Port Glasgow joined them in October 1981.) By June the SDP and the Liberals had issued a joint statement entitled 'A Fresh Start for Britain' setting out areas of policy agreement. By mid-September Scottish Liberals meeting in Glasgow approved the principle of an electoral pact with the SDP.

The *Scotsman* reported my contribution: 'I am fed up with the party forever being second. We have the opportunity to convert a lot of dreary footslogging into genuine and sustained political influence.'

The pace of development was rapid and, for me, an exciting fulfilment of Jo Grimond's vision of a non-doctrinaire, non-socialist, radical party of the centre left.

A few days after the Glasgow gathering, members of the Liberal National Assembly were due to meet in Llandudno, North Wales, to approve an alliance with the SDP. Roy Jenkins and Shirley Williams were to speak at a fringe meeting. As I was packing to go, the telephone rang. It was my mother or my sister, I cannot remember which, telling me my father had died. My conscience told me I should go to my mother in Argyll where my parents had lived since my father's retirement in 1974. But every political fibre in my body yearned for the excitement and drama of Llandudno.

I rang my mother to discuss my dilemma and we agreed I should go to Llandudno. I remember driving as far as Carlisle and pulling into a service station for petrol and waiting there for half an hour as I debated with myself whether I should turn back. I kept on driving south. At Llandudno, I told no one of my father's death apart from George Mackie.

On Wednesday, 16 September the Liberal Assembly backed an electoral alliance with the SDP by 1,600 votes to 112. I remember well the assembly's strong and intoxicating revivalist atmosphere. I left Llandudno in the middle of that night to drive to Manchester to catch an early morning flight to Glasgow and my father's funeral service. Elspeth picked me up from the airport to drive me to Cumlodden in Argyll, near Inveraray Castle. I walked down the aisle of the little church there holding my mother's hand. After the service we drove to Cardross where my father's body was to be cremated. Elspeth's parents were supposed to join us but they went in error to the crematorium at

Clydebank and stood at the back of the chapel until her mother suddenly realised they were at the wrong funeral. Then, Elspeth drove me to the airport to catch my return flight to Manchester and Llandudno. I arrived back after my day trip to my father's funeral to hear David Steel capture the conference mood of the moment with a closing speech that would come back to haunt him.

'I have the good fortune to be the first Liberal leader for over half a century,' he said, 'who is able to say at the end of our annual assembly: "Go back to your constituencies and prepare for government."'

I rang my mother on my return and wondered aloud whether I might have a look through my father's fishing equipment to pick something as a reminder of him. He had enough equipment to stock a shop. She said, 'Oh, there's a chap in the village we're quite friendly with and I just told him to come and take it all away.'

Despite the enthusiasm at Llandudno, the electoral alliance with the SDP suffered considerable birth pains. Deciding which party's candidate should fight in which seat was always going to be contentious and so it proved. An SDP branch had formed in my constituency, the newly named and redrawn North-East Fife, and insisted it had a better chance of winning the seat than the Liberals. The local SDP activists suggested I make way for their candidate. I fought back successfully by lobbying the leaderships of both parties. (The SDP leaders liked me because I backed the Alliance and because I did not belong to the 'beard and sandals' wing of the Liberal Party.)

I went into the 1983 general election campaign with a strong feeling I could win. Our canvassers reported enthusiasm for the Alliance cause. As many as 400 people turned out for my adoption meeting, and we were never short of campaign helpers. With a week to go, we felt the tide was with us. Then, suddenly, it turned Thatcher's way and its ripples lapped against North-

East Fife. The mood on the doorstep and at our public meetings subtly changed. The questions became more sceptical. The doorstep reaction to us was more suspicious. I went to the count on election night with a sense of foreboding. Barry Henderson, the Conservative, won by 2,185 votes. I had slashed his majority by 7,000 votes, but I had lost.

Hardly any of Henderson's supporters stayed to cheer their victory. I felt deep disappointment. When it came to my turn to address my supporters, I didn't repeat what I'd said four years earlier: that I would seek the candidacy again. It was a deliberate omission. I wanted to go home and consider my next move. I had become a QC the year before. Why was I wasting so much time and effort at politics when my ambition was still to become a judge? I wondered whether I should withdraw from North-East Fife.

The decision was nearly made for me. A group in the constituency party favoured a change of candidate. Their nominee was Derek Barrie, the hard-working Liberal Chair of North-East Fife District Council. My comment back in 1979 that it would take two elections to wrest the seat from the Conservatives came back to bite me. My detractors said it showed I never intended to fight more than two elections. The atmosphere in the constituency party suddenly changed, I thought for the worse. Did I really want to fight for the nomination?

My uncertainty encouraged Derek Barrie's supporters to rush the adoption meeting. They hoped to take advantage of my indecision. At 5 p.m. on the evening of the adoption meeting I rang the local party chairman to withdraw my nomination. My QC's practice had taken a lucrative departure into large-scale planning inquiries. I was often away for weeks at a time, and the preparation and work involved were enormous. How could I do my clients justice and nurture a constituency?

I had tried to ride two horses, the law and politics, for years. I thought I could do so no longer.

The adoption meeting began without me. When the members were told I had withdrawn from the contest, one of the most respected members, Alec Russell, immediately protested and insisted the meeting be postponed to give me an opportunity to change my mind. A majority of other members agreed. David Steel and George Mackie then leaned on me to stand again.

They said, 'Only you can win this seat because you can take the soft Tory vote.'

I was susceptible to persuasion despite the reservations I had about balancing politics with my legal practice. A bit of me felt, to use John Smith's famous phrase about Scottish devolution, that North-East Fife was my 'unfinished business'. At the reconvened adoption meeting in Bell Baxter School, Cupar, I agreed to be nominated. I won it with 75 per cent of first preferences. Even my supporters were surprised at the margin of my victory.

Despite the support for me in the constituency I had one more wobble before the general election in June 1987. David Steel put me forward in 1986 for a CBE 'for political and public service' in the next New Year Honours List. I was concerned. If I accepted it, wouldn't I have a moral obligation to fight the seat? My legal practice was now going so well I wondered whether I could afford to be an MP. I was QC of first choice in Scotland for George Wimpey, the house builders, and for Argyll Foods which was then pursuing an aggressive expansion of its Safeway super-market chain. I acted for Livingston New Town Development Corporation and other local authorities. I was in demand as one of the few QCs with specialist knowledge of liquor licensing. (I had been a member of the Clayson Committee, which led to the liberalising Licensing (Scotland) Act in 1976.) I told David I was having second thoughts about North-East Fife. An MP's salary was then £18,500 a year. I said to him, 'My mortgage will take a third of it. I'll give Elspeth another third of it. How the hell do I live in London during the week on the remainder?'

The crisis came to a head at a one-day Liberal conference at Candleriggs in Glasgow. David and George Mackie, who was now president of the Scottish Liberals, ushered me aside. The only private place we could find to talk was the janitor's room among the brushes and the floor-cleaning equipment.

I told them, 'I'm not sure I can do this. I can't afford it.'

I learned later that David went home to Cherrydene, his home in Ettrick Bridge in the Borders, and told Judy, 'This is one of the most depressing days of my life. Ming says he doesn't want to stand.'

In the end I recanted, partly because of a sense of duty towards the party and constituency but also because David offered me a deal: if I stood in the general election I could do all the legal work I wanted if I became an MP. I took him at his word.

I rang my mother before the publication of the New Year Honours List at about 11 p.m. to let her know about my CBE. I asked her to tell nobody but she was so proud that she spent the next hour ringing her friends, I discovered later. She died a week after the public announcement. A message was brought to me at a planning inquiry where I was representing a company that wanted to open an amusement arcade in the centre of Glasgow. A group of elderly ladies with string shopping bags were there protesting that prostitution, gambling, vandalism and every other urban ill known to man would follow in the wake of the amusement centre. They looked disapprovingly at me, a smart-alec lawyer from Edinburgh in a black jacket and striped trousers, but when they heard the case was being adjourned because of my mother's death their attitude softened. 'Ach, son,' 'Puir soul,' 'It's a terrible thing,' they cooed in sudden and genuine sympathy.

The funeral and cremation services were an echo of my father's six years before. The house in Argyll was sold and I spent some of the small amount of money I inherited on something tangible to remember my mother by. I bought a painting by an up-and-coming Scottish artist called Hugh Buchanan whose work now sells in London for many times more than it did in 1987. The picture hangs at home and every time I pass it I think of her.

I went into the 1987 general election campaign knowing it would be my last if I lost for a third time. My consolation prize, I understood, could be a seat in the House of Lords to fill an embarrassing gap on the Liberal benches. The party had no Scottish lawyer among its peers. When Scottish bills with a strong legal content came before the Lords they had to be handled by non-lawyers or, worse still, by English lawyers. I cannot remember how I knew about my possible elevation to the peerage. It was never expressed explicitly. These things never are. Nor was it guaranteed. Our early soundings in the constituency made it seem an unnecessary contingency.

By now Scotland was turning strongly against Thatcher and the Tories. There were campaigns for a 'Tory-Free Scotland' and, coincidentally, the once strong Conservative organisation in North-East Fife had begun to crumble. The Tory agent was head-hunted away to a safer seat in Norfolk. Everything seemed set, at last, for my entry into the House of Commons but I had not foreseen what would happen next.

One day in May, just a month before the election, I received a telephone call in the court buildings in Edinburgh from a *Daily Express* journalist I knew slightly. He said, 'I think I ought to tell you that everyone's talking about a story which the *News of the World* is running on Sunday. It's going to say David Steel and your wife are having an affair.'

I remember repeating like a mantra, 'Thank you, thank you, thank you,' and putting the phone down. I rang Elspeth, who by then was a volunteer worker in party HQ in Edinburgh, and said, 'For God's sake go to ground.'

Then, frantically, I tried to ring David. When I tracked him down he said he had been taken aside at a press conference and questioned about Elspeth. Later that day a woman reporter caught me at home. I came to the door and in my naïveté thought nothing of the tweed overcoat she was wearing even though it was a warm early summer's evening. I presume now her coat concealed a microphone and tape recorder.

I was polite to her. I said, 'Gosh, it must be a nuisance for you being here this evening and not at the Thatcher rally at the Scottish Tory Party conference in Perth.' It was the beginning of a media storm which I had never experienced before. The following morning, a Saturday, the *Daily Star* published a single column on page two under the heading: 'David Steel: Agent Speaks Out'. The *Star* tried the old journalist's trick of running the story as a denial in the hope it would give it some measure of legal protection.

The story began: 'Liberal leader David Steel's agent issued a statement last night denying allegations that Mr Steel had had an affair with the wife of a leading Scottish Liberal.' The story was only five paragraphs long and ended with a dismissive quote from me: 'I have never heard of anything so preposterous in my life.'

Reporter after reporter came to our door in the *Star*'s wake. That evening the woman reporter with the tweed coat turned up with a ferret of a man wearing a blazer and white-grey nylon trousers. I made the same denials as the day before.

We waited for Sunday and the *News of the World* with mounting alarm. At breakfast-time I walked to the nearby paper shop to buy it. There were three so-called articles making allegations about politicians: Roy Hattersley living with someone called Maggie Pearlstine (she is now my literary agent and Roy's partner); Peter Mandelson living with a male friend; and the allegation about Elspeth and David.

There were lots of phone calls of support from friends. Margo MacDonald of the Scottish National Party rang to say, 'If you need a safe house come here.' It was typical of her generosity of spirit. Hugh Morton, my old devil-master, also rang. We went to his home for a cup of tea. The television news was on in the background when we arrived. Nicholas Witchell was reading it and there were clips of Bryan Gould, who was running Labour's election campaign, and of Norman Tebbit both deploring the election's descent into dirty tricks scandal reporting. I remember Witchell saying that David Steel had denied allegations involving a woman called Elspeth Campbell from Edinburgh. Elspeth became tearful when she heard it and we went back home. It was a very bruising encounter for her.

The media storm blew over almost as quickly as it had started. David's lawyer, now Lord Phillips of Sudbury, had spent all Sunday warning off other papers. 'We're issuing a writ tomorrow. Stay away from the story or you'll be added to the writ,' he warned editors. It worked. The *Star* printed an instant apology on page two of its Monday edition. The apology was three paragraphs longer than the original story. 'We intended to help Mr Steel stop the lies. We also wanted to inform the public that a smear campaign had been launched,' it said disingenuously. 'We inadvertently repeated an allegation about Mr Steel's private life in our genuine attempt to explain to readers why Mr Steel was issuing his denial statement. We apologise to Mr Steel and his wife and Mr and Mrs Menzies Campbell for our error.'

By the end of the week the *Star* had also agreed to pay 'substantial' damages. Peter Bowsher, QC for David and Elspeth, said the *Daily Star*'s editor and publishers accepted 'there was not a word of truth in this disgraceful rumour upon Mr Steel and Mrs Campbell, each of whom is very happily married'.

The *News of the World* played a game of brinkmanship. The trial date was fixed for November. The *News of the World* offered a small sum and an inadequate retraction which was rejected. Then Elspeth learned that her father had cancer and had three months to live. He was expected to die in November just when Elspeth would need to be at her strongest under cross-examination by News International lawyers in court. We went to see our QC in this case, Patrick Milmo, and told him we had strong reservations about Elspeth going into court. The *News of the World* blinked first. It settled with David and Elspeth. With David's damages he was able to buy Aikwood, his Borders fortified tower house home. The exact amount of the damages to them both has remained confidential because of the terms of the out-of-court settlement.

Campaigning for the general election began in earnest straight after the stories appeared in the *Star* and the *News of the World*. I was concerned about their impact in North-East Fife. As a public display of unity between the Campbells and the Steels, we asked Judy to come to my adoption meeting. She spoke wonderfully, even making a joke about the allegations. David visited in his battle bus later in the campaign. We made sure the photographers did not get pictures of David and Elspeth campaigning together. As we canvassed the constituency, our hopes of winning it rose. Everywhere we went we found supporters. This time round our optimism did not dissipate with a late Tory revival in the last week.

Elspeth and I went alone to have dinner in the Peat Inn near Cupar on election night. We were nervous but also confident. Before going to the count we dropped in at an election party at the home of Fay Black, David's sister-in-law, in the village of Ceres. One of the first results was Cheltenham. The BBC was forecasting a Liberal win but I could see by the slumped shoulders of the candidate, my old friend Richard Holme, that he knew he had lost. (He later became a life peer and remains a close confidant.) Had the Alliance been too confident in its predictions of a breakthrough? I left the election party to take soundings from our scrutineers at the count. We drove to Cupar with a growing sense of dread. When we pulled up outside County Buildings Iain Smith, my agent and now a member of the

Scottish parliament, came out and told me I had won, predicting the majority to within 100 votes.

I felt relief and elation before my thoughts turned to my victory speech. I had prepared nothing because I thought it bad luck to do so. As we went into the hall I noticed the Tories looking ashen-faced. My supporters were wreathed in smiles. The margin of victory was 1,447 votes, representing a swing of almost 5 per cent to me. After the returning officer had finished reading out the votes, Elspeth and I went to the balcony on the first floor of County Buildings to wave to our cheering supporters filling the street below. A celebratory party followed before I managed to creep off to bed in the early hours of the morning. I had three hours' sleep before I was taken to Dundee in a chauffeur-driven limousine to appear on breakfast TV. My shock at winning was obvious for all to hear. I remember saying, 'I've got a new job. I don't know what the salary is. I don't know if I've got an office and I don't know when I'm supposed to start work.'

Ken Livingston, another new MP appearing on the same programme, had no such novitiate's doubts. He said, 'I know all about the job and exactly what I've got to do.'

After taking Iain Smith for a celebratory lunch in Cupar's best restaurant we returned home happy and exhausted to Edinburgh. The phone rang all evening. One of the callers was David Alton, the Liberal chief whip, inviting me to a meeting of new MPs four days later. David Steel was there to greet us. Afterwards he asked us all to dinner and I remember his face falling when I said, 'I'm sorry, I've got to catch the last flight to Edinburgh. I'm in court tomorrow.'

I was engaged in a big planning inquiry involving a new shopping centre at the western edge of Edinburgh. It had been in my diary for months. I had an outstanding junior, Colin Boyd, now Lord Boyd who became Scotland's Lord Advocate, but I was leading the case. He could not be expected to assume my responsibility. My client, a public authority, was understanding but understandably anxious. For my first weeks as an MP, I shuttled backwards and forwards between London and Edinburgh, between the House of Commons and the public inquiry. Sometimes Elspeth would pick me up from the inquiry at 4 p.m. to take me to the airport. I would fly to Heathrow, go to the Commons, vote that evening, then rush to Euston Station to catch the sleeper back to Edinburgh to attend the inquiry at 10 a.m. the next day. David must have been regretting his deal with me.

7

Coming of age

I rose to make my maiden speech at 9.21 p.m. on Monday, 13 July 1987, in a debate on local government finance. I paid tribute, according to tradition, to my defeated Conservative predecessor in North-East Fife. Barry Henderson was, I said, 'a courteous opponent; generous and gracious in defeat'. I went on to ask the assembled MPs to forgive 'the Liberal benches some small self-indulgence from the realisation that the constituency that returned Mr Asquith for so many years has once more returned a Liberal Member of Parliament.'

The mood among Liberals and our SDP partners in the Alliance was anything but self-indulgent in those early weeks of the parliament. The general election had returned Margaret Thatcher with a working majority of 100. Neil Kinnock, fighting his first election as Labour leader, had reduced her lead but insignificantly. More importantly for me, the Liberals and the SDP in alliance had not only failed to make a breakthrough, they had managed overall to lose one seat in the process. (The fact it was an SDP one did not make it any better.) *The Times*'s post-election analysis could have been written by any of us: 'A movement that rests on the declared intention of 'breaking the mould' must, above all, retain momentum – and this the Alliance has lost. It is further away than ever from replacing Labour as the principal party of opposition. Its leaders face another four or five years in the political desert with little realistic prospect of power after that.'

The Alliance died in the ballot box. What would replace it? The nine months following the election were poisonous. Friends and colleagues fought and fell out as the parties edged towards merger. My election-night elation at winning North-East Fife at the third time of trying soon dissipated. It was replaced by foreboding. The Liberals and the Alliance were so low in the opinion polls that my majority of 1,447, which had sounded miraculous when the returning officer announced it in the County Buildings, Cupar, now seemed slight and vulnerable. My inability to feel secure and settled in my new surroundings was compounded by continuing clashes between my two careers. Even the night of my maiden speech ended with a high-speed dash to Euston Station to catch the sleeper to Edinburgh for a court commitment the following morning. I slept fitfully as the train rattled north. Something had to give. I knew I would have to cut back on the law even though it was so much more reliable than my new political career.

A critical letter from a constituent stung me into action. 'I understand you never go to the House of Commons,' it said, 'because you are too busy doing your legal work.' It wasn't true but it was close enough to the truth.

My growing unease at my frequent absences from parliament was made worse by publication of MPs' voting records from mid-June to the summer recess in July. I had voted in only 40 per cent of the divisions. Once my hang-over, pre-election legal obligations ran their course, I cut back my legal work dramatically (and my income). Clashes between the law and politics still happened occasionally but I bowed to the inevitable. My legal career gave way to my political career, though I didn't regard politics the more important. My long-term ambition remained the same: I still wanted to become a Scottish Supreme Court judge. At times, particularly when the merger negotiations with the SDP seemed hopeless and unbearably fractious, I contemplated standing down after only one parliament as an

MP. What would people think? I knew the answer; but I feared committing for longer than five years to the uncertain prospects of politics if it meant placing in jeopardy the chance of elevation to the Bench.

As my legal commitments diminished so my life took on a new and companionable routine. I would fly to London mid-morning on Monday with other MPs and peers. David Steel would frequently give me a lift from Heathrow to central London. I would return home on Thursday nights, often by sleeper after voting at 10 p.m. in the Commons. The Scottish MPs and peers would gather in the buffet car for a nightcap (in my case, coffee and a biscuit) before going our separate ways for the weekend. If the Commons rose early on Thursday nights, David would drive two or three of us helter-skelter to Heathrow to catch the last flight, the 8.40, to Edinburgh. On Fridays or Saturdays I would hold surgeries in the constituency an hour's drive north of my home in Edinburgh. Sometimes Elspeth and I would stay the night there. We had bought a converted Victorian farm worker's cottage in the village of Gateside, on the north bank of the River Eden and twenty-five miles west of St Andrews. We had driven past it soon after the election and stopped when we saw the 'For Sale' sign outside.

'This'll do,' Elspeth said decisively as we looked it over. It has been our constituency home ever since. We later discovered that my agent Iain Smith's grandfather had been born in it.

By now Elspeth had become my secretary, working from an office in Scottish Liberal headquarters in Clifton Terrace, Edinburgh. 'Give it six months and see how you feel,' I said. She enjoyed it, abandoning with some reluctance her proposal to do a PhD at Stirling University on the Shropshire-born novelist Barbara Pym. (Previously, she had taken an honours degree in English Literature at the Open University, gaining a first. Contrary to popular myth, which I have inadvertently reinforced, she didn't do her dissertation on *Coronation Street*, her favourite television programme. She wrote a single essay on it for a course on popular culture.)

In London, I lodged at the National Liberal Club before becoming a tenant of Teresa Gorman, the Conservative MP, in one of her houses in Lord North Street. It was conveniently close to the House of Commons but politically awkward when we were on opposite sides of an argument in the chamber, as often we were.

My office arrangements were more congenial. I shared with Alex Carlile, now Lord Carlile of Berriew and the independent reviewer of Britain's anti-terrorist laws. Like me, he was a lawyer, a quick-witted QC at the English Bar who took a delight in teasing Paddy Ashdown. Our little office up a spiral staircase had a third tenant – Cyril Smith, the larger-than-life MP for Rochdale. We hardly ever saw him. He came rarely to parliament by this time. I doubt I encountered him in the office more than fifteen times in five years, but when I did he always had pungent opinions to offer.

By the end of the summer recess I had reconciled my legal practice to the demands of my political career. The bigger and unresolved question was whether the Liberals and the SDP could reconcile themselves to a merger. The Liberal Assembly at Harrogate that September proved the first step in a process that would leave most of us bloodied and bruised before the end. We set out to make our small mark on British political history with cheers and applause as the assembly voted by 998 to 21, with 9 abstentions, to open talks with the SDP about merging and forming a new party. In all the euphoria we paid too little attention to a strong undercurrent in the debate that opposed our negotiators making detailed policy commitments for the new party. Three and a half months later the merger almost foundered on the conclusions of the policy group. Then I would see David Steel almost cry with emotion and frustration. It would be momentary. His voice would catch and stop in mid-sentence. A tear would well up in his eye. And, as quick as a flash, he would compose himself.

As we left Harrogate we were filled with optimism, perhaps naïvely. Did we have any choice but to believe in the curative powers of merger? As separate parties we were floundering. Together we might at last fulfil Grimond's doctrine of radical realignment. I hoped so.

I returned to parliament for the autumn session with a sense of purpose assisted by becoming Liberal spokesman for the arts, broadcasting and sport. David had asked me to be spokesman for Scotland but I refused, fearful of becoming typecast by tartan. I explained my concerns at a meeting at David's home at Ettrick Bridge in the Scottish Borders. Archy Kirkwood, then the Liberal MP for Roxburgh and Berwickshire and a near neighbour of David's, was also there. I presented my case for the arts, broadcasting and sport portfolio: I told them I was chairman of the Lyceum Theatre in Edinburgh (although soon to give up); I had just finished a three-year stint on the BBC Broadcasting Council for Scotland; and I was a former Olympic athlete. David conceded after wringing from me a compromise. I would also shadow the two Scottish law officers, the Lord Advocate and the Solicitor General for Scotland. In November, I introduced my first private member's bill outlawing anabolic steroids, used in sport against the rules for building muscle bulk. When I was an athlete I had grown accustomed to seeing my name on the sports pages of the newspapers. Now I was on the news pages. *The Times*, then edited by Charles Wilson, followed my anabolic steroids campaign. I discovered it took more than a populist bill in parliament and some easy publicity to come of age in politics.

If Liberal MPs ended 1987 in hopeful anticipation of merger (mixed with varying degrees of reservation about the prospect of sacrificing too many of the party's historic and distinct traditions), they began 1988 in abject despair. Wednesday, 13 January was the bleakest day. The Jubilee Room at the House of Commons was booked for a big media conference at noon for David Steel and Robert Maclennan, leader of the SDP after David Owen, to announce the merger terms. The night before there had been walk-outs (Michael Meadowcroft of the Liberals in protest at the constitution containing a commitment to NATO) and conflict (over the name of the new party). By 4 a.m. the negotiators had at least agreed a new name for the merged parties, the Social and Liberal Democrats. Eight hours later as the gathering of television, radio and newspaper journalists waited abuzz for the party's triumphal launch, one of Bob Maclennan's aides called Simon Coates addressed them instead.

'The two leaders have not had the chance to consider the final draft of the policy declaration with their parliamentary colleagues, and they wish to do that before this press conference is reconvened at 5 p.m.,' he said.

The postponement happened too late to stop the release of the policy prospectus, a copy of which was already in each of the journalist's hands. What Simon Coates omitted to say was that the Liberal MPs had only seen the proposed joint policy programme that morning and they hadn't liked it. Much of it was electoral suicide: there was even a plan to levy VAT on children's clothes. Liberal MPs had taken collective fright.

Instead of the press conference David and Bob Maclennan, accompanied by the young SDP MP Charles Kennedy, met us at a tense meeting in a Commons committee room. Bob Maclennan was obviously and understandably emotional about the day's disastrous events. We feared he might leave the meeting and declare the merger over to the journalists waiting outside. Simon Hughes and Malcolm Bruce sat between him and the door to prevent him escaping. David took the chair. Nancy Seear, the Liberal leader in the Lords, sat beside him. The meeting ebbed and flowed with our frustrations and anger at the mess we found ourselves in. How could we rescue the situation? Some of the MPs were making suggestions when David blurted out, 'I think I've let you all—' The word 'down' never came. His voice cracked. Nancy Seear held out her hand and placed it comfortingly on his leg. David composed himself and moved on. The moment had passed. I had never seen David cry before or since.

It was my first intimate glimpse of the extraordinary pressures of political leadership. In this room were the leaders of the Liberal and SDP parties and both of them were on the edge of breakdown.

The meeting ended with agreement for the policy talks to be reconvened the following day. Bob Maclennan was sufficiently composed before leaving and trooped off with David to the 5 p.m. media conference in the David Lloyd George Room at the National Liberal Club. Despite the tensions we had to put on a show of unity, though none existed. We stood behind them both at the press conference. What else could we do? The journalists were not fooled. The papers the following day gleefully told how the much-vaunted 'third force' in British politics had turned into the 'third farce'. We cringed.

A week later the merger was back on track after negotiators from the two parties agreed a new document. Effectively, it left policy-making to the machinery of the new party even though the SDP's opening negotiating position had been to avoid policy 'blank cheques'. The papers reported Bob Maclennan leaving a meeting with Liberal MPs 'grim-faced'. He snapped at journalists: 'No comment means no comment. I am not making any comment today.' Bob and Charles Kennedy went to David Owen's house in Limehouse in a final attempt to persuade him to join the new party. They were inside for only five minutes. Owen rejected their visit as a 'set up' and described the policy document as 'a fudge'. David Owen was determined to go his own way with what he regarded as the real SDP but the momentum for merger was unstoppable. In a few days a special Liberal Assembly would meet in Blackpool and the SDP conference in Sheffield a week later to ratify the merger process. I travelled with David by train from London to snowy Blackpool to give him moral support. It was clear to me he would resign immediately if the assembly failed to vote for merger. Elspeth was waiting for us at Blackpool Station. She kissed us both with photographers all around us. I remember my nervousness at one of the papers printing a picture of Elspeth kissing David. The scalding by the *Star* and the *News of the World* the previous summer had not been forgotten. David needed a two-thirds majority approving the merger motion. In the event the assembly voted for it by 2,099 votes to 385, with 23 abstentions. I was pleased by the vote but frustrated I had been unable to speak. The debate lasted five hours. MPs had been given speaking slots throughout it, but I had not. Clearly, I wasn't thought to be important enough.

My pique disappeared as I drove north with Elspeth, David, Judy and their son Rory. The mood in the car was good. David was buoyed up by the result. Even though I knew the strain he was under, I assumed he would stand as leader of the new party. I hoped he would. We took David and Judy to Ettrick Bridge and stayed for a celebratory dinner. Judy pulled a large leg of lamb out of the freezer and David opened some very good red wine. The following weekend, the SDP conference voted for merger.

The final hurdle before merger was a ballot of both parties' members. The results were announced to champagne at the beginning of March. The Liberals voted for it by more than seven to one; the Social Democrats by almost two to one. The turnout was less impressive. Only 52.2 per cent of Liberals and 55.5 per cent of Social Democrats bothered to vote. The new party was born on 3 March 1988. The joke was that the new Social and Liberal Democrats had a party but no leader: the Owenite rump of the SDP a leader and no party. The May 1988 council elections in England were the first chance to gauge how damaging the long merger process had been. The SLD, the new abbreviation for the party, lost 63 seats of the 3,500 it held. Labour gained 107. Would this be our low point? The new party's opinion poll ratings were so bad everyone's attention turned to the leadership election, hoping it would provide a consequential burst of good publicity.

A week after the council elections David let it be known that he would not be a candidate. At a meeting of the party's MPs on the rules of the coming contest, David said he would be making an announcement to his constituency party executive the following evening. We knew what it would be since leadership candidates were forbidden from declaring themselves before the beginning of June. He would not be standing. I sympathised with his decision having seen at close quarters the strain he was under. He had fought the party for so long over so many issues: unilateralism, the Lib-Lab pact in 1977–8, the merger with the SDP. He held the party together during and after the Thorpe affair. He was exhausted by leadership.

With David out of the contest, the leadership election was between Paddy Ashdown and Alan Beith, the brightest mind by far in the parliamentary party. My colleagues assumed I would support Beith. Alex Carlile and Cyril Smith, with whom I shared my Commons office, declared for Beith. David Alton, in the next-door office, declared for Beith. Our two offices were a Beith enclave, except for me. I backed Ashdown because I thought the party needed to take risks. Ashdown, an ebullient, energetic former unit commander in the Royal Marines Special Boat Section, was nothing if not a risk-taker. How could I tell Alan Beith whom I both liked and respected?

I thought he would be embarrassed if I told him to his face. Instead I wrote him a letter telling him of my support for Ashdown and left it in his House of Commons pigeon hole. Alan regarded my behaviour as less than frank. He was right. My commitment to Ashdown was very public. I campaigned with him when he visited Scotland, chairing a press conference for him at the North British Hotel in Glasgow, and accompanying him to my old student haunt, Glasgow University Union, where he made a speech. My lack of candour with Alan made for a difficult relationship between us which was later happily repaired.

When the leadership election result was announced at the end of July, Ashdown emerged the winner by 41,401 votes to 16,202. Alan Beith was disappointed, as Paddy's first volume of diaries, published in 2000, records. What the diaries underplay is how acutely bad the party's financial affairs were. The day after his election the party's chief executive told Paddy there was hardly enough money to pay the wages on Friday. Paddy had to hit the phones to ask supporters for loans, and managed to get the money to tide us over.

Later he called me in and asked me to be the party's Treasury spokesman. I tried to turn it down because it was unfamiliar territory for me. 'I'm way out of my depth,' I thought. Paddy sent Richard Holme, successively a close adviser of David Steel's and of Paddy's, to see me. He persuaded me to change my mind.

Soon after, Elspeth and I flew to Italy for a holiday on the banks of Lake Como. Every day, at 2 p.m., I would walk through the hotel gardens to a café and newspaper seller in the village of Bellagio to buy the *Financial Times*. I spent my holiday trying desperately to acquire a rudimentary knowledge of my new economics brief. When I returned to Britain, Paddy rang me.

'Of course I want you to be Treasury spokesman but Alan Beith wants the Treasury. The only thing he'll take is Treasury.'

'Well,' I replied. 'If it's necessary to get him on board, I'll give up Treasury.'

'What else would you do?' asked Paddy.

'Defence,' I offered.

The possible obstacle was Jim Wallace, the MP for Orkney and Shetland. He combined chief whip with defence, which Paddy persuaded him to give up to me. My new portfolio meant I would be thrust into one of the most contentious issues exercising the new party's members. Should the merged party, like the Liberals before it, be sympathetic to unilateralism or should it, as I believed, be multilateralist? The SDP strain within the new party possibly tipped the balance in favour of the multilateralists. But no one was sure. It was an issue of such critical importance that Paddy became anxious on the eve of the vote at conference the following year. I soon learned how critical an issue it was for me too: my political coming of age depended on the outcome.

I started my defence spokesmanship catastrophically. By tradition, soon after parliament returned from the long summer recess, there was a two-day debate on the defence white paper. It was my first big debate in the defence portfolio but I contrived to miss the start of it, or rather a chapter of accidents contrived to make me miss the start of it.

I was in court in Paisley. My case was supposed to start at 9 a.m. I was assured it would do so. I expected it to take half an hour and be on my way to nearby Glasgow Airport soon after 9.30 at the latest in plenty of time for the debate. But everything that could go wrong did go wrong and I made it to the airport after 3 p.m. to find the shuttle to London running late. When, eventually, I arrived in the Commons the debate was well under way. I was so embarrassed I wrote letters of apology to the Speaker and to George Younger, the Defence Secretary. Both of them understood but it taught me a lesson.

In my defence role, I became a member of a Lib Dem (the party became plain Liberal Democrat in autumn 1989) working group dealing with the touchstone issue of unilateralism v multilateralism in the Gorbachev era. Paddy had led the charge against the deployment of Cruise missiles during the first half of the 1980s and again at the Eastbourne conference in 1986 which gave the party the wrong policy for the 1987 general election. Now, he wanted it reversed. The rival camps in the party appeared finely balanced. Many members of the old Liberal

Party harked back to unilateralism as a mark of their political purity. The new SDP strain wanted rid of it because it was an electoral liability. The two sides were characterised as the 'brown sandals' and the 'black brogues'.

The working party was chaired by Lord (Mark) Bonham Carter, grandson of Asquith. Laura, his sister and Jo Grimond's wife, was also a member. They were trying to steer the group towards multilateralism but it was always going to be a close-run thing. Meeting by meeting the multilateralists gradually gained the upper hand until the working party agreed to abandon unilateralism as party policy. I remember the final meeting of the group in a Commons committee room before its recommendations went to the Brighton conference in September 1989. I was trying to buttress multilateralism as much as I could to make it stick at conference when I said, 'Well, how the hell am I going to defend that on TV to Robin Day?' and one of the group's members retorted tartly, 'That's what you get paid for. You'll just have to.'

The day before the debate, Paddy warned the party's delegates that a vote for multilateralism was 'as crucial as any in our history.' He said, 'Our party's credibility in this area rests on us not only being sincere about disarmament, but also serious about defence.' This was my first big test in the party. On the eve of the debate Geoff (now Lord) Tordoff canvassed the bars and reported back to Paddy: 'It's difficult. We may lose.' Paddy became even more anxious. He telephoned Jim Wallace, the chief whip, in his hotel room in the middle of the night. In a remarkable foretaste of my subsequent leadership, he announced he would speak in the debate because it was too important to be left to me.

Jim woke me at 7 a.m. 'Paddy wants to speak,' he said.

'Well, if he speaks I won't. Either I'm defence spokesman or I'm not,' I said.

I told Jim that Paddy's tactics were misguided. If he spoke and the unilateralists won his leadership would be undermined, possibly fatally. If I spoke and they won, it would not be. It was better that he left it to me. Jim went to see Ashdown to explain my opposition to his plan. I made no effort to contact him because I knew how determined and persuasive Paddy could be. I put the final touches to my speech, not knowing if I would deliver it, and went to the conference hall for the start of the debate.

Paddy was seated on the platform. Would he make an un-scheduled speech and risk weakening his leadership? I didn't know the answer. Mark Bonham Carter opened the debate. He was calm and rational. Reformist leaders in the east like Gorbachev, he said, didn't want a weak west, the dissolution of NATO or unilateral disarmament. Paddy stayed in his seat as I walked to the podium to wind it up. I felt his eyes on my back. Arms reduction, I said, was best achieved by the hard-headed rather than the warm-hearted. 'We now know the conditions exist in which multilateral negotiations can and will be successful.' The vote was overwhelmingly in favour of retaining the Trident missile system. The 'black brogues' were jubilant. Paddy rushed over to me and pumped my hand in congratulation. Mark Bonham Carter and Laura Grimond hugged me. Roy Jenkins heaped praise on me. My face was all over the evening news bulletins. *The Times* reported the following morning: 'Mr Ashdown had hazarded his authority as leader on the outcome of the vote, which came after a powerful speech from Mr Menzies Campbell, the party's defence spokesman, which some delegates were saying stamped him as potential leadership material.'

Jim Wallace told me later that Paddy went on to the platform with a prepared speech in his pocket. Jim had deliberately sat beside him. 'If he made any attempt to get up and speak I was going to grab him and hold him in his seat,' Jim told me.

My next big political test came when Saddam Hussein invaded Kuwait on 2 August 1990. I was on holiday in Italy when I switched on my radio and tuned in halfway through a report on the unfolding crisis. By the time I returned to Britain, Paddy and David Steel, now Lib Dem foreign affairs spokesman, had swung in behind the government for the expulsion of Iraqi forces from Kuwait. Our party conference was the following month in Blackpool. The plan was that David would introduce a motion supporting military action to evict Iraq and I would wind it up. Despite my success at conference the year before, Paddy again was anxious about the outcome. He persuaded Roy Jenkins to speak in the debate. Belt and braces, he said. I felt slighted and made my views known. The conference voted 6–1 for a motion that gave the party freedom to support military action even if China, Cuba or Yemen exercised their veto to prevent UN support for it. One paper the next day said my speech and the vote 'marked the consolidation as a conference star of the defence spokesman, Menzies Campbell'.

In November, in the middle of the Tory leadership election campaign following Margaret Thatcher's departure, I went with the Defence Select Committee and other senior politicians from the Lords and Commons, including Francis Pym, former Foreign Secretary, to Saudi Arabia and Bahrain to visit our troops in the desert and to talk to ministers in both countries. We had our own RAF VC10 to fly us there. On the last night, as we all slept in our hotel in Riyadh, the Saudi capital, the number two in the British Embassy came round our rooms banging on the doors. It was 2.30 a.m. 'Please get dressed as fast as you can. The king will see you now.'

We tumbled into our clothes, suits and ties, and went downstairs to find a fleet of chauffeur-driven Mercedes outside. There were police outriders front and back.

The convoy swept away into the black of night, eventually stopping at one of the royal palaces. We were ushered into a room almost filled by a rectangular table surrounded by ornate golden chairs. A number of princes were already there. Suddenly King Fahd came in and we all sat. Without introduction he

1. Aged 3, a 'Polyfoto' taken at a department store called Lewis's Polytechnic in Argyle Street, Glasgow.

2. My mother. She was a great weekend walker before she met my father: history doesn't relate what she was doing at the wheel of this rather racy sports car.

3. Early athletics honours: the author, back row, third from left, with members of the Hillhead High School athletics team, 1958.

4. 'Ming on the wing' – with the Edinburgh Wanderers team who were runner's-up at the Middlesex Sevens tournament in 1969. I'm standing next to the referee and the Scottish rugby international, John Douglas, is standing next to the touch judge.

5. On the cinder track at Glasgow University's training ground.

6. Preparing for the Olympic relay with Ron Jones: split second timing is
everything at the handover – just like politics!

7. Winning the AAA 200 yards championship in 1964 at the White City stadium in a new championship best time, one of the performances that led to my selection for the Olympic team.

8. With Olympic gold medal winner Mary Rand in 1964, modeling our specially designed Olympic team uniforms. It's hard to understand from this picture how the Daily Mail could have described me as the 'James Bond of British Athletics'!

9. Back from the Olympics, a little older, a little wiser, and wearing a stetson I had swapped with the American 400 metres runner Ulis Williams.

10. 1965, President of the Glasgow University Union.

11. The beginning of a proper career at last as a Junior Counsel.

12. Wedding Day, 12 september 1970.

13. The seventeen Liberal MPs elected in 1987 outside the House of Commons. From the left, Cyril Smith, Sir Russell Johnston, Alex Carlile, Alan Beith, Paddy Ashdown, Ray Mitchy, Archy Kirkwood, David Steel, the author, Ronald Fern, David Alton, Malcom Bruce, Simon Hughes, Jim Wallace, Richard Livsey, Geraint Howells and Matthew Taylor.

14. With Liz Ribbans, Paddy Ashdown, Archy Kirkwood, George Wintle and Bria Linch on a sponsored run - 'Democrats against Apartheid' – at the party conferenc in Brighton, September 1989.

began a forty-five-minute speech, with our interpreter providing an English translation as he went. The king finished as abruptly as he had begun and left the room. We waited, wondering what would happen next when he reappeared. Protocol required replies from each of the political parties represented. Michael Mates, chairman of the Defence Select Committee, spoke for the Conservatives; Martin O'Neill, shadow Defence Secretary, for Labour; and me for the Liberal Democrats. I went last but remembered to describe the king as 'the keeper of the two holy places', a reference to Mecca and Medina and his preferred form of address. I had passed my diplomatic baptism of fire at 3 a.m. in a Saudi palace.

Paddy proved himself to be a skilled war leader for the Lib Dems. We had our own war cabinet: himself, David, me, Admiral Sir James Eberle, former Fleet commander-in-chief, Major-General Sir Jeremy Moore, commander of land forces in the Falklands, Major-General Julian Thompson, who led 3 Commando Brigade in the same conflict, and Sir John Moberly, a former British ambassador to Iraq. We met once, sometimes twice, a week in Paddy's office. It was a lesson to me in how to manage a party at a time of national crisis.

If winning the multilateral argument at the 1989 conference was when I came of age in the party, the first Iraq war was when I came of age at Westminster. I was arguing the party's standpoint in the Commons and on television and radio. It was a crash course in political crisis management.

By degrees I moved more and more into Paddy's inner circle. He shared confidences with me and seemed to value my advice. Elspeth and I stayed with Paddy and Jane at their home in Somerset and they stayed with us in Edinburgh. Elspeth was always impressed by his habit of hand-writing a thank-you letter which arrived without fail within three days of his visit.

As we approached the general election in 1992 I looked back on my first five years in parliament with a sense of achievement.

Would the next five years be better for me politically than the last five? Liberal Democrat hopes rested on Labour beating John Major's Conservatives but without a working majority. We prepared ourselves to lever whatever influence we could from holding the balance of power. It was a strategy we came to regret.

John Major surprised everyone by winning with a majority of twenty-one, while Neil Kinnock lost his second election and the leadership of his party.

Elspeth and I again had dinner at the Peat Inn on election night. I can't remember what we ate. We left earlier for the count than we intended. Iain Smith, my agent, met us outside. 'You're back,' he said, 'with a majority of 3,500.' He had overestimated by 192 votes. I was re-elected in North-East Fife with a majority of 3,308, an increase of 1,861. I was relieved. My Conservative opponent Mary Scanlon, who later became a member of the Scottish parliament, had run a personal campaign against me, and Major's stubborn revival nationally in the polls had left me wondering whether the Tories might even unseat me. Mrs Scanlon was so dismayed at losing she couldn't bring herself to congratulate me after the results were announced.

It was a disappointing night for Liberal Democrats. We returned to parliament with two fewer seats and no prospect of holding the balance of power. I had been put on standby to fly to London the day after the election to join up with Bob Maclennan, Alan Beith and Richard Holme to negotiate if necessary a power-sharing deal with Labour. Our opposite numbers would have been John Smith, Donald Dewar and Peter Mandelson. Richard Holme rang me at about 3 a.m. 'You can stay in Scotland,' he said.

Instead of flying to London, I celebrated my victory with Elspeth.

8

My friend John

By chance I met John Smith on the plane down to London four days after the election. We sat together with an empty seat between us and spent the next hour and a half gossiping about the result. We shared our gloom at its outcome and our views on the weekend speculation about Neil Kinnock's prospects of holding on to the Labour leadership.

Would John stand if Kinnock resigned quickly as expected? (In fact, Kinnock resigned later that day.) John avoided answering my question but it became clear to me he would stand as our conversation carried on through the flight. Any lingering doubt about his intentions disappeared when we landed at Heathrow. I wandered off to catch the underground into central London as usual; John was swept up by minders and put into the back seat of a car. His leadership campaign managers were already looking after their man. He launched his candidacy two days later.

From then on, chance encounters between us grew fewer: the commitments of campaigning and then, after July, of leadership packed his diary. We ran into each other occasionally in the House of Commons tearoom and on the plane to and from Scotland. Our friendship had often been like this since leaving university.

Although we worked together at the Scottish Bar as young advocates, John's presence there became irregular after his election to parliament in 1970. I followed him seventeen years later. During all those years when he was in parliament and I was not, we met in a formal political capacity on a number of occasions. In 1977, during the Lib-Lab pact, I went to the Cabinet Office in London to help negotiate the bill for Scottish devolution for the abortive, post-legislative referendum in 1979. I was Scottish Liberal chairman at the time. Sitting at the other end of the table from me and the small Liberal team from Scotland, led by Russell Johnston, was John Smith, then minister of state at the Privy Council Office and the minister effectively in charge of devolution legislation. John was very businesslike and formal.

If politics kept us distant, domestic geography kept us close. We maintained our friendship in Edinburgh where our homes were never more than two miles apart. Elizabeth, John's wife, would organise large and generous parties in their comfortable house in Morningside, a district famous for its staid reputation. John was anything but staid. He could, and often did, start a party in an empty room, as Donald Dewar joked two years later at his funeral.

We also met at dinners and events in Edinburgh, particularly in August at Festival time. Elspeth and I would sometimes end the evening with John and Elizabeth talking and gossiping politics. John would berate me sternly. 'What the fuck are you doing in the Liberal Party? Why aren't you in the Labour Party like your mother and father?' he would say in a mock serious attempt at converting me. (In fact my mother followed me into the Liberal Party towards the end of her life after a brief post-Labour flirtation with Scottish Nationalism. One of my aunts remembers her putting up SNP posters in Scotstoun and shocking her mother and the neighbours.)

I would reply to John: 'I'm not in the Labour Party because I'm a Liberal.'

The expression on John's face let me know my answer was woefully insufficient and that he expected better from me.

We would also meet in the Highlands: John joined a small group of advocate friends with whom I went hill-walking occasionally. I remember climbing Ben Lomond with him, Lord McCluskey, the life peer and Scottish judge, and Ranald Mac-Lean QC, a founding member of the group and later one of the Scottish judges at the Lockerbie bombing trial.

Our next venture in the Highlands was more adventurous. We walked the Lairig Ghru, an old cattle drovers' trail through the Cairngorm Mountains. Half of us started at one end of the twenty-three-mile walk and half of us at the other. When we met in the middle we swapped car keys so we could drive to join up the next day. Hill-walking became an enthusiasm of John's and, with typical gregariousness, he wanted more and more people to walk with him. By now the group was known as the 'Radical Ramblers'. I thought of the name on the ferry from Ardrossan in Ayrshire to Brodick on the Isle of Arran off the west of Scotland. There were about twenty of us on the walk up Goat Fell, Arran's highest mountain, including Gordon Brown, Murray Elder, Gavin Laird, John and Elizabeth with their three daughters Jane, Catherine and Sarah. I took my stepson James, who, with the energy of youth, practically ran up the mountain. As usual on these outings, the conversation was anti-Tory. On our way back down someone suggested us tackling another hill nearby. Gordon Brown and I were the only ones who didn't want to do it. We carried on down Goat Fell to Brodick. It was my first proper conversation with Brown. We talked about life, politics and sport. He told me about the rugby injury to his eye. I talked to him about athletics and my experience at the Olympics. We were very easy in each other's company. I have liked him ever since.

Enthusiastic as ever, John was one of those who climbed the nearby hill. His love of walking the Highlands transformed him into a Munro-bagger (hills in Scotland of 3,000 feet or higher) after his first heart attack in 1988. It was good, healthy exercise for him and an antidote to the stress and pressure of politics. Sadly, it did not keep him alive for long once he became leader.

My phone rang soon after 8.30 on the morning of 12 May 1994. Alison Suttie, who worked in the Lib Dem whips office and became head of office after my election as leader, said, 'I think you ought to know there's a report on the radio that John Smith has been taken ill.' I went to the House of Commons where shock was etched on the faces of all the Labour MPs I met. Some MPs put their arms round one another when they heard the news confirming John's death. We were all stunned. John had been at a Labour fund-raising event the night before for the European elections in June. He had seemed so well, according to those who were there.

After the party leaders had spoken, I paid a brief and, for me, emotional tribute to John in the Commons before business was adjourned for the day.

> Throughout my adult life, I have had the privilege of calling John Smith my friend. We were students together at Glasgow University, we were struggling advocates at the Scottish Bar and we even climbed a few Scottish mountains together.
>
> It seemed to John Smith's friends that he never failed at anything to which he set his hand. He could easily have reached the top of the legal profession. He led his party and he might well have led the nation. He was a devoted father and husband, and he derived great strength from the warm and loving embrace of his family.
>
> In his recreation, he was a fierce, if not particularly elegant, tennis player, but it was in the Scottish mountains that he found a great deal of satisfaction. He used them to restore him after the trials and tribulations of his life. It is typical of John Smith that he was well on the way to climbing all the Munros in Scotland . . .

He had an overwhelming sense of duty which was the product of his upbringing. His political beliefs were based on an unyielding Christian belief which was the firm foundation for all that he said and did. However, it was typical of the man that that Christian belief was never paraded. It can fairly be said of John Smith that he had all the virtues of a Scottish Presbyterian, but none of the vices. For those of us who had the privilege to be his friends, some of the light has gone out of our lives. For his family, the sense of loss is incalculable.

I still have the scribbled notes I wrote before standing up to speak. They covered four pages of House of Commons writing paper. I had written and crossed out that John's death 'left a gaping hole in the fabric of Westminster'. Maybe I thought it was self-evident and didn't need saying.

I did one or two interviews for television on the Green outside parliament, repeating to one TV reporter my comment about John having all the virtues of Presbyterianism and none of the vices. My tribute to him came back to bite me. My postbag became swollen with outraged letters from Presbyterians.

'How dare you say we have vices,' they protested in unison.

John would have laughed at my predicament. 'Serves you bloody well right,' he would have said.

I flew to Scotland that evening to take part in a special *Question Time*, chaired by David Dimbleby. Quite by coincidence it was scheduled to be in Edinburgh. I had been on the programme the week before. Apart from the presenters, I am one of the very few people to have been on the programme on two consecutive weeks. The format was changed to turn the programme into a tribute to John. Ludovic Kennedy, the broadcaster, stood down from the panel to make way for me. The panel included Malcolm Rifkind, then Secretary of State for Defence, George Robertson, shadow Secretary of State for Scotland, and Alex Salmond, leader of the SNP. A mood of shock pervaded the programme. I went home saddened at the death of a good friend.

I wanted to pay my condolences to Elizabeth but felt awkward at intruding on the family. Eventually Meta Ramsay, now Baroness Ramsay who had been John's foreign policy adviser and another of our group from Glasgow University, rang to say Elizabeth would like to see me and Elspeth. The Smith family home in Morningside was defiantly welcoming: outside it was bathed in bright May sunshine; inside there were tears, hugs and fond memories. As the afternoon wore on, more and more people called in. Tea, cake and drink appeared. It was like a funeral wake, except before the funeral. Everyone thought John would have enjoyed it.

I went home to write an article for the *Sunday Times* on the consequences of John's death for Scotland and Scottish devolution in particular. I had written 600 words of eulogy but was asked for 250 more. Instead of my later addition running on at the end of the original article, it was put at the beginning. It made it look as though I was using John's death to score political points. The published opening paragraph was: 'John Smith could not and would not have avoided making a Scottish parliament a priority in the next election. A Labour leader representing an English constituency may not feel the same obligation.'

The article went down like a lead balloon with my Labour friends. They regarded it as a pre-emptive attack on Tony Blair. George Robertson spoke so sharply to me about it that I felt I had to write him a note saying it had not been my intention to cause offence.

The funeral on Friday, 20 May was a sombre and impressive occasion. The political establishment, particularly the Labour one, turned out in force. So did Morningside. The street outside Cluny Parish Church, where John had been an elder, was lined with mourners. Paddy Ashdown and David Steel joined Elspeth and me for the short car journey from our house in the New Town to Morningside. James, my stepson, abandoned his tractor (he was running his father's farm in East Lothian) and came to drive us.

After the service the oak coffin was taken out of the church to begin its journey for interment the following day in St Oran's graveyard on the Hebridean island of Iona. The mourners went to the funeral wake in the Signet Library, built in the nineteenth century as a library for advocates in the Supreme Courts next door to the Court of Session and the historic hall where Scotland's parliament last met in 1707 and where John had practised law.

The whole building was buzzing with memories of John and of who would come after him. Everyone assumed Blair would stand, but would Brown? I spoke briefly to both of them. James Naughtie, in his book about Blair and Brown, *The Rivals*, records a 'leading Scottish Liberal Democrat figure' speaking to Blair and deciding to talk frankly.

'When you win, don't forget the Liberals,' insisted the un-named Liberal Democrat.

Naughtie said Blair's response was decisive. 'Don't worry. I can assure you that I won't.'

The leading Scottish Liberal Democrat figure was Elspeth.

9

The project and Paddy's resignation

Elspeth's conversation with Blair seems now, with the benefit of hindsight, to have been remarkably prescient. Little did she know that a highly confidential political relationship was developing between Blair and Ashdown which would lead to conversations about coalition and even merger between the Liberal Democrats and Labour. By May 1994, the Ashdown-Blair relationship was already nine months old, but neither Elspeth nor I had any inkling of it, nor of its possible ramifications.

Elspeth's question and her concern about Blair's attitude to the Liberal Democrats sprang from a different and uniquely Scottish context. Beneath the radar of most London-based political commentators, a body called the Scottish Constitutional Convention had been meeting to draw up proposals for establishing a parliament in Edinburgh. Its membership was drawn from the Labour, Liberal Democrat and Scottish Green parties, the Scottish Trades Union Congress, local authorities, the Scottish churches and others who could loosely be described as civic Scotland. Though the Scottish Conservative and Scottish National parties did not participate, the convention was a rare example of making common political cause to achieve a shared policy objective. Rarer still, the convention reached decisions by consensus, not by majority vote. It had joint chairmen: Harry Ewing, a Labour peer, and David Steel, recently knighted, for the Lib Dems. In similar spirit, Labour committed itself to legislating for a Scottish parliament in its first year of government, whenever that might be, and to base its Scotland Bill 'on the framework set out by the Scottish Constitutional Convention'.

John Smith had been a supporter of this cross-party approach to what he described famously as Scotland's 'unfinished business'. After his death Elspeth was concerned that a new Labour leader might take a very different view of cooperating with the Liberal Democrats in Scotland. Her comment to Blair on the day of John's funeral was testing where the shadow Home Secretary and the politician most likely to succeed John stood.

With the benefit of hindsight, I suspect Tony Blair's unexpectedly emphatic response sprang more from his secret knowledge of shared political interests with Paddy Ashdown than his enthusiasm for the ethos of the Scottish Constitutional Convention, of which he would have been only dimly aware.

Whatever source his answer sprang from, its significance became clear to me within months. Over the next four years, Paddy and he formed an unprecedented relationship which would take the Liberal Democrats to the brink of coalition government, and me to the brink of Blair's cabinet as Secretary of State for Defence. It would also lead to Paddy's resignation as leader and pose a threat to my friendship with him.

It is easy now to forget the political context of the mid-1990s. Those of us on the left were united with a grim determination to end the long and demoralising run of Conservative governments since Thatcher swept into Downing Street in May 1979. John Major's surprising election victory in 1992 with a majority of twenty-one and his subsequent harrowing term of government provided a tantalising opportunity to replace the Conservatives as the 'natural party of government'. This sense of opportunity was tempered by a dark fear that all of us on the progressive left shared: if we failed to beat John Major next time, could we ever beat the Conservatives again?

Paddy's frustration at yet another Conservative government after the 1992 election led him to reassess his party's strategic position of studied neutrality between the Conservatives and Labour. In May, in the immediate aftermath of Major's victory, he made a speech in the town of Chard in his Somerset constituency signalling the end of so-called 'equidistance' between the two bigger parties by the Liberal Democrats. (He abandoned it finally in May 1995.) He proposed a 'new forum' open to all wishing to see a 'viable alternative to Conservatism' and a national electoral reform commission to consider the best form of proportional representation for Westminster. Paddy had put down his marker though Blair, at the time, seemed unlikely to pick it up. Perhaps his reaction to Paddy's speech was edited to the point of misrepresentation but newspapers made him sound dismissive and closed to the idea. He saw 'no point' in a forum, nor in Paddy holding talks with Labour, one paper reported. Nonetheless, a meeting of minds there was.

'The whole thing started,' Paddy wrote in his leader's hand-over notes to Charles Kennedy in 1999, 'at a dinner at Anthony Lester's house on 14 July 1993, before John Smith died. We got on well and agreed we would need good relationships between the parties if there were ever a hung parliament.'

Paddy continued: 'Since then we have met very regularly. My diaries and notes from these meetings amount to nearly half a million words! When Smith died, the relationship took off and we worked very closely together, co-ordinating our campaigns, including attacks on Major at PMQs, to a much greater extent than anyone has ever realised.'

Such a relationship with John Smith would have been impossible had he lived. John was more dyed-in-the-wool Labour than Blair. His favourable attitude to limited cross-party co-operation in Scotland stopped abruptly at the border. As far as the House of Commons was concerned, he would have done a deal with the Liberal Democrats only to secure the keys of

10 Downing Street for Labour. He was quite open about his impatience with the Liberal Democrats. Blair, it emerged, seemed to be motivated like Paddy by a philosophical attachment to a partnership of the progressive, social democratic left. He doubted Labour's ability to win power at the 1997 election without Liberal Democrat MPs but with him it went further. He wanted to build enduring partnerships of interest to ensure the twenty-first century belonged to the left (though certainly not the far left) as the twentieth century had belonged to the right. His philosophical attachment to the idea seemed to stretch beyond emergency electoral expediency. After the 1997 election, with a majority so big he needed no helping hand to power from the Liberal Democrats, he carried on with what became known as 'The Project' and his conversations with Paddy about bringing the Liberal Democrats into government.

Such a relationship between Ashdown and Smith as Prime Minister with a big majority would have been inconceivable. Their dealings with each other had been lukewarm at best. I remember them sharing the back seat of a car after appearing together on BBC Radio 4's *Any Questions*. Each told me about it afterwards. Paddy thought their conversation had been constructive; that it left open the possibility of cooperation between their respective parties. John's account of it was very different and dismissive. 'He doesn't understand rough politics,' he said. John's politics were tribal; Blair's, to the eventual dismay of his own party, were not.

Paddy's private dealings with Blair even came to have a coded vocabulary of their own: 'crossing the Rubicon' was Paddy's and Blair's veiled description for the Liberal Democrats and Labour becoming partners in government; 'The Full Monty', abbreviated to TFM, and Our Mutual Friend (OMF) were Paddy's private codes for, respectively, coalition and Blair. They were disguises with which I became familiar after Paddy set up a small team of close colleagues to advise him on his talks with Blair. It was called the 'Jo Group' after Jo Phillips, then the head of press in Paddy's office. The first impromptu meeting was in September 1994, less than two months after Blair became leader of the Labour Party. Its membership eventually included Archy Kirkwood, then chief whip, Bob Maclennan, Tom McNally, a founder member of the SDP and one of Paddy's advisers, Paul Tyler MP, who became chief whip, Tim Razzall, party treasurer and adviser, Richard Holme, an adviser to both David and Paddy, and me. It met weekly in Paddy's office in the House of Commons. We would advise him on the limits of his conversations with Blair before they met, and we would review the products of his conversations afterwards. All of us were sworn to secrecy.

The sensitivity of the meetings was apparent to us all. Many of our MPs, particularly those with slim majorities over Labour rivals, would have been horrified by the intimacy of Paddy's discussions and their subject matter. Paddy knew he was walking through a minefield. The Jo Group's job was to guide him on what step to take next and often what step not to take. Blair was also flirting with danger. As he was to discover after he became Prime Minister in 1997, big Labour beasts like John Prescott were never prepared to share power with the Liberal Democrats. Even with his landslide majority, Blair did not command the support of his party for the Project. And so, eventually, it foundered to varying degrees of disillusion in our ranks. Blair talked progressive but he wasn't prepared or able to take all the necessary practical steps to achieve his long-term ideal of a realignment of the left if it meant taking on his own party (which it did).

But in those pre-election days, when the conversations were known to no more than a dozen people in both parties, the promise of coalition tied to proportional representation for the House of Commons seemed to me not only possible but even from time to time probable. Between 1994 and 1997 I was astonished the secret had been kept so well. I remember an event at Westminster Hall attended by all the party leaders and their wives before any of their conversations started to seep out into the public domain. The Ashdowns and the Blairs greeted each other like the close personal friends they had become. The body language was clear. I was amazed that no one else saw it for what it was.

The first example of public cooperation between senior Labour and Liberal Democrat politicians happened by accident, not design as is sometimes inferred now. It was over the report by Lord Justice Scott into the arms for Iraq scandal. Scott's inquiry, commissioned in 1992 after the collapse of the trial of three Matrix Churchill executives charged with illegally export- ing defence-related equipment to Saddam Hussein's regime, held 500 hours of public hearings. Robin Cook and I sat through many of them. We queued together in the rain in competition with the public for seats (none was reserved for MPs). We played a double act with television news interviews when the inquiry adjourned for lunch or at the end of a day. We discussed each drama, each development in the unfolding story of government sleight of hand. When Scott's report was completed in February 1996 we were each given three hours pre-publication privileged access to it in the basement of the Department of Trade and Industry. Robin read it in one room, I in an adjoining room.

We agreed that after two and a quarter hours we would confer on what we had unearthed. Robin knocked on my door earlier. He said he had seen all he needed. I wondered how he could have: the report ran to 1,800 pages. Robin implied later he'd been tipped off about which chapters to read. Then we went separately to the House of Commons to do our individual responses to the government's statement on Scott's report by Ian Lang, the president of the Board of Trade. When his statement was over we went from radio studio to television studio continuing our attacks on the government. Malcolm

Rifkind had been put up to give the government view. It was a national issue but was being argued by three Scots MPs who lived within a few miles of each other. It was a powerful illustration of the Scottish impact on Westminster. We all ended up together at the BBC at 10 p.m. for *The World Tonight* and *Newsnight* programmes. In between broadcasts Robin and I carried on running discussions with our press officers about the timings of our respective press conferences the following day. It had become obvious to me that my press conference would have to be before Robin's otherwise I would just be blown away by the coverage he was bound to attract.

After we finished *The World Tonight*, Robin said to me, 'Can I have a word?'

I thought, Oh, God, does he think I've got it wrong in some way?

He took me down the corridor and round a corner, stopping outside the gents'. 'Instead of having two press conferences why don't we have one?' he said.

I was surprised but enthusiastic. 'I'll have to check with Ashdown,' I replied. 'Will you need to check with Blair?'

'No,' said Robin, seemingly surprised I had asked. The speed and certainty of his response illustrated how powerful his position in the shadow cabinet had become after his brilliant dissection of the government throughout the arms to Iraq affair.

I rang Paddy to discover he was at a passing-out dinner for the latest batch of recruits to one of the security services somewhere in England. My call had to be passed through two anonymous switchboards before I reached him. Paddy's instant reaction was 'I'll come back to London' but when I explained Robin and not Tony Blair would be leading for Labour he agreed I should go ahead.

At 9 a.m. the next morning I walked with a Liberal Democrat press officer, Judith Fryer, through the rain and the wind to Labour's headquarters at Millbank for a pre-press conference briefing. We were wet and dishevelled when we arrived. As we walked up the stairs I had a sinking feeling of entering an organisation much more sophisticated than our own. The first room we walked through seemed to contain about sixty people and rows of computers. Waiting for us in the next room were Robin himself, Dave Hill, Labour's director of communications, Pat McFadden, one of Blair's advisers now an MP and minister, Alastair Campbell, in charge of Blair's press operation, Peter Mandelson MP, Blair's fixer, and Charlie Falconer, Blair's former flatmate and lawyer. They had already produced three well-argued documents setting out the case against John Major and his government. My damp press officer and I had a flimsy press release on a single sheet of A4 paper. If Labour's operation was a Rolls-Royce, ours was an old banger. I learned a lesson that day about the connection between a good party head-quarters organisation and political impact.

Once we had sorted out the camera angles to cut out the big 'Labour' sign embedded in the floor in front of the raised platform, the press conference went smoothly. Afterwards George Foulkes, then the Labour MP for Carrick, Cumnock and Doon Valley, said to me, 'A lot of my Labour colleagues are very suspicious of you but we were all pleasantly surprised that Robin and you were able to combine so well.'

It seemed that our joint press conference had made some Labour MPs suddenly realise: 'We can work with these guys.'

Little did they know then how closely Paddy and Blair were already working together. Nine months later, the first official fruit of their conversations was revealed, though only those few in the know like me understood its proper significance. On 29 October 1996 Labour and the Liberal Democrats announced joint talks on constitutional reform. The Joint Consultative Committee was chaired by Robin Cook, shadow Foreign Secretary, and Robert Maclennan, the Liberal Democrat constitutional affairs spokesman. It established areas in which the parties could work together after the general election in 1997, including the adoption of proportional representation for elections to the European parliament and the establishment of a commission to consider electoral reform for Westminster (which Roy Jenkins would eventually chair).

These were interesting, dynamic times for the Liberal Democrats and, particularly, for me working so closely with Paddy. We had recovered a sense of purpose and momentum under his leadership. Not only were we speaking to Blair about coalition government, we were also leading the attacks on the government over the crisis that unfolded in Bosnia between 1992 and 1996. The government's slow-footedness and evident fear of being sucked into a brutal and bloody ethnic war offended Paddy. He pursued John Major relentlessly over it. Some of these exchanges in the House of Commons were brutal and the correspondence that followed was incendiary. I thought Paddy was right to oppose the government so strongly but was less enamoured of his derring-do in Bosnia itself. His repeated visits, including crawling through the tunnel into besieged Sarajevo, gave him extraordinary knowledge and credibility but I worried about the unnecessary risks he was taking. He was so critical of some of the players in Bosnia I thought there was a danger of him being shot at by one of the many snipers infesting the country. I had a concern too that his focus on Bosnia made it look as though he cared for little else, which was most certainly not the case.

Sometimes I felt minor irritation at being displaced by him on broadcasts when I added foreign affairs to my defence brief in 1994 after David Steel announced his intention to retire from the House of Commons. However, Ashdown was so expert on Bosnia my resentment never amounted to anything more than fleeting pique. His knowledge of Bosnia was encyclopaedic, his contacts extensive.

I visited Bosnia on several occasions with the Defence Select Committee and always returned home overwhelmed with frustration at the mess I had witnessed. The UN mandate was dangerously inadequate. Here was a population desperately in need of protection and the UN mandate allowed it only to protect itself. I remember visiting the Royal Highland Fusiliers, my father-in-law's old regiment, in Vitez. We had a hearty three-course dinner in the refectory of a dilapidated school where the soldiers were based. Suddenly there was a noise at the door and two regimental pipers in dress uniform marched in, kilts swinging and silver buttons gleaming. They marched round the tables playing a selection of pipe tunes. It was an emotional occasion. The commanding officer, beside whom I was sitting, asked me what I would like them to play. I asked for the classic 'Barren Rocks of Aden', a nineteenth-century march originating from Aden's annexation to British India in 1839. In Vitez, in these extraordinary surroundings, it sounded wonderful. The next morning the Royal Highland Fusiliers put up a spit-and-polish sergeant-major and two soldiers to talk to the members of the committee. Their uniforms were immaculate and so were their answers. 'Why are you here?' we asked. 'We're here to implement United Nations mandate such and such . . .' Then, after a few more anodyne questions and well-rehearsed answers, one of the privates cracked. His frustration was palpable. In a familiar Glaswegian accent, he said, 'Just let us get at the bastards, sir. Gie us a chance and we'll fuckin' sort them oot.'

The problems of the UN were not confined to the mandate. Some countries assigned troops without providing them with boots, equipment or weapons in the hope that the UN would equip them free. The UN itself was hardly beyond criticism either. I remember looking down on a car park in Zagreb and wondering aloud why there were so many UN vehicles parked there. The Scottish army doctor in command of a field army ambulance unit told me with weary disgust how UN officials of a certain grade were entitled to a Toyota land-cruiser. They drove to work every morning from their comfortable billets in the Intercontinental Hotel, parked and then drove back again at the end of work at 5 p.m. The colonel was incensed at so much unused UN transport since he had been trying for six months without success to get authorisation from New York for spares for one of his Land-Rovers.

By now there was some background chatter about me as a potential leader. I heard it mostly in the context of Paddy's talks with Blair. If there was a leak there was a risk of the party turning against Paddy and forcing his resignation. As a precaution I was afforded what was called 'deniability' so that someone from Paddy's wing in the party could be a credible candidate to succeed him. Although I continued to attend the Jo Group, I was kept away from other meetings that would associate me too closely with Paddy's initiative. For example, Archy Kirkwood ensured that I stayed away from a dinner at Derry Irvine's house in March 1996 in case it was discovered that senior Liberal Democrats and senior Labour people had met for private discussions there. Roy Jenkins reinforced my sense of momentum within the parliamentary party when I sought his advice on an unexpected offer of a job in Edinburgh.

Lord Mackay of Drumadoon, the Lord Advocate and senior Scottish law officer, invited me to become a Scottish Supreme Court judge. I was tempted, sorely so. Did I want it now that my political career showed signs of movement? I was torn between fulfilling my legal ambition and the excitement of politics; between a comfortable judicial salary and pension and the insecurity of being an MP. Elspeth was another consideration. If I gave up politics to become a judge, Elspeth would lose her job as my secretary which she had come to value. Would that be fair?

There was something else nagging at me. I thought I smelled political skulduggery. Was I being offered the Bench to remove me from North-East Fife and give the Tories a better chance of winning it back at an unpopular by-election? Michael Forsyth,

Thatcher's Scottish protégé, was then Secretary of State for
Scotland and Lord Mackay was his Lord Advocate. It was the
kind of political game the Tories were capable of playing. The
Conservative Party was facing the prospect of annihilation in
Scotland at the next election. Was this a covert way of
providing a Conservative candidate with a winnable seat?
In the febrile atmosphere ahead of the 1997 general election
it didn't seem impossible. Michael Forsyth has since told me
my fears were unfounded, that I was offered the judge's job
because I was the obvious and best candidate. At the time
however I felt I needed advice and sought out Roy Jenkins. He
persuaded me to stick with politics. He reminded me how he
had turned down the editorship of the *Economist* and eighteen
months later became Home Secretary. The implication seemed
clear to me: turn this down and you might be a cabinet
minister in eighteen months in a Labour-Liberal Democrat
coalition. I rejected Donald Mackay's offer, but with a sharp
pang of regret. I took a gamble on politics. Had I made the
right decision?

As we went into 1997, election year, I thought I had. Even
though the Major government lurched from crisis to crisis,
everyone still assumed that Labour could not win outright
and would need the Liberal Democrats to take power. As in
1992, I was put on stand-by to fly immediately to London
after polling day to be part of the Liberal Democrat team
negotiating terms with Labour. However, on the Sunday
before polling day it became clear something remarkable was
happening. We realised Blair would win by a landslide.
Oddly, I was neither disturbed nor disappointed by this.
Like so many others on the centre-left, the end of almost
twenty years of Conservatism was something to celebrate no
matter that the prospect of a coalition between the Liberal
Democrats and Labour had all but been buried in the
landslide.

For a Scot and a Liberal Democrat, Labour's victory would bring with it a number of likely bonuses. A Scottish parliament in Edinburgh was chief among them. Another would be its election by the additional member system (AMS), a type of proportional representation.

For some inexplicable reason I had started my constituency election campaign full of the usual anxieties. After the first week, Elspeth turned to me and said, 'I don't know what's going to happen in the rest of the general election but I can tell you that you're going to win North-East Fife and by a substantial majority.' She was right. My majority rose by 7,048 to 10,356. It was a long way from the marginal I won in 1987. Our candidates also did well elsewhere. We had forty-six MPs, an increase of twenty-eight, and more than any third party since Lloyd George's Liberals in 1929, though we paled into insignificance compared to Labour's legions.

What influence would we have on Blair? I resigned myself to the knowledge that I would not now be a cabinet minister. It seemed a minor disappointment by comparison to evicting Margaret Thatcher's heirs. Little did I know then that Blair rang Paddy Ashdown just after he had been to see the Queen on the afternoon of 2 May. Paddy records the conversation in the first volume of *The Ashdown Diaries*. Blair told him: 'I really do want to seize this opportunity, to demonstrate that we can follow a programme . . . which will (form) . . . the basis of cooperation in the future . . . But I need you to know that I see this as a means of transition to an end position where you come into the show.'

As I was to learn at the first Jo Group meeting after the election, Blair was still talking coalition and so, by the end of May, was Paddy.

During the Whitsun holiday at his home at Irancy, in Burgundy, Paddy wrote a post-election position paper for the party and faxed a confidential letter to Blair. In the position paper he set out what he saw as Liberal Democrat guiding principles for the next five years. He wrote: 'Our first and overriding aim is to secure PR for Westminster and, if possible, for Europe as well.' His second conclusion was: 'We have a vested interest in the success of the first term of the Labour government.' Number three was: 'Our relationship with Labour and our clear opposition to the Tories at parliamentary level should not change.' The priority given to PR would not be controversial among our MPs and local councillors. The other two principles most certainly would be. Some of our MPs and many of our candidates who failed to win seats just weeks before had fought bruising battles with Labour's election machine. Now, with the smell of election cordite still strong in their nostrils, their leader was saying their party's best interest lay in Labour's success.

Paddy went further in his faxed letter to Blair, which he records in his diaries. 'I think it would be right, at our forthcoming meeting, to reconsider all the options before us including full-blown partnership in the present parliament,' he wrote. His conditions were the electoral reform commission proposed by the pre-election Cook-Maclennan constitutional talks, Blair's personal commitment to it and PR for the European elections in 1999. When Paddy returned from France he canvassed the views of the Jo Group. The dangers to his leadership were huge as he admitted when he saw me at 4 p.m. on Monday, 2 June.

'I could go down on this,' he said. 'I do not think you should openly support me. It is more important for you to be available to stand for the leadership if I fail.'

Yet again I was being offered 'deniability'. I refused it.

According to Paddy's diary, I replied: 'What nonsense! This is what I came into politics for. If you go down I wouldn't want to lead the party anyway. I am absolutely with you. We must tackle this now.'

The following day Paddy met Blair again, going into Downing Street by the back door as had become his routine. He left feeling

Blair had shifted ground over PR for Westminster. Paddy recorded Blair saying: 'Look, I must tell you that if I give you guys PR, without getting from you a guarantee of merger, or at least some bottom line assurance that you won't break away later, my party will think I have lost my marbles.' Paddy didn't want to sell merger to his party and anyhow his party would never have bought it. He wanted coalition and PR for Westminster.

This was to be the rhythm of Paddy's talks with Blair over the next eighteen months. Hope was followed by disappointment. Blair's attachment to the idea of amalgamating the forces of the social democratic left seemed to loosen as soon as he thought of confronting the dark forces of Old Labour with it.

Some significant progress was made. By mid-July the government announced proportional representation for the European elections in 1999. The following week Blair announced a joint cabinet committee (JCC) of senior Labour ministers and five Liberal Democrats led by Paddy. I was one of the other Lib Dems. One newspaper said the committee 'marks the strongest alliance between the two parties since the Lib-Lab pact was created to prop up James Callaghan's Government some 20 years ago'. As with the Cook-Maclennan talks the significance of the JCC was underplayed because so few people knew the context of its birth. By now though, news of Paddy's Downing Street assignations had begun to seep among senior Lib Dem MPs outside the Jo Group. Paddy was taken unawares by the explosion that resulted.

Six days before Blair's announcement of the JCC, Paddy met Jim Wallace, then the Lib Dem MP for Orkney and Shetland and the leader of the Scottish Liberal Democrats. He erupted with anger as he challenged Paddy with the details of his discussions with Blair, including the talk of possible coalition. Paddy asked him to keep it confidential but in his diary Paddy reported Jim shouting, 'What's in it for me? What's in it for Scotland?'

Paddy had been so disturbed by Jim's reaction that he rang me. 'Can you come now?' he said with urgency. When I walked into his office, the window was open and he was smoking, something he did rarely during the day. He was shaking.

'I've just had the most awful exchange with Jim,' he said.

There was another difficulty with Jim over the first meeting of the JCC in the Cabinet Room at 10 Downing Street on 17 September 1997. Jim heard that Donald Dewar, the Secretary of State for Scotland, was going to be on Labour's side. Jim with justification said he ought to be there if Donald was going to attend. Paddy asked me to drop out to make way for Jim which I refused to do. I said, 'Bloody hell, I've supported you right from the beginning . . .' In the end Jim helpfully accepted a compromise: if the JCC did anything more than note home rule a parallel meeting between Donald and Jim would be held later.

The JCC meeting was on a lovely sunny afternoon. Our group – Paddy, Alan Beith, Bob Maclennan, Richard Holme and I – posed for pictures outside Downing Street after we came out, having made a little bit of history around the cabinet table. The Labour group included Blair, Robin Cook, Jack Straw, Ann Taylor and Peter Mandelson. (Holme and Mandelson were both fixers by nature and had been in regular contact to facilitate Paddy's and Blair's conversations about the Project.) It was typical Blair: jackets off, 'hi, guys' and tea. The meeting went well. Perhaps we could work with Labour at the cabinet table!

An unexpected postscript to the meeting occurred a few days later one Indian summer evening as Elspeth and I were having a cup of tea in the garden of our house in Edinburgh. Robin Cook rang me.

'This conversation isn't taking place,' he said.

I mumbled something indicating I understood.

'When you talk to Ashdown next,' Robin said, 'would you ask him to raise with Blair the export of Hawk aircraft to Indonesia?'

I said I would and Robin rang off. It was a fascinating glimpse of the tensions within government. In opposition Robin had pursued the Tories over the contract to sell Hawks to Indonesia. (There was anecdotal evidence they were being used against the rebels in East Timor.) Everyone expected Labour to cancel the contract and refuse to supply the remaining aircraft because Robin had publicly committed the government to a foreign policy with an ethical dimension. But the Prime Minister felt legally bound to honour the contract even though there was a QC's legal opinion in circulation saying the government need not do so and could escape damages if it did. Robin hoped to put pressure on Blair to change his mind by enlisting Paddy clandestinely as an ally.

I passed on the message to Paddy, who had already begun to fear an ambush at our party conference at Eastbourne the following week. A motion banning talks about coalition was mooted but Paddy departed the conference with his discretion for movement still intact. When he came to stay with Elspeth and me in Edinburgh at the beginning of October we discussed what would have happened if the motion had been put to the conference. We reckoned a majority of the parliamentary party would have voted for it. We also discussed coalition, with Alan Beith and me in the cabinet: Beith as Chief Secretary to the Treasury, me as Defence Secretary. Would the party accept it?

Paddy records his view to me in his diaries: 'I thought . . . it would be quite difficult for the Party to reject a coalition if it was based round policies with which we agreed and if its most senior and talented people – Roy Jenkins, Shirley Williams, Bill Rodgers, Ming Campbell, Alan Beith, Bob Maclennan, Ralf Dahrendorf – all argued for it.'

On Monday, 1 December 1997, the Electoral Reform Commission chaired by Roy Jenkins was announced, another step in our slow choreography with Labour. Spring 1998 came and went as a possible deadline for going the Full Monty or coalition, then

November was pencilled in. But by then Jack Straw had done a 'hatchet job', in Paddy's view, on the Jenkins report when he appeared on *Newsnight* the day it was published. I went through the year never quite knowing whether I would be in the cabinet or not but inclining to the view I wouldn't. By late autumn the signs were not good: Gavin Strang and David Clark, the two cabinet ministers who were to make way for Liberal Democrats, were understandably outraged when news of Blair's plan began to leak out. They and their supporters, among them John Prescott, successfully dug in their heels against coalition and Liberal Democrats in the cabinet.

In mid-December 1998 Elspeth and I went to lunch with Roy Jenkins and his wife Jennifer at East Hendred in Oxfordshire. Their legendary lunch parties always had an eclectic mix of people with all the political parties often represented. Talking confidentially about the latest political developments was sometimes difficult. So, after lunch, when the other guests were leaving, Elspeth and I hung back to have a private conversation with him.

Roy said, 'The most surprising thing happened last weekend. Paddy sent me a fax saying he was about to resign.' Roy then asked me if I knew anything about it. I told him I did not. The news left me stunned. Why would Paddy want to resign? The Project was still alive, albeit faltering. A month previously Blair and Ashdown had issued a joint statement widening the work of the JCC and reiterating their determination to work together to ensure the 'ascendancy of progressive politics in Britain'. I knew the statement was not quite what it seemed. The decision to extend the remit of the JCC was, as far as I could see, a tacit admission by both Paddy and Blair that their private conversations were beginning to run into the sands. Would Paddy resign over that? Hadn't he grown used to false dawns over shirt sleeves and mugs of tea in Blair's Downing Street office?

By coincidence Paddy came to stay with us almost immediately after the Jenkins lunch. We attended a Liberal Democrat business dinner together at the New Club on Princes Street, Edinburgh. Afterwards, over a drink in our drawing room, Elspeth asked him abruptly, 'Are you going to resign?'

I remember his reply clearly.

'No. Not in the foreseeable future.'

I didn't mention our earlier conversation with Roy Jenkins, nor our knowledge of the fax Paddy had sent him. We let the conversation die and Elspeth and I went to bed reassured.

When I returned to the House of Commons after Christmas the whispers about Paddy resigning became ever more insistent. Paul Tyler, the chief whip, would say obliquely to me, 'I'd watch this if I were you.' At other times he would be quite enigmatic. He would make reference to him being my friend as well as chief whip, suggesting the obligations of the latter were somehow in conflict with the duties of the former. It was obvious he knew something but felt unable to tell me. Archy Kirkwood, a confidant of Paddy's, also seemed to know. I began to feel excluded. Did I mind? I minded more that Paddy might be considering resignation though I didn't believe it. After all, Paddy had recently assured me he would stay for the foreseeable future. My inclination was to accept Paddy's word for it, particularly as he had always displayed loyalty and friendship to me. For example, in early December I had received a confidential letter from Tony Blair asking me whether I would accept nomination to the Privy Council in the New Year Honours List. I knew I had Paddy's powers of persuasion with the Prime Minister to thank for it. Why should I doubt his word over resignation?

I decided to speak to Paddy about the rumours. On Wednesday, 13 January I took him to dinner at the Reform Club in London. I asked him if he was going to resign. His answer was the same as before. I left dinner with the impression that he planned to stay on as leader and I told Paul Tyler about his response. The following Wednesday, I was sitting in my House of Commons office after lunch when the phone rang. It was Paddy.

'I think you'd better come and see me,' he said.

There was something in his voice that made me wonder. I went to his office and sat down.

Paddy handed me a letter and admitted he had misled me: 'I'm announcing my resignation at five o'clock this afternoon.'

I remember little else about the encounter. I find it hard to describe my emotions. I felt a mixture of anger for myself and anxiety for the party. My anger became mixed with embarrassment at my gullibility. How could I have allowed myself to be so easily diverted? The signs had been there: the whispers that became louder as December turned into January; a growing realisation that the Project might have run its course despite the JCC's extended remit.

Our meeting lasted only a few tense minutes. I left his office grey with shock and seething with anger and emotion. Back in my office I rang Elspeth who was in Edinburgh. She was aghast at Paddy's decision and admission. 'Who will be leader?' we asked each other.

I went to the parliamentary party meeting at 5.30 where Paddy read out his letter of resignation. The rest of the evening passed in a blur with occasional voices intruding on my troubled introspection with queries about whether or not I intended to stand as leader.

It was only when I read Paddy's published diaries some time later that I understood the full context and chronology of his resignation and his decision to keep it secret from me. The fax Roy Jenkins had referred to after that lunch was also sent to Archy Kirkwood and Richard Holme. It was headed 'How and When to Finish' and was a point-by-point explanation of his reasons for resigning. These included his wish to spend more time with his family and to do something else with his life before retiring: 'write a book, do some TV, get involved in foreign affairs or just make a little money'. Paddy thought he had substantially achieved the targets he set after the 1997 election and added: 'A leadership contest fought now would probably be fought by all the serious contenders on the basis of a confirmation of the present strategy (or a close variant of it).' He planned to announce his resignation on Wednesday, 9 December but the date slipped.

Roy Jenkins must have told Paddy about our snatched post-lunch conversation at East Hendred because Paddy wrote in his diary on Friday, 18 December: 'I was absolutely livid with Roy. He knows that I do not want this. I have also specifically told him that the very people I do not want to know about my probable resignation are those who may go for the leadership, since it would give them an unfair advantage. I rang Archy, who confirmed that Ming had also spoken to him about this. I told Ming in a further conversation that naturally I was reviewing my position, but I had taken no decisions yet. I'm not sure I convinced him but I tried.'

Paddy's explanation for keeping me in the dark was unconvincing. I would have kept the confidence and avoided any campaigning until his decision was made public. I was by no means certain to stand in any event.

Paddy also recorded our dinner at the Reform Club.

'Ming met me at 8.15 . . . he questioned me closely about my intentions. I am afraid I threw him completely off the scent by saying that if I was to go it would be around June. At one stage he asked if there wasn't an option for me to announce and go later. I said that was one option I would have to consider, but I gave him the strong impression that nothing was going to happen. He later reported back to Paul that I had seen sense and wasn't going to go. I had deceived him, of course, but it had to be done.'

Paddy's diary described our tense encounter in his office a week later.

'At 2.15 the meeting I was dreading. Ming. I sat him down, gave him the letter and said, "Ming, I am afraid I pulled the wool over your eyes when we dined at the Reform Club the other night. I am so sorry."' Apparently I replied, though I cannot remember my words, 'That is dreadful news. Just dreadful. This is a disastrous way of doing it.'

My friendship with Paddy cooled but not for long. We had done so much together. The crisis in Kosovo was under way. A dysfunctional relationship between the foreign affairs spokesman and the departing party leader was in nobody's interest. Our friendship was soon entirely mended. Although Paddy was put out when I stood for the leadership seven years later, in January 2006, and mentioned these events to the *Guardian* newspaper. Archy Kirkwood had to act as conciliator between us.

As soon as Paddy announced his resignation publicly, speculation about who would succeed him ran riot. Charles Kennedy, then the thirty-nine-year-old rural affairs and agriculture spokesman, became favourite immediately. Every conversation was Kennedy, Kennedy, Kennedy. Charles himself cleverly stayed in the shadows saying little or nothing, allowing others to talk up his candidacy for him. It was good tactics. He avoided any risk of opprobrium by ensuring that there was no campaigning openly before the European elections in June, a prohibition imposed on potential candidates by Paddy. In spite of his propriety Charles's campaign quickly gathered momentum. Nobody seemed to doubt he would be standing even though he had not said so himself. I knew he would.

Fifteen months earlier, at the post-general election Liberal Democrat conference Charles and I had dinner. Elspeth and Jane Bonham Carter, the chief press officer in the 1997 election and now a Lib Dem peeress (the third generation of the family to be nominated to the House of Lords), ate with us at a restaurant in the conference hotel. We discussed the possibility of Paddy resigning and what we should do about it if he did. We struck a deal. If Paddy resigned early in the parliament I would stand for the leadership and Charles would support me. If Paddy resigned late in the parliament, Charles would stand for leadership and I would support him. It was, if you like, our 'Granita' moment except that Tony Blair and Gordon Brown probably had better food.

As it happened, Paddy resigned in the middle of the parliament. But I knew Charles would stand: indeed my impression was that his campaign was ready and waiting before Paddy's announcement, although some of his closest advisers deny this. By comparison I felt (and was) flat-footed. The manner of Paddy's resignation had knocked some of the stuffing out of me. By the time I had regained my composure Charles already seemed unbeatable. If I could not beat him was there any point in standing? I decided to keep my options open for a few weeks to see what happened. (Paddy criticised me for it later, saying I looked too obvious.) Part of me wanted to stand but another part of me was concerned by the burdens of leadership which I had seen at close quarters with David Steel and Paddy. There were other considerations. When would I see Elspeth and my family? Could I afford it?

There was also a distinct mood in the party for change. Ashdown's policy of cooperation with Labour which had run into the sand was even less popular now with the membership, every one of whom would have a vote for the new leader (as had been the case since the formation of the Liberal Democrats in 1988). Why should they vote for me when I had been so closely associated with Ashdown and his strategy?

A minor health scare added to my uncertainty. A blood test to detect prostate cancer recorded a higher reading than normal. My doctor arranged a biopsy. The intrusive procedure, without anaesthetic, was so painful I fainted in hospital and had to be taken to the recovery room. Thankfully, there was no cancer.

Elspeth and I wrote all the 'pros' of leadership in one column and all the 'cons' in another. The list of 'cons' stretched down the page. The 'pros' did not. Elspeth now says that I didn't have any 'glint in my eye' for leadership. She is right. The knowledge that Charles had so quickly become the front runner was a powerful disincentive. I could not envisage beating him. He was much closer in age to Tony Blair whose freshness had worked so well electorally for Labour. Charles had been consistently sceptical about Ashdown's policy of cooperation with Labour. He matched perfectly the mood of the party.

Despite my private doubts I kept open the possibility of my candidacy, listening to any opinion that allowed me to gauge my chances of success. The Liberal Democrat spring conference in 1999 was, coincidentally, in Edinburgh. All the possible candidates were discreetly taking soundings, me included. Elspeth and I tried to ask a group of journalist friends to dinner at home: Robin Oakley, the BBC political editor, Elinor Goodman, Channel 4's political editor, Michael White, political editor of the *Guardian* and others. One by one they told us they had a prior invitation. Charles had got to them first. It was another sign to me that his campaign was well organised and, probably, unstoppable.

Two days after the conference Elspeth and I went to dinner with Roy and Jennifer Jenkins at their flat at Kensington Park Gardens, London. Roy had a justifiably high opinion of Charles because of his political bravery when the SDP merged with the Liberals. Without Charles and Bob Maclennan the merger would never have happened. As I rang the doorbell, I wondered whether Roy would support me if I stood against Charles. I remember two things about the dinner. One was the magnum of claret that we drank. The other was Roy giving me his support. I was flattered, though still uncertain about standing.

Another influential Liberal Democrat figure who gave me his private support was Tom McNally, now leader of the Liberal Democrat peers in the House of Lords. His backing surprised me because he had been a close confidant of Charles Kennedy's. Tom took me out to lunch and said, 'My heart's with Charles but my head's with you. If you run I'll support you.' Tom's backing for me leaked to Charles's group of supporters who were not pleased.

In the middle of May, Elspeth and I went to spend a weekend with Michael Jopling, the Conservative peer, and his wife Gail, at their home in Yorkshire. Elspeth and he are co-godparents of the daughter of mutual friends and our friendship long predates my election to parliament. We had intended to take the train back north to Edinburgh on Sunday afternoon. Paddy rang and urged us to take the train south instead so we could have dinner with Jane and him in London. It was just the four of us round the kitchen table at their house in Kennington. Paddy declared his support for me but balanced it by telling me about the disadvantages of leadership: the end of family life and so on. Elspeth asked Jane about the life of the leader's wife. 'Hell' was Elspeth's shorthand translation of Jane's more colourful answer.

The longer the phoney campaign lasted the more I became aware that most of those urging me to stand were outside the Westminster village. My parliamentary colleagues were noticeable by their silence. Their endorsement mattered even though the electorate was the Liberal Democrat membership across the country. Various camps silently sprang up backing different candidates. Don Foster, the education spokesman, Nick Harvey, the spokesman for the English regions, and I met several times in an attempt to agree on a single candidate to fight for Ashdown's legacy. We failed.

On Thursday, 27 May I announced I would not be standing. I said in a letter to Anthony Garrett, my constituency chairman, that 'having consulted political colleagues, family and friends, I have reached the conclusion that I should not put my hat in the ring. I have decided to make my intentions clear now to avoid further speculation.' I wrote also to Tony Blair. He replied by hand the following day. 'It was very thoughtful of you to write,' he said. 'I entirely understand your decision. I happen to think you would have done very well as leader. But my view matters less than yours that you could not win! I do hope co-operation continues in the future. And I agree strongly there are lessons to be learned from Scotland.' (Labour and the Liberal Democrats had agreed a coalition deal to form the first administration in the newly devolved Scotland.)

My withdrawal gave Charles a boost although he hardly needed it. *The Times* reported he had become 'the runaway favourite' after my decision to stand aside. Campaigning officially started in the middle of June, and Nick Harvey, Don Foster and I declared our support for Charles to the TV cameras on the Green outside the House of Commons.

The election, by proportional representation, went Charles's way though less easily than everyone had predicted. He needed 50 per cent of the vote and it took four rounds of eliminating three of his four rivals and transferring their votes before he achieved it. Charles won 28,425 votes (56.6 per cent) compared to 21,833 (43.4 per cent) for Simon Hughes. Charles generously praised Simon's 'magnificent, positive, inspiring campaign'. *The Times* reported his victory speech as 'a masterpiece in the doublespeak that has characterised his leadership campaign'.

Very soon Simon Hughes would be expressing the same concerns in what was reported as the first rift in Charles's leadership. We had swapped hyperactive Ashdown for a leader with a very different style.

10

Kennedy's party and I'm leaving

What happened to the clever, youthful and gregarious politician who became our leader? His public image of easy-going charm, informality and approachability grew to be at odds with the demeanour of his private office. A wall was built. A moat was dug. A drawbridge was raised. I thought my close association with Paddy might be why his office kept me at a distance, though MPs more distant than me from Paddy began to complain of similar feelings of remoteness. We were mystified by it and speculated on its cause whenever we gathered in the tearoom or in the dining room where the Liberal Democrat group usually ate together. Charles never came to either. The public knew and liked Charles as a relaxed and friendly extrovert, a new style of popular politician whose constituency included the audience of fashionable television programmes like *Have I got News for You?*. We felt we knew him less and less.

Only much later, after I became deputy leader in February 2003, did I begin to understand why Charles's office behaved as it did. They were protecting him. They did their job well. There were rumours linking Charles to drink in the first six months but nothing out of the ordinary for Westminster, which is, after all, the palace of rumours. Did I begin to regret my decision not to stand against him? The received wisdom now is that I did, based largely on an incomplete quotation in the *Guardian* published in November 2002. I said I regretted my decision for '10 minutes every day' but the newspaper should have added, as I did in the interview, the qualification 'until common sense kicks in'.

My attitude to Charles when he became leader was supportive. I had known him as a parliamentary colleague for twelve years and regarded him with affection and respect for his political bravery over the SDP's merger with the Liberal Party. He was a good companion. Save for the Project, we had been on the same side of pretty well every issue in the party from merger onwards. We shared a common Glasgow University heritage. If I had reservations about him as leader they were selfish ones about the independence of action he would allow me in my twin portfolios of defence and foreign affairs and whether he would agree to me retaining both. I remember discussing it with him when he flew helpfully to North-East Fife for the day to support the Liberal Democrat candidate at an important council by-election soon after he became leader. We had planned to talk about my role after campaigning but Charles had the chance of catching an earlier plane back. I was determined to keep him for an hour or two longer so we could have our discussion. We went for supper in a restaurant in the village of Upper Largo owned by a Liberal Democrat supporter who gave him a warm welcome.

'Do you think it's time we split foreign affairs and defence?' he asked.

I replied, 'I don't think we should for the moment.'

He was inclined to give defence to Paul Keetch, the MP for Hereford, who had entered parliament in 1997 and who was keen to have it. I thought him then insufficiently experienced. There was an amicable compromise. Charles agreed to delay the separation of my portfolios and I agreed to have Paul as my deputy. The discussion between us was friendly. Charles seemed to respect my judgement and knowledge. I remember giving him advice like an old uncle. 'Make sure you have your own advisers,' I said. We parted on good terms.

Others were less happy at their treatment in Charles's first reshuffle announced in October two months after he wrote to the party's MPs asking them what portfolios they wanted. One MP discovered he had been sacked when his local paper rang him to question him about it. Others remarked on the delay in the reshuffle. Charles gave the impression of losing enthusiasm for it halfway through, leaving everyone on tenterhooks. It was clear he disliked having to sack colleagues or to disappoint them. I later came to realise how difficult it was to do either.

He began his first conference speech as party leader by saying, 'Have I got news for you!' and continued with a string of other puns which played well as comedy sound bites on the television news but left many MPs still wondering where he was leading them. Two days before his speech Simon Hughes, his main challenger in the summer leadership election, publicly expressed his concern. He said party members had 'not seen the same definitive leadership . . . Paddy stuck his head out, went out front and everybody knew where he was going. With Charles that isn't clear and he will have to answer some of the questions.' *The Times* reported it as 'the first rift in Charles Kennedy's leadership'. I voiced my own frustration at Charles's office at a dinner at the Atrium restaurant beside the Thames at 4 Millbank. The Lib Dem shadow cabinet was there in force. I remember it as a clear-the-air meeting with Charles. My unhelpful contribution was to tell Charles his office was a 'fucking shambles' or words to that effect. I remember I said 'fucking' because it was uncharacteristic of me at such a gathering. The reaction to my outburst was muted, like bombing blancmange I thought at the time. By now, Mark Oaten, who was Charles's parliamentary private secretary, started obliquely to express anxiety about Charles to me.

Two other episodes at different times left me feeling unsettled and wondering whether my time in politics was drawing to a close. One, which is still vivid in my memory, involved a visit to

London by the Palestinian leader Yasser Arafat. Charles and I were scheduled to meet him. First I was asked to join Charles in his office. Then I was told to meet him in his car. When I got to the car, the driver said he had been asked to pick Charles up from his flat. On the way there a mobile phone rang. Charles wanted us to buy him a can of Lilt and a packet of cigarettes. We sat outside Charles's flat waiting for him to come out. Were we going to be late for our meeting? Eventually, Charles climbed into the front seat and we drove off to the hotel where Arafat was staying. On the way Charles opened the can of Lilt and raised it to his lips, but he was shaking so much he had to use both hands to hold it steady. I thought, How the hell are we going to get through this meeting?

When we arrived at the hotel we were told Arafat was running late. Charles said he needed to go to the loo and disappeared. Arafat arrived before Charles returned. Eventually, Charles came back and we were ushered into a suite where Arafat and his entourage awaited us. Charles asked one question and then fell silent for the rest of the meeting leaving Jackie Rowley, his press secretary who was extremely knowledgeable about the Middle East, and me to keep the conversation going. After twenty to thirty minutes, as were saying our farewells to Arafat, Charles said he had a 'call of nature' and left us standing there as he disappeared once more to the loo.

When we returned to the Commons I went to see Andrew Stunell, the chief whip, to complain. Charles's people were horrified at what they regarded as my disloyalty. Was Charles the worse for drink? Was he sick? I had no way of knowing since I had never seen Charles behave like that before but I presumed it was drink.

I took a group of Liberal Democrat MPs to the UN in New York in January 2000 as I had done under Paddy's leadership. The group should have included MPs from all the strands of opinion within the party but late cancellations turned it accidentally into a group closely associated with Paddy. Don Foster, Paul Tyler, Michael Moore and Nick Harvey went to New York with me. No sooner had we arrived than Don Foster told a journalist from the *Guardian* that 'Kennedy had only six months' before he would be judged, adding, 'Anyone expecting an instantaneous miracle, with Charles hitting the stage with great fanfare, is crazy.' A *Mail on Sunday* story about our New York itinerary including a concert, a musical and a visit to a gallery made it look as though we were junketing in New York while criticising our leader back home. The impression could not have been more false but it gained currency within the parliamentary party. By now we had been dubbed the 'Manhattan Five', much to the mirth of our colleagues who met for a parliamentary party meeting during our absence in America. Charles presided over the laughter with 'amused detachment'. When I returned from New York I went to see him to explain the reason for the group's composition and its purpose in making contacts at the UN. Charles seemed uninterested and I left with the impression that he was still enjoying the joke.

The withering away of the joint cabinet committee under Charles also made me wonder what else was left for me in politics. I knew Charles's view was different to Paddy's and more in tune with the party's. Nor did I blame him for making no attempt to resuscitate the process after the last JCC meeting on 27 July 2000. His behaviour was understandable. Paddy had come to the same view. He explained his thoughts in an interview in the *Journal of Liberal History* published in spring 2006. He said: 'With the benefit of hindsight it is obvious now that until about November 1997 all of the things we wanted were possible but that beyond that Blair's power was already diminishing. Then came Jack Straw's performance on *Newsnight* over Jenkins [the Electoral Reform Commission chaired by Roy]. If I had remained as leader beyond 1999, I would have killed the whole relationship sooner rather than later.'

The demise of the JCC, inevitable though it was, meant for me the end of a political opportunity that had promised so much. My two closest colleagues and political allies – Steel and Ashdown – had either left parliament or were about to. (David had gone to the Lords, became a member of the Scottish parliament and its first Presiding Officer or Speaker; Paddy left the Commons for the Lords in 2001 and was appointed High Representative for Bosnia and Herzegovina in 2002.) Any ambition I had of leading the party had died with Charles's election. A young leader would surely serve at least ten years.

I reached the conclusion my future lay elsewhere. I began to wonder again about becoming a judge in Scotland. My route was blocked initially by having to wait for the formation of a new Judicial Appointments Board for Scotland. My old friend Donald Dewar, who had become First Minister of Scotland after devolution in 1999, was adamant I must submit myself to the appointments board because he would be accused of cronyism if he made me a judge. Jim Wallace, Deputy First Minister and Justice Minister in the Liberal Democrat and Labour coalition government, agreed with Donald. While I waited patiently for the board to begin work, Betty Boothroyd announced her intention to stand down as Speaker. Frank Field, the Labour MP for Birkenhead, encouraged me to become a candidate to replace her. Word got out that Blair allegedly looked favourably on my candidacy, which probably damaged my chances. MPs like to choose their own Speaker without prods and hints from the executive. Seven candidates stood, including Alan Beith, the Lib Dem deputy leader, which split our supporters. Donald Dewar alerted me to Michael Martin's considerable support on the Labour benches.

'Don't underestimate him,' said Donald.

Archy Kirkwood, who ran my campaign, picked up the same feeling. I thought of pulling out but Paddy advised me not to. He warned me: 'You didn't run for the leadership against Charles. If you don't run for this people will say you chicken out.'

I spoke to Donald again after newspapers had run a contrived story of two Scottish Labour MPs attacking him about my candidacy. 'The Labour Party in Scotland will not understand it if Donald Dewar votes for his old crony Ming Campbell as Speaker,' it warned. Donald laughed it off. 'The Labour Party in Scotland hasn't understood me for the past thirty years. I see no reason to try to change that now,' he said. It was to be my last conversation with him. He died ten days later.

Elspeth and I were bereft. Donald had become entwined in our lives. He used to visit us for lunch or dinner every couple of months, sometimes leaving at midnight to drive back home to Glasgow. 'For God's sake stay the night,' I would say but he would ignore me. He spent the night only once and emerged the following morning, a long, gaunt scarecrow of a figure, in a funny little pair of boxer shorts. Sometimes he joined us on Christmas Eve at our cottage at Port of Menteith but refused to stay for Christmas Day. He preferred, or so he said, to be at home in Glasgow by himself 'reading a book and eating fish fingers'. My friendship with Donald had spanned forty years; Elspeth's for almost thirty years. They were firm, if unlikely, friends given their different backgrounds. She treated him like a brother, teasing him and laughing at the embarrassments he suffered because of his acerbic wit. She often rang him on Sunday nights for a gossip. Donald seemed to enjoy the conversations because they would be on the phone for half an hour, laughing together.

Five months before he died Donald fell ill with heart disease. An operation to replace a faulty heart valve had gone well but his friends worried he had returned to his duties as Scotland's First Minister too quickly. I remember him coming to lunch a few weeks before he died: His skin was alabaster white and sepulchral; his demeanour one of fragility. During his recuperation, I visited him at his new flat in Glasgow where he was installed in front of a large television set watching test cricket (sport was one of his passions). I settled down to watch it with him. As we chatted, he gave me the impression his intention was to resign as First Minister at the next Scottish parliament elections in 2003 and probably retire from politics at the same time. If only he had felt able to resign there and then. He returned to work in the middle of August, only three months after his operation. And two months later he was dead. He slipped on the pavement outside Bute House, the First Minister's official residence in Charlotte Square, Edinburgh. He complained later of feeling unwell and he was taken to hospital where doctors found bleeding in his brain. He became so ill he was put on to a life-support machine.

I heard of his critical condition while I was attending a fiftieth birthday party in London. Elspeth bleeped me and when I rang her she told me the sad news. Politeness made me return to the dinner table – I was sitting beside my hostess – but I felt distracted and wanted to go home, to my flat in Dolphin Square. When I got outside it was raining so hard there were no taxis. Luckily, an acquaintance from the House of Lords saw me and offered me a lift. By now the press office was ringing, passing on requests for me to do interviews about Donald.

'I'm not doing anything,' I said. 'I don't know whether Donald's going to live or die.'

I went to sleep hoping the morning would bring better news. My phone went at 6.30 a.m. It was Jim Naughtie from the *Today* programme. The news was bad. Donald was still on life support. It seemed hopeless. Jim asked me to do an interview on the telephone. 'We'll approach it very gently,' he reassured me. I agreed to do it but cannot remember what I said except my conclusion which was: 'Scotland is holding its breath and praying for a miracle.' I flew back to Scotland immediately. The announcement of Donald's death came soon after. The rest of the day went in a blur of television and radio interviews. Huw Edwards presented the six o'clock news from Edinburgh. I did a live interview with him, just managing to get through it. David Steel, the Presiding Officer of the Scottish parliament, Jim Wallace, who had immediately become acting First Minister after Donald's death, and I met up and went off to a French bistro near my home to have dinner. We were distressed at Donald's death and tense from doing so many live interviews and trying so hard to pick the right words about his significant place in Scottish political history. After a few drinks we began to relax and to remember the fun of knowing Donald. I told the story of Donald plucking a card from our mantelpiece one Sunday lunchtime before Christmas and expressing horror at its profusion of Christian imagery. There were angels and Madonnas everywhere.

'This card is the most pretentious thing I have ever seen,' he said with glee at so vulgar a discovery. 'Who could have sent it?'

His long, bony fingers grasped it and were on the point of opening it so Donald could delight in scorning the name of the sender when a quiet voice behind him said, 'I did.'

Donald turned with a look of disconcerted amusement and embarrassment on his long face to meet the gaze of another of our lunch guests, Angus Grossart, Edinburgh's leading merchant banker who had been at school with Donald and Glasgow University with us. Donald reddened with embarrassment and twisted his legs and flailed his arms like a schoolboy caught being naughty.

David, Jim and I laughed happily and affectionately at Donald's memory until we began to grow self-conscious about the scene we were presenting to the restaurant's other customers. There we were, the acting First Minister, the Presiding Officer and the Lib Dem foreign affairs spokesman, all in our different ways good friends of Donald's, laughing and joking on the day of his death when flags in Edinburgh were flying at half mast and the Scottish football team playing that night were wearing black armbands. We calmed down. Two days later the Scottish parliament mourned Donald's passing in a dignified debate preceded by a minute's silence. Elspeth and I sat beside John Smith's widow, Elizabeth, and her daughters. Afterwards we went to a pub nearby called McGuffie's to exchange more stories about Donald and to recall the fun he brought to all our lives.

I remember drinking too much and telling Jimmy Gordon (Lord Gordon of Strathblane) about it afterwards. He was another of our old university friends who had been close to both John and Donald.

He joked: 'You should know by now that going drinking with the Smith women is a dangerous pastime.'

Elspeth dictated an article for the *Sunday Times* that weekend which Roy Jenkins described as the best one about Donald he had read. It gave a flavour of the wonderfully comical side to Donald's personality and his solitariness since the dissolution of his marriage to Alison twenty-seven years before.

Elspeth wrote:

A few weeks ago he turned up at the house. Unusually, it was just the two of us. The steps up to our door seemed an effort for him on that occasion. He had long since given up taking a technical interest in his operation and his illness, all of which had intrigued him in the beginning. He said he was fine, though I knew he hadn't been sleeping well.

I didn't often let him in the kitchen. I preferred to put him somewhere safe in a chair, where he couldn't knock things over. Once I remember him sitting in a window seat and pulling down the curtains and the rail around him.

That night we sat up talking till well after midnight. I asked him why he hadn't found someone special and he said he was simply alone, not lonely. He said he couldn't bear the thought of getting used to someone and their ways all over again. He didn't want to adapt.

The funeral at Glasgow Cathedral on Wednesday, 18 October 2000 was an occasion of sadness as well as a moving display of Glasgow's huge affection for Donald. John Smith was a great Scotsman but Donald was a great Glaswegian. He loved the city and on the day of his funeral the people of the city reciprocated. They crowded round Glasgow Cathedral and clapped the funeral cortège as it travelled through the streets; Glasgow firemen carried the coffin. Elspeth and I sat beside Roy Hattersley and Maggie Pearlstine, his partner and my agent. Roy was in tears throughout. I doubt he sang any of the hymns. Donald and he had been very close, sharing a love of books and the Labour Party. I managed to keep my composure until the celebrated Scottish traditional musicians, Aly Bain on fiddle and Phil Cunningham on accordion, played the Internationale as Donald's coffin was carried from the cathedral. Neil Kinnock sang along to it lustily in his strong Welsh voice as if he meant every word of it. I left the cathedral tear-stained and hugged Fiona Ross, the daughter of the former Scottish Secretary Willie Ross and another great friend of Donald's. We parted when we realised we were holding up the other mourners behind us. On the way back to the car people kept on leaning over to shake our hands. Charles Kennedy, Archy Kirkwood, Elspeth and I arrived at the wake at Kelvingrove Museum soon after Tony and Cherie Blair. There were cups of tea and shortbread but no alcohol. The mourners shuttled back and forwards to a pub across the road to have a drink. Whether in the art gallery or the pub the conversation was all about Donald and what I call his 'magnificent obsession' with Scottish constitutional reform and the parliament in Edinburgh. Occasionally, in my case, the conversation would also turn to the impending election for Speaker and my candidacy. Labour, with its 170 majority, voted virtually en bloc for Michael Martin despite Labour MPs proposing and seconding me.

I was disappointed rather than heartbroken. I thought another opportunity, perhaps a job abroad, might eventually come my way. Lesley Bonham Carter, the widow of Mark who died in 1994, told me my decision to turn down the judge's job in 1996 to keep the Project on track was well known in government circles. I knew Roy Jenkins had also told Tony Blair about it. Blair was sympathetic, Roy told me.

By the turn of the year my enthusiasm for politics was diminishing. The next general election was looming. Did I want to fight another campaign and spend another five years in parliament without a fresh challenge? I asked Anthony Garrett, my constituency chairman, and Andrew Arbuckle, a prominent member of my local party, to lunch in Edinburgh. I told them I was considering leaving parliament.

'I don't want to sit on the backbenches and spend the next five years a member of the travellers' club.'

I confided also in Roy Jenkins who said I might have a chance of becoming the next British ambassador to the UN. He told me I should stay in parliament because my chances of an appointment like that depended on me staying visibly on the public stage. 'If you leave the mainstream your chances will be much reduced,' Roy persuaded me.

I rang Messrs Garrett and Arbuckle to inform them of my decision to seek re-election. Others who were unaware of my previous uncertainty confided in me their worries about Charles Kennedy and the forthcoming election campaign.

Andrew George, MP for St Ives and disabilities spokesman, said to me, 'I hope you'll be ready to take over if anything goes wrong in the general election.' In the event the June 2001 general election was a very good one for the Liberal Democrats and for Charles himself. I told him he need not visit me in North-East Fife during the campaign because I was confident of winning without the leader's assistance. I did so by 9,736 votes, a reduction of 620 in my majority but an increased percentage of the vote. We went back into parliament with fifty-two MPs, six more than at the 1997 general election. Charles had shown, as he would again, his capacity to do well in elections and to charm the electorate. In the post-election reshuffle I relinquished my defence spokesmanship with equanimity (by leaving me with it since 1999 Charles had honoured his agreement with me) and retained foreign affairs.

I headed off for the summer holidays in July 2001 hoping for a door to open on a new career. Paddy had pressed my case with Tony Blair. He faxed Jonathan Powell, Blair's chief of staff, on 14 August, prodding him for an answer. It came when Elspeth and I were staying with Paddy at his house at Irancy in Burgundy. Powell rang and said words to the effect that 'the Prime Minister thinks a lot of you but no'. He slammed the door gently on my ambassadorial ambitions with practised politeness and civility. 'If there's anything else you're interested in just let us know,' he added. Elspeth and I went for a walk in the village by Paddy's home. She remembers our feeling of disappointment. I remember being disappointed but not really surprised. I felt I had over-reached myself. I remember, too, feeling envious of Paddy, and guilty about doing so. He had finished his parliamentary career as leader of the Liberal Democrats and now seemed destined for a high-powered UN job. I contemplated going to work for him as his deputy. We had a half-joking conversation about it. Paddy seemed to like the idea. I got cold feet. Was it a good idea for me to work in his shadow again? There was a possibility of a job with the Organisation for Security and Cooperation in Europe (OSCE) in Warsaw, leading its human rights programme. I didn't want to spend fruitless years visiting boot-faced ministers of the interior asking them impotently to stop their police beating up prisoners.

After our stay in France with Paddy I flew to Australia with a Commonwealth Parliamentary Association delegation of British MPs. We were there when the 9/11 hijackers attacked the Twin Towers in New York and the Pentagon in Washington. The television pictures left me horror-struck. They were beyond belief. I arranged to return to Britain for the recall of Parliament on September 14 and to speak in the debate. On my flight home rolling footage of the hijacked planes crashing was screened continuously. I went by way of Singapore. When we touched down I rang Elspeth in Edinburgh. She sounded anxious. 'I've just talked to Paddy who's been up to Charles's office and he thinks they're trying to cut you out of the debate.'

The explanation was that Charles's advisers wanted to project him as a good leader in a crisis like Paddy during the first Iraq war in 1991. They wanted him to speak twice, once in response to the Prime Minister's opening statement and then again in the debate to follow.

Elspeth told me she had rung Charles's office and had spoken to Dick Newby, his chief of staff: 'If Ming comes all the way back from Australia with a speech in his pocket to find he's been cut out when Straw and Michael Ancram [the Tory shadow Foreign Secretary] are speaking he'll resign.'

Newby tried to assure her; 'It'll be all right; it'll be all right.'

She said, 'If you think that you don't know Ming.'

My flight arrived at Heathrow on time at 7.30 a.m. The debate in the Commons was scheduled to begin at 9.30 a.m. I rang Charles as I waited for my luggage at the carousel.

'What's all this?' I asked.

'We think it's better I should make the speech and you should go to the memorial service.'

'What's Blair doing?'

'Blair's going to the memorial service,' he said.

'Well, I regard this as a resignation matter,' I warned him before ringing off.

I travelled into London by taxi, changing into a suit as I went – to the discomfort of the driver. When I walked into the chamber of the House of Commons with my speech in my pocket Charles was not in his seat. It was 9.25 and I had no idea whether I would be speaking or whether I would be resigning.

'Probably just as well you make the speech,' Charles said as he came in. It was a crucial moment in our relationship.

Charles spoke after Tony Blair and Iain Duncan Smith, who had been announced as Conservative leader only the day before, and remarked on the 'breathtaking nature of the savagery that we have witnessed in the United States'. He went on to ask Blair not to rule out a further recall of parliament should British troops be involved in any military response to the 9/11 attacks. Afterwards he left the Commons to accompany the other party leaders to the memorial service at St Paul's Cathedral. I spoke later, deliberately striking a pro-American position while trying to place the attacks on the Twin Towers and the possible consequences in a wider context. My scribbled words, composed on the long flight home from Australia, seemed to strike the right chord with my Lib Dem parliamentary colleagues. My conclusion was:

> Retaliation is not self-defence by any legal measure with which I am familiar. The United States as our oldest ally is entitled to our support, and we have heard already of the unique invocation of article 5 of the North Atlantic treaty.
>
> But this is a sovereign House of Parliament, and this sovereign House of Parliament and this nation, even accepting the letter and the spirit of the article 5 requirement, cannot give a blank cheque for military action. NATO operates by consensus and if there is to be any NATO action and implementation of the article 5 obligation it will be only because it is supported by all the nineteen members of that organisation.

I suggest that any response should be based on clear and unequivocal intelligence, that it must not be disproportionate and that it must be consistent with the principles of international law. I do not rule out for a moment the use of United Kingdom forces and material for the purpose of such a response if that be appropriate.

There is a risk – a risk of what is sometimes called rich man's justice – lest, by the overwhelming zeal with which we pursue the perpetrators of these terrorist acts, we give the impression that the lives of citizens of the richest countries are worth more than the lives of citizens of the poorest. In the past ten years, we have seen in Rwanda hundreds of thousands, incalculable numbers, massacred – that is a form of terrorism – while the world looked on and the United Nations uniquely had to make a formal acknowledgement of failure.

In Srebrenica, in the name of Christianity, 8,000 Muslim men and boys were massacred, while units of NATO – the most successful military alliance in history – looked on and the skies above were quiet, and empty of the aircraft that a short time before had bombed Iraq into a wasteland.

Perhaps the events in New York and in Washington are a watershed. Perhaps they reflect a new beginning. Perhaps they are a defining moment. They will be such if they achieve the apprehension, in accordance with justice, of those who were the perpetrators of the terrible acts of this week. But they will also constitute a defining moment if they make the Srebrenicas and the Rwandas much more difficult to achieve.

I sat down feeling I had made my best speech to the House of Commons. These were themes I returned to often over the next five years as the Bush administration, aided by Blair, went to war in Iraq. My speech to the Liberal Democrat Party conference in Bournemouth ten days later set out similar principles: those who committed crimes against humanity should be brought before an international court which, ironically, America had declined to endorse; any military response to the 9/11 attacks must be precise, proportionate and seeking justice, not revenge.

'I want you to understand that in committing forces in this way, we are accepting the risk of casualties,' I told the conference. 'Easy to say in the autumn calm of a seaside town; more difficult to explain to grieving relations in the dawn at RAF Lyneham.'

The conference passed an emergency motion supporting an armed response to the attacks provided it was lawful, precise and proportionate. There were no dissenting voices.

The pace to war quickened: NATO formally invoked its mutual defence clause for the first time on 2 October after the US produced evidence linking Osama bin Laden and al-Qaeda to the attacks; the House of Commons backed military action against al-Qaeda on 4 October; and Cruise missiles and bombs fell on the Afghan cities of Kabul, Kandahar and Jalalabad on Sunday, 7 October. A month later Kabul fell and on 7 December, two months after America and Britain began their attack, Mullah Omar slipped out of Kandahar with a group of his most loyal supporters. The infamous Taliban regime collapsed.

I flew into Kabul with Jack Straw in February 2002. He had generously invited Michael Ancram and me to accompany him. Michael had obligations he could not break but I was able to accept his invitation. We arrived by C130 Hercules aircraft at night, plunging steeply towards the darkened airport at frightening speed to present for the shortest possible time a target for Taliban surface-to-air missiles. Our RAF pilots flew using night-vision goggles. We sat tensely, strapped into canvas seats, in the plane's cavernous hold lit only by a dim red glow and filled with the roar of its four propeller engines. We were given earplugs but I had previous experience of the cacophony on board a Hercules and brought my own ear muffs with me from Edinburgh. The familiar bump of wheels on tarmac was reassuring but only comparatively so. A squad of muscular men in their mid-thirties with cropped hair and wearing jeans hurried us with professional efficiency across the tarmac to the terminal building. Were they British troops? Why were they making us move so quickly? We discovered the answer when we reached the building that passed for a terminal. The Afghan minister of air transport and tourism had been beaten and stabbed to death at the airport only four hours before we arrived.

We spent the night at the British Embassy, unoccupied for so long under the Taliban. Jack had his own room. I shared with Ed Owen, his political adviser. Very senior Foreign Office officials had to sleep on rows of camp beds in the down-at-heel public rooms. There was a 'London in the blitz' atmosphere. The embassy had no running water but breakfast was an unforgettable experience. In the wreckage of Kabul, we had ham and eggs served on silver with a white cloth on the table. The elderly Afghan caretaker had kept the embassy's treasures hidden from the Taliban. We spent the remainder of the day visiting ministers including lunch with Hamid Karzai, chairman of the transitional administration who became President of Afghanistan two years later. Jack invited me to go everywhere with him except the embassy's high-security communications centre. One of the meetings was with a group of Afghan women who worked for NGOs in Kabul. They were dressed in black hoods and robes but underneath they wore high-heeled sandals. I noticed one of them wore fishnet stockings and had painted toenails.

Jack Straw and I flew back to London together where the rhythm of politics for the remainder of 2002 was set by the quickening drum-beat of George W. Bush's rhetoric against the 'Axis of Evil' and Iraq in particular. My working life was dominated by President Bush's challenge to international law with the new doctrine of pre-emption and the attack on human rights in the prosecution of the war on terror.

The mood in the parliamentary party was helped by Charles's wedding to Sarah Gurling on 20 July in the chapel of St Mary Undercroft at Westminster. It was a happy occasion attended by the Prime Minister and seemed to bind us all together. I commented on the effects of Charles's marriage at our conference in September. He was more confident, I said, and more comfortable. He was 'providing a much more obvious sense of leadership and that's because he's growing into the job'.

I remained unsettled. By now the Judicial Appointments Board for Scotland had begun operating. I asked for a judge's application form and filled it in by hand at home. I wrote 'confidential' all over it.

Margaret Peattie, the board secretary, wrote back reassuringly: 'The concerns you express will be brought to the attention of the Board at the earliest opportunity.

'For my own part, I can assure you that applications are dealt with in strictest confidence and no-one other than myself is involved in handling application forms and referees reports for this particular exercise.'

On 16 August I received a letter from Sir Neil McIntosh, chairman of the appointments board, thanking me for my application but regretting I would not be required for interview. I was taken aback. Six years before I had turned down a judge's job. Now I couldn't even make it to an interview. I wrote to Sir Neil asking for a meeting to discuss his letter 'face to face'. He agreed to my request but the encounter left me none the wiser. He made a remark at the end about how I was obviously not used to filling in application forms. I presumed it was a reference to my handwritten application. The deliberations of the board were confidential but I discovered later my application failed because I was thought to be out of touch with the European Convention on Human Rights which was introduced into

Scottish Law in 1999. I found the whole episode extraordinary. I had been crown counsel. I had shadowed the Lord Advocate and the Solicitor General for Scotland between 1987 and 1999. I had sat in parliament as the legislation to create the Human Rights Act had been passed. Its provisions were familiar to me. One of my legal friends wrote to commiserate with me afterwards: 'The party owes you a great deal for your self-sacrifice in 1996. I hope they see you right and soon.'

Then Jack Straw asked me if I was interested in being Governor of Gibraltar. The post was becoming vacant in May 2003. This was not quite the diplomatic posting I had in mind. I doubted it would suit me or Elspeth. I thanked the Foreign Secretary but declined to be considered.

By now I had another private worry. Since the early summer of 2002 I had felt an intermittent pain in my leg. It hurt most if I kept my right leg stretched out for long periods, for example on long-distance flights. One particular weekend in the middle of June sticks out in my memory. Elspeth and I travelled up to Aberdeenshire to spend the weekend with our friends Bill and Maggie Williams. I drove from Edinburgh and began to feel a niggling pain in my back. When we arrived my leg felt sore and I was stiff at the hip. The pain lessened gradually as I walked around to stretch and loosen it. I changed for dinner but after we had eaten my leg flared up again and I started to feel quite unwell. I left the room, giving the impression I needed to go to the loo but I went to bed instead. Elspeth was indignant when she found me there. She said it was bad manners, which it was. 'At least you might have said you were feeling ill,' Elspeth protested. I apologised to our hosts the following morning.

By August the pain was so constant I could stand it no longer. I made an appointment to see an orthopaedic specialist who had treated James, my stepson, for a disc problem. I had a scan at the Western General Hospital in Edinburgh. The consultant was reassuring when he saw it.

'I bet you played rugby when you were young,' he said.

'Yes, I did.' I told him about my athletics as well.

He said, 'Well, it looks to me as if you've got some osteoarthritic change in your back like many men of your age who threw themselves about the rugby field in their youth.'

He did not think it looked too serious and advised me against an operation but would keep me under review. The pain, though, was getting worse and becoming more constant. My leg was so sore by the beginning of September we cancelled our annual holiday in Italy. Although I was having regular physiotherapy it made little or no difference. The parliamentary recess was interrupted by the recall of parliament on 24 September for a debate on the growing Iraq crisis right in the middle of the Liberal Democrat conference at Brighton. It happened on the day the government published a fifty-page dossier which was delivered to Charles Kennedy the night before and which I read with him on the train up to London under strict embargo. It detailed, according to Blair in his opening remarks to the House, 'the history of Iraq's weapons of mass destruction programme, its breach of United Nations resolutions and its attempts to rebuild that illegal programme'.

When I rose to speak, in response to Jack Straw, I began by outlining the principles that should be guiding Britain's policy as I had done for the 9/11 recall of parliament the year before. I said: 'No country should ever exclude the use of military force if that is the only way to protect the security and safety of its citizens but as both the Prime Minister and the Foreign Secretary have already confirmed today, to be consistent with the principles of international law, war must be a last resort, after all other diplomatic and political alternatives have failed. There is no principle of international law that authorises regime change by means of military force. Indeed, article 2 of the UN charter expressly prohibits it.'

A few minutes into my speech, I said, 'What are the answers to those lethally eloquent questions of Mr John Major last week, which, surprisingly, were not taken up today by the leader of the Opposition? What is the exit strategy? Who will replace Saddam Hussein? How long would coalition troops be required to remain in Iraq? Will Iraq split up?'

My mention of the leader of the Opposition brought Iain Duncan Smith to his feet. Party leaders seldom rise to respond to foreign affairs spokesmen. I knew my questions had hit home. He tried to suggest that Charles, in an interview on the *Today* programme that morning, had a different position to mine. 'Is not the real question the position of the Liberal Democrats with regard to military action?' he said.

I rounded on him and his own record over using British troops at times of international crisis.

> If the right hon. gentleman is now concerned about a willingness to commit British troops, let me remind him of the occasions when Lord Ashdown challenged the government . . . to commit troops to Bosnia, to support the so-called safe haven of Srebrenica and was shouted down by the serried ranks of Conservative members, most of whom are no longer in the House.
>
> Let me remind the right hon. gentleman that when he and I were covering similar responsibilities, there was, shall we say, a certain reluctance on his part about Kosovo. Let me remind him that his Conservative spokesman said that we should not send a battalion of Ghurkhas to East Timor.

By now I was in full flow, saying all the things I had wanted to say for so long about the short-sightedness of Conservative foreign policy. 'When it comes to committing military force for clear political objectives,' I said, 'we will take no lessons from the right hon. gentleman.'

I silenced him and felt a flush of excitement. I finished by setting out once more my view on military force: 'I do not shrink from the conclusion that military action may be required, but I am firmly of the view that it must be the last resort. It must be consistent with international law and must be authorised by the United Nations and endorsed by the House of Commons.'

As many MPs congratulated me for my speech as asked me why I was limping so badly. I returned to our conference in Brighton to face the same question time and again. I didn't really know the answer.

The following week I went to see a different specialist in Edinburgh. Another x-ray was taken. It showed osteoarthritic change in the hip, my new consultant said. In his view I needed a hip replacement operation. I debated whether I should have it done over Christmas and New Year or wait until the following summer. The pain became worse and worse. I was still doing some legal work – about twelve days a year – and I remember representing clients at a planning inquiry in the Borders while the House was still in recess and the pain in my leg becoming excruciating.

I rang my doctor. 'Look, this is getting really very sore and I'm beginning to lose weight.'

I was summoned to the newly built Edinburgh Royal Infirmary. The consultant said I should have another x-ray and when I returned to his consulting room there were three other doctors with him.

'This is more serious than we thought,' I was told. 'We'd like you to go to the old Royal Infirmary tomorrow for a more detailed examination.'

The next day one of the technicians there raised my suspicions. 'How long have you been having trouble with your prostate?' he asked.

'I'm not having any trouble with my prostate,' I replied, but wondered whether that was what they had found.

When the tests and a scan were finished a doctor took me into a small room in the basement which had a pile of fax rolls in one corner and nurses' shopping in Safeway bags on the floor.

'I'm afraid I've got bad news for you,' he said. 'You've got a tumour on your hip.'

I think I said to him, 'Is it malignant?'

He said, 'Yes.'

'Could there be any mistake?'

'No.'

11

Cancer

Nothing prepares you for the shock and the physical and emotional reactions that follow a diagnosis of cancer. I felt faint and suddenly hot. Sweat trickled down my forehead. I put my head between my knees. A motherly nurse asked me if I was all right and offered me a glass of water. I sipped at it but felt faint again and almost collapsed. I made up my mind to leave the hospital as soon as I could, as if by doing so I would also leave cancer behind. I stood up and said something about leaving. The nurse asked me if I wanted transport. 'No, no, I don't need transport,' I replied hurriedly. I had to get away as quickly as possible. I walked along the corridor thinking of nothing but trying to escape from cancer. I remember the cold, refreshing feel of November storms as I walked out of the hospital's exit. It was raining, pouring. Every so often the rain turned to sleet. I shivered uncontrollably. My fingers felt numb and clumsy on the buttons of my mobile phone. I rang Elspeth. She was at the check-out at the Safeway supermarket two miles across Edinburgh.

'I've got cancer,' I said.

'Oh no,' she said plaintively.

Her voice was so full of distress that someone in the supermarket asked her what was wrong. I heard her replying, 'My husband's got cancer.'

Then Elspeth said to me, 'Where are you? I'll come for you.'

I told her where I was but said, 'It'll take ages.'

'No, no. I'll come for you now. Wait there.'

Elspeth hurried to her car, leaving her shopping scattered across the checkout desk unpaid for.

I must have walked up the hill from the hospital entrance towards the main road (though I have no memory of doing so) because that is where Elspeth found me. She seemed to get there in a minute or two. I remember wondering how she could have driven across the city centre so quickly. I climbed into the passenger seat soaked from the rain and still shivering. I can remember little else of that day except the pain in my leg seeming altogether more menacing now I knew it was caused by a growing tumour and not, as I had previously thought, by wear and tear on my hip. The weekend passed in a haze of worry and fear at what lay in store for me. We talked or thought of little else though we knew almost nothing. Our knowledge amounted to three words: cancer, malignant, tumour. We did not know what type of cancer nor whether it was curable. The pain in my leg reminded me constantly of its destructive potency.

I returned to Edinburgh Royal Infirmary on Monday morning for more tests and examinations which lasted most of the day. Elspeth sat with me to keep me company. We were subdued and worried. I tried not to let my anxiety show to Elspeth and I am sure she did her best to hide hers from me. I thought back to that weekend when my leg had been so sore after driving up to Aberdeenshire. How long ago had that been? Four months. When did I start to feel the pain? Five or six months ago. We kept private our concerns about late diagnosis and decided to tell no one about the cancer until we knew more about it ourselves. A consultant would contact us, we were told, after the tests. We went home little the wiser about the disease or the treatment I would have to undergo.

Even at this early and uninformed stage I knew I had a choice: I could let the cancer and my worry about it overwhelm me or I could fight it and refuse to let it dictate the course of my life. I chose to fight. I fixed my mind on doing so. Elspeth and I would deal with it. Her attitude was the same. She strengthened my resolve.

I flew to London the next day to keep my diary commitments and to leave my office in order for what, I presumed, would be a long absence from the House of Commons. I told no one. The following evening Elspeth answered the phone at home. A voice said, 'I'm Dr Michael Mackie and I'm your husband's consultant haematologist at the Western General Hospital.'

'What's a haematologist?' Elspeth asked, because she had been expecting the consultant allocated to my case to be an oncologist.

'I treat blood and bone cancer,' replied Dr Mackie. 'I would like to see your husband as soon as possible.' It was the first clue about the cancer. Elspeth made an appointment for me at the end of the week.

Before I returned to Edinburgh I went to the *Spectator* magazine's Parliamentarian of the Year Awards lunch, where a number of people mentioned or noticed my pronounced limp. I sat beside Martha Kearney, then *Newsnight*'s political editor. Jonathan Dimbleby, the broadcaster, came up to me after lunch and said, 'I hope you're not going to let up in your opposition to military action against Iraq.'

I flew back to Scotland that evening to attend the funeral the following day of David Steel's father at St Michael's, Linlithgow, where he had been the Church of Scotland minister. Michael Moore, the Lib Dem MP for Tweeddale, Ettrick and Lauderdale in the Scottish Borders, came to collect us, because he knew the pain in my leg meant I could no longer drive. By now I was in agony. I was walking with a stick. My face was grey with pain and worry. People kept on coming up to me at the funeral and asking me when my hip replacement operation was to be done.

My first appointment with Dr Mackie was the following day. Before we went to the Western General Hospital in Edinburgh, about a mile north of our home, I jotted down some questions in a black, hard-covered, ruled notebook which I had taken with me to a disarmament conference in Beijing the previous April. After pages of notes in black ink about tactical nuclear weapons, Ukraine's obligations under START 1 and global ballistic missile problems, I wrote on separate lines:

What is it?

When arise/ how arise?

What treatment?

How long treatment?

Link to hip?

Hip first or second?

Stick

Medicine

Pain relief – night?

Normal life?

Dr Mackie had a dry and expert manner which we grew to respect and trust. I noted down his matter-of-fact, academic explanations of my illness that first day. For the next ten weeks my notebook became a diary of my cancer treatment and my reaction to it as I embarked on a course of chemotherapy. Reading it again now is an emotional experience. What I did not realise was that Elspeth also kept a diary in a notebook from the start of chemotherapy at the end of November 2002 until the middle of March 2003. She, like me, finds it difficult to read her diary again.

At that first meeting, I covered six A5 pages with words and phrases from Dr Mackie's explanation. He told me I had non-Hodgkin lymphoma, which is a tumour that affects the lymph glands or, as in my case, an extra nodal site. My hip would probably need pinning and the cancer might weaken the whole area. While Dr Mackie couldn't provide any miracle cure, he was cautiously optimistic.

Dr Mackie then explained my chemotherapy regime would be accelerated because of my physical fitness. In most cases it was repeated every three weeks but I would have it done every fourteen days. The mnemonic for my treatment was CHOP14. I would also have injected growth hormones from the fourth to the tenth day of every fourteen-day treatment cycle. (To my surprise I learned to do this injection myself, overcoming my usual squeamishness about needles.) With Elspeth's help I listed the names of relatives and political colleagues I should ring and Dr Mackie assisted me to draft a press release which I scribbled hurriedly.

'NE Fife Liberal Democrat MP MC has been diagnosed with non-Hodgkin lymphoma and will shortly undergo a course of chemotherapy, a spokesman for MC said today. The spokesman added that the prognosis was optimistic and that Mr Campbell would continue to fulfil his obligations as an MP so far as his treatment would allow. He also requested journalists to respect the privacy of Mr Campbell and his family.' I asked Greg Simpson, a close personal friend then working in the party press office, to take it round to the Press Gallery in the House of Commons.

The meeting drained me. I felt like fainting again. Back at home, Elspeth and I hugged in the hallway and she said, 'Don't leave me yet.' We drank champagne to pick up our spirits.

The newspapers published stories about my illness the following morning. *The Times* insensitively placed my news at the end of an article about John Major's son-in-law dying in hospital from an inoperable form of brain cancer. Another newspaper, I cannot remember which, quoted a medical expert on the odds of beating non-Hodgkin lymphoma. I resented it doing so because I didn't want to read anything adverse about my condition. For the same reason I didn't look up non-Hodgkin lymphoma on the Internet. The publicity also brought dozens of letters from friends, acquaintances and well-wishers.

One came from the Kuwaiti ambassador to Britain who said how sorry he was to hear of my illness and he would pray to Allah for my recovery. My old university friend Brian Gill, now Scotland's second most senior judge, wrote promising a novena for me, which in Roman Catholic tradition involves nine days of public or private devotion to obtain special graces. Michael Martin, the Speaker of the House of Commons, rang to express his good wishes. He is also a Catholic and when I told him about the prayers to Allah and the novena he said, 'I'm not sure about a novena for you, but I'll light a candle!' We laughed together.

A House of Commons debate on Iraq was scheduled for Monday. Should I go? I considered it but I worried that my presence in parliament would focus more attention on my health than on the Liberal Democrat arguments against military intervention in Iraq. I talked it through on the phone with Charles. Should he speak instead of me? he wondered. I thought not. Charles and I discussed whether Michael Moore, my deputy foreign affairs spokesman, should stand in for me. Was he experienced enough? He had been an MP since 1997. I told Charles that Michael was as well read on Iraq as anyone else in the party, apart from myself, and should be given the responsibility in my absence. Charles agreed. When Michael stood up in the Commons, he said: 'I preface my remarks by apologising on behalf of my right hon. and learned friend the Member for North-East Fife for his unavoidable absence. We trust that he will be back in his rightful place on these Benches before too long.'

Michael continued, stepping into my shoes with confidence: 'This is an important debate on perhaps the most significant issue facing the country and the international community at this time. It involves not simply Saddam Hussein's evil regime and the nature of the threat posed by it to world peace, but how the world in general and this country in particular deal with the consequences of that threat.'

Over the next few months Michael and I would speak almost every day, sometimes two or three times a day, as we developed our party's policy against war in Iraq. I installed Sky television at home and from an armchair in my study kept myself briefed on developments around the world. I talked through policy with Ben Rawlence, the party's foreign policy adviser, and with Charles also on a daily basis. All four of us were determined to maintain our opposition to military action unless it was demonstrably legal and the last resort. As I told Sue Lawley on *Desert Island Discs* two years later: 'I was determined not to be out of it. It was my way of coping . . .'

Though I could not take part in Iraq debates in the House of Commons I decided to play as full a role as my treatment would allow in the intense public debate about British and American policy. My diary is a record of my treatment as well as a log of my many media appearances. I did radio interviews by ISDN link from my study and television interviews from the BBC studios in Edinburgh. I tried to maintain an unchanged public profile despite my weakening voice and depleting hair, both the consequences of chemotherapy. I discharged one last legal commitment before my treatment began. It was a one-day planning case for a company that had been one of my best clients over the years. I didn't want to let the company down and travelled to Aberdeen and back for it in the day.

My chemotherapy began on Friday, 29 November preceded by a further meeting with Dr Mackie who provided a detailed explanation of the treatment and the various medicines I would be taking. These included steroids (twenty a day), anti-sickness pills, a mouthwash to prevent mouth ulcers and the four drugs in chemotherapy, dripped into a vein in the back of my hand from different brightly coloured plastic tubes like the fluorescent tubes of the Slush Puppies children drink. He also asked for a bone marrow sample and for a blood test every fourteen days just before the next course of chemotherapy began. He warned I might suffer from tingling in my fingers and toes, one of the side effects of my treatment.

Dr Mackie introduced me to Lesley Shepherd, the nurse who would always administer my chemotherapy. As with Dr Mackie I liked, respected and trusted her instantly.

'No immediate after-effects of chemotherapy,' I wrote that evening after my first course. 'Bloody painful sample of bone marrow,' I added. This was an understatement. Even though a local anaesthetic had been used I lay on the hospital bed gripping its iron stanchions willing myself not to scream.

I was well enough to go on Radio 4's *Today* programme the following morning to talk about the bombing of a hotel in Mombasa, Kenya, which had been blamed on al-Qaeda and Osama bin Laden. I wrote down preparatory briefing notes for the interview in my diary and added afterwards: 'John Humphrys asked about health – I think I coped quite well – positive/optimistic etc.' I remember saying to him, 'I'm one of those people who don't like talking about private things in public but I've begun the chemotherapy treatment and the prognosis is optimistic and so am I.' And so I was; and scared.

It is easier to tell the story of my treatment through extracts from my own and Elspeth's diaries, adding explanatory notes where necessary. Both of us wrote matter-of-factly about my treatment and my reactions to it. Emotion occasionally reveals itself but for the most part our diaries reflect our attitude throughout my illness. We were determined to deal with it and revert to normal life if at all possible. What the diaries do not properly reflect are our private moments of doubt and fright. Everyone with cancer has them. I was no different. Some nights I lay awake crying with pain or too scared to sleep. Every day brought anxieties. Would my temperature still be 98.4F? I had to check it daily and if it moved up significantly I had to contact the hospital immediately. Living out your life so insecurely, even for a few months, is exhausting physically and emotionally.

1 Dec: Up at midday. Feel fine. Still think it's too good to be true. Quiet day. Eating well.

Elspeth: v good night's sleep. No pain. 2 teaspoons morphine. Bed all morning.

2 Dec: First injection. Self-administered OK!! [A nurse called Susie Power taught me how to inject the growth hormone under the skin of my stomach.] Slept like a log. No after-effects. No sickness. Will I look back at this with envy after the 4th or 5th [course of chemotherapy]?

5 Dec: [I did early morning radio interviews with the *Today* programme, Five Live and Radio Wales and then went to visit the orthopaedic surgeon who had examined me before my cancer diagnosis. There were two other consultants with him. I wrote down their comments.] Keep weight off hip. Crutches – I resisted. Tumour first, hip later. I said June before finished. No one demurred. Rather disappointing.

6 Dec: One more injection (£50 a time!). Feeling a little stiff but morale remaining good. V touching letter from David Blunkett – replied today to PM who wrote by hand as ever.

7 Dec: Slight back pain – second last injection. Headache relieved by Anadin and E [Elspeth]. Dinner Douglas-Homes [Mark, then editor of the *Herald* in Glasgow, and Colette, then a columnist for *Scottish Daily Mail*]. Got a bit tired. Home before 12. Drank sparingly. Ate well, 2nd helping of beef.

Elspeth: Slept till lunch time. Brian and Tari Lang for tea [Principal of St Andrews University and his wife Tari Hibbitt] and out to dinner for first time in quite a few weeks. Jack McConnell [then Scottish First Minister] there. M ate well but got tired. So we were home by midnight.

11 Dec: Quiet day. Getting ready mentally for chemotherapy on Friday. Funny sort of limbo. Wrote dozens of letters and paid bills.

13 Dec: Nervy in advance of chemo. Judy Grant rang up [the widow of Sir Alistair Grant, former chairman of the Safeway

group and governor of the Bank of Scotland who died in January 2001] – I do find it difficult to talk to the widows of my friends who have died of cancer. They are so sympathetic but you can't help feeling that the conversations are very painful for them. Chemo over. Slight headache. Queasiness around 11/11.30 p.m.

Elspeth: 2nd dose of chemotherapy. Dr Mackie seems v pleased with M. All-over checks for lumps. Stacks of steroids/injections/anti-sickness to take home. M felt a bit sick before bed so started anti-sickness pills.

14 Dec: [I did an interview with the *Today* programme on National Missile Defence.] Pretty sick in morning. Held surgery [for constituents in North-East Fife] – not too many clients. Slept in chair for 3 hours before going out to dinner with James and Sarah [Elspeth's son and daughter-in-law].

15 Dec: [I wrote 'feeling much better' but added later in brackets 'bit of a wobble late at night'. I had two 'wobbles' during my treatment. During this one I lay awake in bed late at night in panic wondering whether I would survive the cancer. The second 'wobble' reduced me to tears. I was watching the film *Rob Roy* and was overcome by emotion at the end of the film when Rob Roy returns home. I didn't tell Elspeth about either of them.]

18 Dec: Generally seedy. Gilmours [David, biographer son of the late Sir Ian Gilmour, former Tory cabinet minister, and his wife Sarah] came in – kind and good fun. Wonderful spag bol from E. Slept much better. Up twice but slept.

19 Dec: *World at One* pre-record 10.45. Sleep has transformed me. Lesson is no drink with steroids. Andrew Wilson [an old friend of mine, a former advertising agency director] came to lunch. News 24.

20 Dec: Weak since treatment – still feel as if I have a hangover. Office lunch in Cupar [with constituency workers] – hair really on way out. I reckon to do one 'event' or 'person' per day.

Elspeth: M ate good lunch but tired on return. Gregor [grandson], dropped in with present which made him weepy. Emotions obviously affected.

23 Dec: Quiet day. Meant to go out but no incentive. Still short of one Christmas present for E.

25 Dec: [Christmas Day with stepson James and his family in East Lothian.] Wonderful Christmas. E very elegant in red suit. Good books to read – good sleep. Roy Jenkins rang. V touching. [Sadly, it was the last time I spoke to Roy. He died on 5 January 2003.]

Elspeth: Lovely lie-in. V good day with all the family. M feeling well. Lasted through until 6 p.m. when we came home – stuffed with good food and wine. David's comment [David is youngest grandson] 'Why haven't you got any hair?' the only sour note!

26 Dec: Elspeth: Boxing Day. Blood test 11 a.m. at Western. Dr Mackie appeared and said – oh joy – he was very pleased with Ming's progress (first cheering thing that's been said to us). Out to lunch of cold turkey. M on good form. D Steel came in 7 p.m. for visit. M dreading chemo tomorrow.

27 Dec: [Chemotherapy day. Dr Mackie told me I would have a CT scan on 9 January to see whether the tumour was retreating.] Resigned to feeling not so good after this treatment. Stronger anti-sickness pills prescribed. Felt tired. Slept reasonably well.

29 Dec: Better in morning – but no doubt this bout [of chemotherapy] is worse and obviously so than last one. Not feeling sick but not feeling hungry either. Ducked out of pantomime with James and Sarah, E et al but joined them in Bar Roma afterwards. Slept for three hours in my chair.

31 Dec: Lot of doubt about Balvarran. [We had been asked to spend the weekend by our old friends Robin and Carola Stormonth-Darling.] Decided not to go – feeling OK but lack

of confidence about being away from Edinburgh. New Year with the Douglas-Homes. Civilised – quiet – bed at 3 a.m.! Read too long.

Elspeth: Pulled out of Balvarran. Too uncertain about M being OK. First injection of cycle. Eating quite well. Weight steady. Trip to Safeway in case we starve. We'll certainly stay slimmer than if we'd gone to Balvarran. Martin O'Neill [Labour MP for Ochil, now Lord O'Neill of Clackmannan] came in to see M. On to Douglas-Homes to see in the New Year – great fun. M going like a train until 1.30 a.m.

1 Jan: New Year. Let's hope it works out. My pain has almost gone [the tumour responded quickly to the chemotherapy. I could feel it shrinking in my leg and as it did so the agonising pain reduced too]. I turn over at will in bed – but use stick whenever I move anywhere. Next chemo only 10 days away. Still peeing every two hours – steroids maybe. We are getting there. Dear God, make it work. The scan will be the big moment on 9 Jan. E is wonderful. If she ever gets down she never shows it. [Elspeth hid her concerns and anxieties from me. She talked them through with her son James.]

2 Jan: To Bigram [Elspeth's mother's home in Perthshire] for lunch. I drove. Fish pie and then Pate de Foie for supper – which may have resulted in my bad night. Slept v badly. Up for an hour in a chair. Then back to bed. CK [Charles Kennedy] rang. Cancelled Kirkwoods (Archy, Lib Dem MP for Roxburgh and Berwickshire, and his wife Ro).

3 Jan: No better in morning. Dr Davies rang – insisted I go in. Room to myself. Blood pressure, temperature, blood sample taken – careful prodding of stomach. Released after an hour. Quickly home. Fiona and Duncan [my sister and brother-in-law] to lunch. Feeling pretty groggy.

4 Jan: Dr Davies rang to say blood fine. Quiet day. E Brilliant as ever.

5 Jan: On the mend. Links Trust for lunch [the St Andrews Links Trust in my constituency] followed by *PM* programme and *Newsnight*. Great sleep into next day.

Elspeth: Excellent night's sleep. Ankle much less swollen. Peeing less frequent. Tingling fingers but still not too troublesome. Roy Jenkins died. He asked for a lightly poached egg and then died in his chair. Media gone mad. M did an appreciation for the *Scotsman* on the phone. I will miss him so much. He's been a friend and mentor to Ming and such fun to be with over many years.

6 Jan: Feel a million dollars. Impatient to be in parliament. Endless phone calls and press statements on Iraq. [My Roy Jenkins appreciation appeared today under the headline: 'Free-thinking scholar with many friends'. I began it by saying: 'I first met Roy Jenkins at the Hillhead by-election in 1982, when he took to Glasgow and Glasgow took to him as if each had been waiting for the other. He came to love the west end and the character of the Glasgow people, and often said that from a political point of view his happiest days were there.']

8 Jan: Feel tremendous. Endless calls to London. Scan tomorrow – a lot riding on this. Apprehensive scan will not be good enough. Back to chemotherapy on Friday. Going to do nothing for 2 days afterwards – just to see what works best.

9 Jan: Elspeth: Most of the day in the Western General getting a scan. Best possible news that evening when Dr Mackie rang up with the results. Tumour shrinking rapidly and bone regenerating 'better than one could have expected at this stage'. Jubilation all round.

10 Jan: Elspeth: Chemotherapy again. Long chat with Dr Mackie in advance. Much more upbeat as a result of scan. Possibility of radiotherapy when chemo over depending on the size of the tumour. Reconstituting hip obviously some way down the line. Hasn't felt sick this evening but only ate soup.

11 Jan: Slept v well. In bed until 1 p.m. Quiet day.

Elspeth: Roy Jenkins funeral. Wish we could have gone. M slept like a log. Determined to have quiet day. Still taking anti-sickness and steroids started again.

15/16/17 Jan: Days merge into each other. Too many people to visit me but they are very kind. Lots of broadcasting – *World at One*, BBC, STV, *Channel 4 News* etc, World Service. By 17th feeling rather sore all over – a consequence of the injections [I was told the growth hormone injections below the skin on my stomach stimulated bone marrow growth in the small of my back which caused back pains].

17 Jan: Elspeth: Talked to Dr Pope [my GP] who said scan results were 'impressive'. He said he was cautiously optimistic. M did *Channel 4 News* live from the street but was wilting by the evening. Getting pain in his back and arms. Went to bed at 10.30 but restless. Gave him two Paracetamol and he slept after that.

18 Jan: Elspeth: Not so well today. Some pain and nausea. Keeping v quiet all day. Deputy leadership worrying him. [Some of my colleagues wanted me to stand as deputy leader after Alan Beith stepped down to chair the new Commons select committee on the Lord Chancellor's Department. They seemed to think I would be a safe pair of hands if things went wrong.] Timing is difficult but if it keeps him engaged and stimulated would be a good thing. Can't really see beyond the end of the chemo and subsequent treatment. Archy and Ro [the Kirkwoods] coming for supper. Successful evening.

19 Jan: V poor night. Rang ward 8. Dr Jones had me on antibiotics because of suspicion of urinary infection. Analgesic because of pain in back.

Elspeth: Stomach, back pain and constant peeing. Call to Western who called him in immediately. Urine test and blood test. Signs of urinary infection so straight on to antibiotics and analgesics for pain. Went straight on to Thorburns [Ronnie and Rosie, old friends] near Peebles for lunch. Didn't arrive until 2 p.m. Had delicious and happy lunch.

23 Jan: [We go to Edinburgh Royal Infirmary to meet Dr Porter, an orthopaedic surgeon. I jotted down his words.] 'Medical miracle.' 'Results are fantastic.' 'Bone practically re-grown.' We're euphoric then emotional. E and I cry in car park – then out to lunch – pink champagne followed by steak.

24 Jan: 5th chemo. Much buoyed up by yesterday. Impatient but determined. E looks elegant in new coat.

25 Jan: Sick last night. Ate very little. Did practically nothing.

27 Jan: [Hans Blix delivered his report on weapons inspections in Iraq to the UN.] Blix day – Sky TV is wonderful help. Tweaked article for *Indie*. Feel v much better.

28 Jan: Slept v well again. Went for walk, further than for several weeks. Managing around house without a stick. Eating well. We seem to be getting thro' this OK. One more chemotherapy then decision time about radiotherapy and/or hip. E is wonderful. Article in *Independent*. (It was published under the heading: 'Let the weapons inspectors take as long as they need'.)

My diary ends there, apart from one further entry on 7 February when I received my last course of chemotherapy. I wrote down questions for Dr Mackie about follow-up radiotherapy and about some of the side effects I was experiencing including the continuing sensation of tingling in my fingers and weakness in my voice which worried me because of all the broadcasting I was doing. Elspeth continued her diary. It was a bleak time. Just as my chemotherapy was ending and I was desperately hoping to be rid of cancer and feeling ill, I became very sick. I lost weight fast. The doctors wondered whether the lymphoma had spread undetected somewhere else in my body. The worry was unbearable. Ironically, this sudden deterioration happened when most people thought I must be recovering. Ten days before I became so ill that I was readmitted to hospital I was elected deputy leader of the Liberal Democrats. The story of the next month comes from Elspeth's diary, with explanatory notes where necessary.

3 Feb: M definitely feeling better. Good night's sleep which helps. Decided not to take pain killers. Still on antibiotics. Went to NE Fife (in the snow) to meet NFU but came back tired. M couldn't face dinner with the Gilmours so I went on my own and had a v jolly evening.

6 Feb: Blood test. M did *Newsnight* live on Iraq – endless phone calls all day. Not feeling his best. Constant sickness therefore not eating well.

7 Feb: Last chemo. Bad news in the afternoon. Dr Yuille was there. Said Ming needed a month of radiotherapy. I lost my cool but of course it has to be done and am now resigned. Chemo went well. Sad saying goodbye to Lesley our nurse.

8 Feb: Most of weekend in bed. Anti-sickness pills worked. M's voice weak.

11 Feb: M decided to stand for deputy leadership.

12 Feb: Off to London. All went well. The train journey was comfortable if cold. Taxis available. Then hustings for deputy leadership. M did splendidly – huge welcome from colleagues – then dinner with Archy and Paul [Tyler, a Lib Dem peer] in Grumbles. M bore up splendidly but couldn't eat much. Got tired towards end of dinner so we went back to [my flat in] Dolphin Square. The news that he had won – 31 votes to Malcolm Bruce's 22 – caused much celebration. Last day of steroids which bolster his spirits and give him an appetite.

[Going back into the House of Commons for the deputy leadership election was very emotional for me. Archy Kirkwood and Nick Harvey spirited me in by a back entrance so I didn't have to deal with a queue of MPs enquiring after my health. I waited in the foyer of Charles Kennedy's office for the hustings in front of the parliamentary party to begin. People kept on coming in to welcome me back. Anna Werrin, Charles Kennedy's head of office, gave me a warm embrace. Malcolm Bruce, the MP for Gordon, made his pitch to the Lib Dem MPs first. Then it was my turn. I remember saying, 'Chemotherapy does two things to you. It makes you cry and makes you pee. If I leave the room urgently I'd like to ask you to assume it is the second.')

13 Feb: Return by train to Edinburgh.

Feb 14: Hans Blix pronouncement. M did several interviews but feeling quite unwell and not eating at all. M spent a lot of time in bed including writing a 1,200-word article on post-Blix for the *Independent on Sunday* until 1.30 a.m. [Published on 16 Feb. 'Quick march to war. Whatever happened to Britain's third way?' was the heading. I wrote: 'Mr Blair's strategy has throughout been to stay close to President Bush in public in order to influence him in private. He can plausibly claim that the approach was successful to the extent of persuading the US President to go to the UN Security Council. But I doubt that he will have much credit in Washington following the apparently scholarly, but in reality deeply political, presentation of Hans Blix to the Security Council on Friday.' The article coincided with the huge anti-war march in London which Charles attended, a decision I opposed according to some commentators. The correct version of events is this: Charles had gone to lunch with the senior editorial team at the *Guardian* who gave him a hard time about not going on the march. When he returned to his office he decided to take part in it and rang me to let me know his decision. I said, 'I wouldn't have done that,' because of the demonstration's strong anti-Americanism and because some of the other groups taking part didn't exactly espouse liberal values. I added, 'But now you've decided to do it it's become the right decision and we must defend it.' Charles sent me a draft of his speech to which I made a few amendments. I watched the march on television and when Charles suddenly appeared on my screen I sent him the pager message: 'Keep to the script, Uncle Ming', because he had a tendency to depart from his text. My message amused him, apparently, and he did keep to the script.]

16/17/18/19/20 Feb: Bad week. Unable to eat. Constant sickness.

21 Feb: Fed up with deterioration. I talked to Dr Pope who came round and in consultation with Dr Mackie told him to go into Western General. Checks in all directions. Haemoglobin down but blood OK. Suggested gastro infection or prostate infection. M stayed in overnight and was offered sausage roll, baked beans and mashed potato for supper – how ridiculous for ill people.

22 Feb: Allowed out of hospital and came home by taxi without drugs which I will have to collect later. Another gloomy, quiet weekend in prospect. Last night my first night off since cancer diagnosed. Feeling very washed out – but must keep going.

23 Feb: Feeling a bit better. M ate small quantities of food but v weak. I went to the cinema with Jan and Elizabeth [Bruntsfield and Fairbairn]. *The Hours*. Wonderful. M was in bed when I got back and stayed there.

25 Feb: Still sick and low. A stone weight loss.

26 Feb: Into Western General, thank God. A kidney scan which was clear. Up and down to hospital like a yo-yo.

27 Feb: CT scanner broken down. They have told us spread of lymphoma can't be ruled out. Sick with worry.

28 Feb: Thank God, CT scan fixed and by 5 p.m. Dr Mackie came in to say it was clear!! Tears all round and a hug for Dr Mackie. Still no reason for stomach complaint. M stayed in overnight. Gave him a blood transfusion which stopped him sleeping well. Eating a bit of hospital food. [Dr Mackie's typically considered and low-key announcement about my scan – 'Well, I am able to tell you that the scan is clear' – was a significant moment for me. It had a huge psychological impact on me because it indicated the cancer had gone. My weight loss and eating difficulties were ascribed to the side effects of chemotherapy.]

1 March: Allowed home. Definite improvement. Relief. Can deal with anything if it's not the lymphoma back.

8 March: M on the way up. Appetite coming back. Not able to go out anywhere.

10/11 March: Regular radiotherapy slot at 11.20 a.m. every day. Swanned through. Still on anti-sickness pills and antibiotics.

Elspeth ended her diary with my improving health. We looked forward again, hardly daring to believe the cancer had gone away. My morning visits to the Western General Hospital for radiation therapy took on a routine that was broken only by one brief visit to the House of Commons to vote against the government over war in Iraq on 18 March. Even though I was still weak from the chemotherapy I felt a compulsion to cast my vote against something that I believed to be so profoundly wrong.

The day before I travelled to London Paddy Ashdown rang me from Sarajevo where he was High Representative in Bosnia and Herzegovina. Jonathan Powell, chief of staff in 10 Downing Street had rung him wondering whether there was any scope for persuading the Liberal Democrat MPs to vote with the government at the end of the Iraq debate. It was a sign of Blair's anxiety in the face of a threatened rebellion by so many of his own backbench MPs. I told Paddy it would be impossible since my name was on the all-party amendment opposing war and also the parliamentary party was united in its opposition. He asked me to ring Powell to let him know my view but I refused. I thought it would damage me and the party if it became public that I had talked to Powell about backing the government, even to dismiss it.

On the morning of the vote I had radiotherapy earlier than normal and flew down to London in time for lunch. I spent most of the afternoon in my flat and in the evening I went to the Liberal Democrat table in the Commons dining room feeling very nervous about meeting all my colleagues again. The dining room was full of MPs for what promised to be one of the most dramatic Commons occasions for years. Robin Cook, the leader of the House, had resigned from the cabinet the previous day by delivering a devastating personal statement doubting the existence of weapons of mass destruction in Iraq. The dining room was buzzing with gossip and anticipation when I walked in. Alan Duncan, the Conservative MP, came over and put his arm round me, to welcome me back. Alistair Darling, the Labour cabinet minister who lives in Edinburgh, did the same. Other MPs asked me how I was and were evidently pleased to see me.

I found it all very emotional and made my entry back into the chamber more nerve-racking still. I asked Paul Keetch, the Liberal Democrat defence spokesman, and Mark Oaten, the chair of the parliamentary party, to escort me in. A ripple of recognition greeted my appearance and a murmur went round the benches. When Tony Blair came in he nodded towards me and smiled. It sounds corny and clichéd to describe my feelings in this way but the reception I experienced that evening was a kind of coming home for me. My restlessness to find another career had disappeared with the spring and my recovery. I was pleased to be back in the Commons even though I was only there to vote. I had decided not to speak because I thought it would be difficult emotionally for me and because I worried I might misjudge the mood of the House on such a fevered occasion after being away from it for four months.

When the time came to vote Paul Tyler, the Liberal Democrat chief whip, mentioned that Robin Cook might appreciate a word with me. I approached Robin in the lobby, congratulated him on the fluency of his resignation statement the previous day and talked to him about his next act of rebellion – voting against his own government at a moment of crisis for his party leader. It was good to see him again though the encounter was an odd one. Here was I, the cancer patient, offering support to Robin rather than the other way round. Blair survived the vote. The amendment insisting the case for war had not been made was defeated

1. A chance remark during a dinner at RAF Leuchars led to an invitation to go 'through the sound barrier' in a Tornado jet fighter piloted by Squadron Leader Alec Yule. As we taxied for takeoff my nerves were not helped by him saying in a very neutral tone of voice: 'Should at any time it become clear that I have succumbed to a heart attack or other such incapacity rendering me unable to fly the plane, you should pull sharply on the yellow lever between your feet. This will immediately eject you from the aircraft'.

2. At the 1997 launch of the 'Yes' campaign for Scottish devolution, with Alex Salmond and Donald Dewar, in the old Royal High School building in Edinburgh, which was to have been the site for the original assembly.

3. With Paddy Ashdown and Nelson Mandela at Buckingham Palace during his State Visit to London.

4. The wonder of modern telecommunications: doing a live interview by satellite phone for BBC Radio Scotland from Kabul.

5. Away from politics, fishing on the River Gruinard in north-west Scotland.

6. An extraordinary coming together of the political great and good at the funeral of Robin Cook at St Giles Cathedral, Edinburgh: I was on crutches from the ankle I broke fishing, but many people assumed it was to do with my cancer. Elspeth is just in front of Charles Kennedy.

7. With Charles Kennedy after I took over from him as leader.

8. An anxious moment at the September 2007 party conference in Brighton, but Paddy assures me we're going to win the vote on taxation.

9. One of the pleasures of being Chancellor of St Andrews University –
congratulating Joanna Lumley after awarding her an honorary degree.

10. With Hilary Clinton.

11. With Gordon Brown at the State Opening of Parliament 2006.

12. Remembrance Sunday 2006. While we were waiting to perform our duties we had been talking about how draining we all found Prime Minister's Question Time

3. Voting on the Trident resolution at conference, March 2007. The tension is clear on all our faces. Ed Dewey, my Chief of Staff is trying to count the votes!

14. Relief as we win the vote.

15. September 2007 Party Conference ovation. To Elspeth's right is my press secretary, Puja Darbari; to my left is Jenny Willott, MP for Cardiff.

by 396 votes to 217, a government majority of 179 despite a rebellion by 139 Labour MPs. All but 15 Conservatives voted with the government.

After the vote Paul Tyler walked with me out of the Commons (Elspeth had told him: 'Whatever you do make sure Ming is looked after'). Paul and I looked for a taxi to take me back to my flat in Dolphin Square but there was none. So we started walking and discussing the debate, the vote and our opposition to the government. Rehearsing it as we walked across London in the dark dispelled any last lingering doubts about whether we had been justified in voting against the government when so many of our troops, including the Black Watch, were on invasion alert in the Kuwaiti desert. Had we done right thing? Would people understand why we had voted against the government on the eve of war? We thought they would because so many of them, perhaps the majority of them, agreed with us.

As I slept President Bush delivered an ultimatum to Saddam Hussein: leave Iraq with your two sons Uday and Qusay within forty-eight hours or else. By the time I flew back to Edinburgh in the morning to keep my next radiotherapy appointment, war seemed inevitable and imminent. It began at 2.30 a.m. the following day with a series of missile strikes on targets in Baghdad. Like everyone else I watched it all unfold on television. In between radiotherapy appointments Monday to Friday and check-ups I carried on as I had done in the previous three months. I talked daily to Charles Kennedy, Michael Moore, Ben Rawlence and others in the party. I continued to table parliamentary questions (I tabled questions during my absence from parliament on subjects as diverse as the British prisoners held at Guantánamo Bay, arms exports to India, contingency planning and, of course, Iraq). My media profile increased as I felt able to do more television, radio and press interviews. I felt so much better.

Then one day I sat in the armchair in my study and a set of keys in my pocket rubbed against my right thigh and burst the skin which had been burned by radiotherapy. I covered the cut with a sticking plaster. It was the worst thing I could have done. When I took the plaster off a section of skin from my thigh peeled off with it, leaving a red, raw expanse of scalded flesh. It looked like a very painful case of sunburn. The district nurse dressed it every morning to prevent infection. As the Easter weekend drew closer we wondered whether we could go away. We had been asked to spend the weekend in Perthshire with our friends Robin and Carola Stormonth-Darling. Could I have my leg dressed by a nurse there? When it seemed impossible Elspeth burst into tears. She went to the kitchen and cried. All the emotional tension of the past six months had pushed her to breaking point. I had not realised how much she needed a weekend away. She had reached the end of her tether. The district nurse saw how much it meant to her and arranged for the district nurse at Blairgowrie, fifteen miles from where we were due to stay, to dress my leg over the Easter weekend. We were so grateful to her.

I returned to parliament after the Easter recess for a statement by Jack Straw on Iraq and the Middle East peace process. When Michael Martin, the Speaker, called my name there was a rumble of approval. Hansard recorded it as 'Hon members: Hear, Hear.'

I rose and said, 'Perhaps I might take a moment, Mr Speaker, to thank you and colleagues on both sides of the House for the messages of support that have meant a great deal to me and my family in recent weeks. However – to the business of the day.' I kept the reference to my health deliberately short to avoid distracting attention from more important issues concerning Iraq which by now was largely under American and British control. 'Can the Foreign Secretary,' I asked Jack Straw, 'give the House some illustration of what the Government envisage as a vital role for the United Nations? Does not a vital role involve more than merely acting in an advisory capacity, or being concerned with humanitarian relief? What progress has he made in his entirely sensible suggestion that there should be a United Nations-sponsored convention to consider the future of Iraq?'

Jack prefaced his reply by commenting: 'May I first say how pleased I am to see the right hon. and learned gentleman in his place and on such good form? I am sure that, in saying that, I reflect the sentiment of the whole House. The right hon. and learned gentleman's wise contributions, which he has made over many years, have been greatly missed by us all.'

I was back.

12

Back to work

I returned to a parliament echoing with the ramifications of war in Iraq. On my first day back, Monday, 28 April 2003, US troops fired on a group of demonstrators in Baghdad killing thirteen and wounding seventy-five. Every day thereafter seemed to bring more news of bloodshed and bombing and, increasingly, disclosure at Westminster about the use of intelligence, its scarcity or unreliability, which led Britain to war. I lost count of the number of times I appeared on news bulletins or political discussion programmes describing Downing Street's case for war as a 'flawed prospectus'. The discrediting of Tony Blair's two pre-war dossiers, Downing Street's ill-judged battle of wills with the BBC, the suicide of the weapons specialist Dr David Kelly and the subsequent Hutton inquiry into his death set the political agenda for months. As before the war, the Liberal Democrats provided the critical commentary in parliament and in the media. The Conservatives neither had the will nor the credibility to do so. They were compromised, hopelessly so, by their previous unquestioning backing for military action in Iraq. Charles Kennedy and I cooperated easily and effectively over Iraq. Our views on the war, its illegality under international law and the government's pre-war manipulation of public opinion were almost identical. We differed sometimes on emphasis and at other times on tactics but never on the principles underlying our opposition to the war. Our relationship was cooperative, informal and amiable. Charles seemed to have little or no concern, or certainly none that I detected, about my public profile over Iraq being so high. As a party leader, he had generous instincts.

The Iraq agenda and my easy relationship with Charles meant my return to day-to-day political life at Westminster was both interesting and compelling. I threw myself back into it with enthusiasm and commitment assisted by my decision to give up looking for a job outside Westminster. (Who would want a recovering cancer patient anyhow?) My enforced absence over the winter coupled with the emotion of my return in the spring made me remember how much I enjoyed the House of Commons, particularly at moments of high political drama like these.

Soon after going back to parliament I met Charles to try to define my new role as deputy leader (Alan Beith, the previous incumbent, had been deputy at a distance from Charles as he had been with Paddy). He was welcoming and friendly, inviting me to become a member of his two strategy groups. There was no trace of the wariness about me that had followed Charles's election four years earlier. I was no longer regarded as a rival for the leadership; nor indeed was I.

The summer of 2003 was good for me personally and for the party. Our stance on Iraq was winning us more and more support. An ICM opinion poll in June put the Lib Dems on 22 per cent, the highest rating for a decade. Charles was the only party leader with a positive approval rating. Everything seemed set fair for us to capitalise on the mid-term unpopularity of the government and the seeming inability of the Conservatives to pull themselves out of their long slump. The only corrosive worry, and one that was known only to a small group within the party, was Charles's drink problem. Like everyone else I had heard the rumours. How could you avoid them? I had listened to Charles's TV grilling the previous summer when Jeremy Paxman on *Newsnight* said, 'Does it trouble you that every single politician to whom we have spoken preparing for this interview has said the same thing: "You are interviewing Charles Kennedy, I hope he's sober." ' Paxman later apologised but the damage was done. Charles's drinking, or at least allegations of it, had moved from private whispers in the Commons corridors to public gossip. What I didn't know was how bad it was. The Yasser Arafat episode had been my only personal experience of anything untoward in Charles's habits since he became leader.

About a month after my return full-time to parliament I had lunch with Anna Werrin, who was effectively the gatekeeper to Charles's office. We met at the Reform Club on a beautiful day. No sooner had we ordered than Anna briefed me in detail on Charles's problem. As I listened to her unfolding story I started to make sense of the past four years: why Charles's office had so quickly thrown a wall around him after he became leader; why he seemed so remote from his MPs; why I, despite holding a key spokesmanship, had felt so excluded from him. According to Anna, Charles's office had tried to provide a shield for him. They protected him in the only way they could. They kept him close. Whenever necessary, and it was frequent by her account, they put up a shield for him. She provided all the missing pieces in the jigsaw and it left me sympathetic to him as well as anxious for the party. I kept my concerns to myself but at least I could better interpret Charles's leadership armed with Anna's inside information. It was not long before I had to act on my newly acquired knowledge.

The big parliamentary event in early June, at which Charles's absence would be unthinkable, was Gordon Brown's announcement on the euro and whether Britain had met his five economic tests for joining the single currency. (It hadn't, according to Brown.) All of us in the parliamentary party expected Charles to be sitting in the leader's seat giving moral support to Matthew Taylor, the Lib Dem's Treasury spokesman, who had the job of responding to Brown's statement. I took my seat in the chamber, assuming Charles would appear before Brown rose to speak. With only seconds remaining it occurred to me that Charles could not be coming and I moved over to sit beside Matthew. Europe was one of Charles's enthusiasms. He had taken the platform with Blair, Brown, Heseltine and Clarke for the launch of the Britain in Europe campaign in October 1999. At his first conference as leader Charles had made a brilliant speech at a Britain in Europe fringe meeting pledging his party to the European cause.

Charles's office made no public explanation for his absence, but it caused speculation among the Lib Dem MPs. I had my suspicions about the cause following Anna Werrin's briefing at the Reform Club. So I asked Mark Oaten, then his parliamentary private secretary, about it.

'Why the hell didn't you just send him down to the chamber to sit there? He didn't have to say anything, but surely he could sit there?' I said.

Mark replied, 'He wasn't capable of it.'

Soon after, I went to the BBC Radio 4 *Today* programme's summer party at the Royal Institute of British Architects building at Portland Place, London. I happened to overhear a conversation in which a well-known female journalist was making allegations about Charles's drinking or his illness as I now regarded it. I said nothing, but her comment troubled me. If someone so well connected in the media knew about it how long would it be before it was splashed all over the newspapers? My attitude towards Charles had changed substantially since my lunch with Anna Werrin. I'd always liked him though I admit he sometimes irritated me as I no doubt did him. Now my irritation became concern for him and sympathy for his predicament. I felt I was watching a slowly unfolding tragedy. What could I do to interrupt its progress? Those around Charles must have been asking the same question.

Late one Friday evening, my pager sounded as I was having dinner with Elspeth and our friends David and Sarah Gilmour in Café St Honoré, a restaurant in Edinburgh.

'Please ring Anna Werrin immediately,' it said.

I rang her on my mobile phone.

'Charles is giving a press conference tomorrow at 1 p.m. and he would like you to be there,' Anna said.

'What about?' I asked.

'Well, he's going to announce he's stepping down to have treatment and he wants to be able to say that you'll take over while he's away and that you're supportive.'

I was so surprised by what Anna said all I managed to offer in reply was, 'Okay, but I'll have to see if I can get there in time.'

The early morning shuttles from Edinburgh Airport to London were fully booked so I decided instead to catch the 6.30 a.m. GNER train from Waverley Station.

I rang Anna to tell her.

'Go straight to Cowley Street [the Liberal Democrat headquarters in London],' she said.

As I hurtled south past Newcastle and Durham I wondered what had happened to force Charles to take such a dramatic step. Had his people rounded on him after he missed the euro announcement? My other concern was my own health. I worried about taking on Charles's role little more than two months after the end of my treatment for cancer.

At Peterborough my pager went again. It was Anna. The message simply said: 'Please ring CK.' I rang Anna instead.

'He's not doing the press conference any more,' she said and explained what had happened. The night before, his office had got together and told him he had to deal with his problem. Charles agreed to the press conference and went home to talk to Sarah, his wife, about it. By the morning he had changed his mind. After speaking to Anna, I rang Charles.

'What happened?' I said.

'Oh well, I talked to Sarah and we don't think it's necessary to make a formal, public announcement. The recess is coming and I'll get help then,' Charles replied.

I reached King's Cross and went straight to Heathrow. I flew back to Scotland mulling over what, if anything, I could or should do. I thought about it constantly over the weekend and decided it was such a serious development something had to be done for Charles's sake as well as the party's. I arranged to meet Jackie Rowley, Charles's press spokeswoman, Lord Razzall, the Lib Dem peer who was close to Charles, and Dick Newby, Charles's chief of staff, in the House of Lords. By prior arrangement we went upstairs to Charles's office. Sarah, his wife, sat in on the meeting which was an awkward and reticent affair. None of us wanted to be there.

I said something like, 'This is painful and difficult for everyone. Perhaps the easiest way for me to deal with it all is to treat you as if you were one of my legal clients and not a friend.'

Then I said, 'This can't go on. The risks to the party are enormous. The risks to you are enormous. You've got to do something about it before it's too late.'

Charles replied, 'I will. I've made an arrangement. I'm going to see a doctor. I promise you everything will be fine.'

We left the meeting relieved the issue had been addressed at last and a possible solution proposed. I was pleased at the outcome. We hoped the summer recess would bring an end to the whispering and restore Charles to health. As the Liberal Democrats' main electoral asset it was vital we had him back at his best for the party conference in September.

The summer rumour mill continued turning. Jackie Ashley wrote in the *Guardian* in mid-July: 'There is a Charles Kennedy mystery. On the one hand there has been a ferocious whispering campaign against him – in trouble with drink; in poor physical shape; bored of the job; hidden away in his shell after a backlash against his anti-war position; always tired; and . . . well, you name it.' It was the same mystery that I had wondered at before I knew about his alcoholism. Jackie Ashley summed up the apparent contradiction in all the rumours about Charles and the party's performance. 'And the mystery?' she continued. 'Well, simply that if it's going so badly why is it going so well? The Liberal Democrats have been polling strongly, consistently above 20%. They did well in local elections. Their position on Iraq, doubting that weapons of mass destruction were such an imminent threat, now looks wise. And Kennedy himself seems to be popular in the country. A recent Populus poll showed his trust rating at +16 against -13 for Tony Blair.'

Ashley's analysis was one we knew only too well. We needed Charles's popular appeal but we also needed him to be fit and healthy.

Why had senior party figures like me been so reticent to confront Charles? Partly, it was natural reluctance to challenge him over something so private and partly because his reputation and popularity in the country and in the party at large had never been higher. It was the big conundrum: those of us who knew about Charles's drinking were concerned, but those who didn't saw Charles as a leader of a party that was strong and strengthening in the polls.

I spent the summer hoping Charles would be able to get fit. I didn't know whether he did or didn't receive treatment, but when the party gathered for its September 2003 conference Charles was justifiably riding high and confident on the back of a spectacular by-election win. Sarah Teather's victory at Brent East was extraordinary: she overturned a Labour majority of 13,047. Charles could take enormous credit for it since he had visited the constituency as often as six times during the campaign. Not surprisingly his welcome at the party's annual conference in Brighton the following week was rapturous. Charles's post-summer buoyancy shone through in his speech.

'Well for me it's been a year of jubilees,' he said. 'I've had the pleasure of representing you all, our party, at the celebrations for Her Majesty the Queen's Golden Jubilee. But more recently another jubilee has played a recurrent part in my life. The London Underground Jubilee line which runs from Westminster Station to Willesden in Brent. Nine stops on the tube. Now renamed the Victorious line. The people there voted for fairness and decency. That's what we Liberal Democrats stand for.' He made a generous and flattering reference to me in his speech.

Charles's success and the headlines that followed it stilled the gossip but it would be back.

After the party conference Charles rang me. 'Would you accept a knighthood?' he said out of the blue. Tony Blair had asked him to ring because he wanted to know my response before including my name in the next Honours List. I said I would accept it and felt flattered by the offer. The citation made it clear it was for 'services to parliament', a reward for being a good parliamentarian, not a reward for anything party political. It was a gesture of considerable generosity on Blair's part since I had spent most of the year providing a critical commentary on his policy towards Iraq.

When my knighthood became public I received many letters of congratulations. Jack Straw wrote saying: 'many congratulations on your knighthood. It is really well deserved.' Jack McConnell, Scotland's First Minister, sent me a card: 'I really admire the way you have continued to intervene so effectively during all your recent troubles. It is really great to see your efforts recognised.'

Elspeth wrote to Blair thanking him for his political generosity in rewarding one of his political opponents and critics. Blair replied: 'I was delighted to be able to recommend to the Queen that Ming be recognised in this way.' (If I had known I was destined to become party leader I would never have accepted it. The knighthood separated me out from other people or so I felt. It was a cause of constant discussion: should I be called Sir Menzies or Sir Ming? I was happier with plain Ming Campbell.)

Prince Charles conducted the investiture at Buckingham Palace and was very friendly to me. He said, 'I do look forward to listening to you on the *Today* programme.'

I thanked him and mumbled something about the programme being required listening.

We celebrated with lunch at Petrus, Gordon Ramsay's restaurant in Knightsbridge.

The knighthood did nothing to still my criticisms of the war and its aftermath in Iraq, nor would Blair have expected it to. Charles and I argued our case against the war to a rather surprised George Bush during his state visit to Britain in November 2003. We met him with Colin Powell and Condoleezza Rice in a room at Buckingham Palace. We expected to be with them for about fifteen minutes, but Bush found our opposition to the war so engaging he debated it with us for twice as long. Normally, at occasions like these, a look passes between the state visitor and someone in his retinue as if to say: 'We must be moving on to our next appointment.' It never came with Bush. Eventually Charles looked at his watch and said, 'Mr President, we've really got to go. We have to vote against Tony Blair.'

Bush looked uncomprehending and startled. 'You gotta go! You gotta vote against Tony Blair!' he exclaimed disbelievingly in his Texan drawl.

On the way back to the Commons we discussed a remark by Bush about the British prisoners held at Guantánamo Bay in Cuba. When we made representations to him about what we regarded as the illegal detention of British citizens, Bush made a throwaway remark: 'As far as we are concerned, if the British government wants the British detainees back again, they can have them. Just send us the airline tickets.' Lawyers for two of the British detainees, Feroz Abbasi and Martin Mubanga, later asked Charles and me for affidavits confirming the details of our discussion with Bush.

Colin Powell was diagnosed with prostate cancer soon after. I wrote to him saying cancer can be beaten as I was lucky enough to know. He wrote back saying: 'Your gracious get well message was a wonderful boost.'

Privately, I was more cautious about my recovery from non-Hodgkin lymphoma. I guarded against over-confidence and became deliberately short-sighted about my political career. I made few assumptions about how long I could carry on and, consequently, left it to the last minute to confirm my intention to stand again in North-East Fife at the next general election. The deadline was 31 December. I notified my constituency party on 29 December. If I had delayed for three more days I would have had to fight a reselection contest against other nominees. My uncertainty stemmed partly from the timetable of my three-monthly post-chemotherapy check-ups in April, June, September and December. Before an appointment I would become nervous, imagining and checking for lumps on my neck, in my armpits, anywhere a recurrence of lymphoma might reveal itself. The week after receiving the doctor's all-clear I would be euphoric which would gradually subside into a feeling of well-being until the next appointment loomed and my anxieties returned. It's a syndrome of behaviour that most recovering cancer patients experience. Dr Mackie, my consultant who has now retired, tried to take the sting out of the check-ups by telling me: 'If non-Hodgkin lymphoma has come back you'll know before we do because you'll be conscious of the change in yourself.' My December check-up found nothing untoward and I felt confident enough to presume I would be well enough to stand for parliament again. Three months later I learned of a side effect of my chemotherapy. I had a long-lasting cold at the tail end of the winter and became breathless when I climbed stairs. I thought the breathlessness might be caused by the cold. I mentioned it at my spring check-up. One of the doctors connected me to an electrocardiogram (ECG).

'Your heart seems to be within the normal range,' she said encouragingly before adding, 'It's not quite right though.'

Its ability to pump had been impaired. I had dramatic evidence of this when my legs swelled up with fluid. Since then I have taken beta blockers, ace inhibitors and a daily aspirin to counteract the damage. My heart functions are now almost back to normal.

Politics in 2004 continued the pattern of 2003. In the House of Commons and in the media Charles and I cooperated to attack the government over its Iraq policy and over the findings of the Hutton report into Dr David Kelly's suicide and the Butler report into the use of intelligence leading up to war. We read the Hutton report together at six o'clock in the morning before its publication and five days later we debated together whether we should participate in the Butler Review. Charles rang me on the first Monday in February and asked me to join him in his office.

'I've just had Blair on,' Charles said, 'and he's going to announce Butler tomorrow and he wants us to have someone on it but I'm not convinced.'

I understood his reservation. The day before on television and radio we had both been calling for the inquiry to have terms of reference wider than merely to investigate the use of intelligence to make the case for war. Blair was not prepared to alter its remit and he had told Charles so.

'Well, if it doesn't have wider terms of reference,' Charles had said to Blair, 'it's difficult for us to join.'

While I sat in Charles's office Downing Street rang again. It was Blair.

Charles said, 'I've got Ming with me. Do you mind if he stays?'

Blair said no. Charles put his speaker phone on and told him again of our unease at joining such a narrowly focused inquiry.

Charles picked up from Blair that Michael Howard, the Conservative leader, had agreed to his party being represented on the review. Consequently, Blair seemed to mind less about Liberal Democrat involvement now he had the fig-leaf of cross-party support.

Charles told Blair we would discuss it overnight and let him know the following morning.

The discussion we had with Alan Beith, who would have been the Lib Dem representative on Butler's committee, was one of those occasions where Charles and I held different opinions about the politics of an issue even though we agreed on the principles. His strong view was that we should not cooperate with Butler. I was more cautious and wanted time to think through all the political consequences of standing on the sidelines. We arranged to meet again in the morning when we agreed not to nominate anyone to the Butler Committee. The judgement was right as Michael Howard realised when he recanted his support for the Butler Review a few weeks later, citing its 'unacceptably restrictive' terms of reference.

I responded in the Commons to Jack Straw's announcement of Butler's committee. I said, 'Let me make it clear that I make no criticism of the members of the proposed committee – not of their integrity, competence or independence.' I went on to explain why the party could not support Alan Beith's membership of it. 'That was not an easy decision and nor is it likely to be universally popular. However our objections relate to the remit the Foreign Secretary announced . . . [It] is confined to intelligence and weapons of mass destruction. It deals neither with the workings of government, nor with political decision making based on intelligence.'

Straw replied, 'I suspect it was a controversial decision among the Liberal Democrats. I believe it is a decision the wiser counsels inside the party, especially, will come to regret greatly.'

We didn't.

Our opposition to the war and our critique of the government played well in the country in 2004 just as it had before. Then a crisis erupted on one of the biggest occasions of the parliamentary year, Budget Day on 17 March. I looked into my office just before going to the chamber for Prime Minister's Questions, which preceded the Budget statement by Gordon Brown. Spencer Grady, my House of Commons assistant, asked me to ring Anna Werrin.

He added, 'I think it's urgent.'

'Anna, it's Ming. You rang.'

'Charles has a stomach complaint and can't do Prime Minister's Questions. Can you do it?'

I remember looking at my watch. It was a quarter to twelve. I had fifteen minutes to prepare myself for one of the most difficult parliamentary occasions of the week.

What questions would I ask? Anna told me two questions had been prepared.

'I'd better come over and get them,' I said.

When I arrived, the door to Charles's office was closed and Anna was standing outside.

I said, 'Can I see Charles?'

Anna said, 'He's very sick. He's in a bad way. It's better if you don't.'

I asked about the Budget response and Anna said Vince Cable, our shadow Chancellor of the Exchequer, had been alerted to stand in for Charles.

'We've rung Blair and Howard to let them know.'

I grabbed the two questions and rushed to the chamber. When I sat down Blair flashed me a huge grin. Luckily my questions were on Iraq and Afghanistan.

'Does the Prime Minister agree,' I said when it was my turn to stand up, 'that irrespective of our attitudes towards military action against Iraq, we now have a continuing moral responsibility to the people of that country, in particular with regard to security and reconstruction? Does he believe that a greater role for the United Nations will help us to implement that responsibility; and what progress is being made in New York to find a fresh UN Security Council resolution?'

Blair agreed it was important that 'we stay in Iraq and that our troops stay in Iraq, working with the Iraqi people'. He accepted a greater role for the UN.

My second question was about al-Qaeda's apparent resurgence in Afghanistan. 'How can we best carry on the campaign against al-Qaeda in Afghanistan and at the same time maintain our commitment to the people of Iraq?' Would there be 'sufficient financial resources for our armed forces to meet those obligations?' I asked and saw Gordon Brown grimace at me.

Blair said there would be and stressed the importance of reconstruction teams to restore order in the majority of the country where the Taliban was weak. Al-Qaeda was trying to get into Iraq and Afghanistan because 'it knows that if we manage to lift these once failed states into . . . prosperity and stability that will be a hammer blow to its fanaticism'.

I sat down, relieved at emerging unscathed after so little time to prepare.

My thoughts now turned to Vince Cable who had the far more daunting task of replying to Gordon Brown's Budget. I sat beside Vince to give him support. Vince acquitted himself well with a clever, intelligent speech but we all knew what would make the headlines. 'Kennedy too ill to attend Budget', said the Press Association. It was also the talk of parliament and the lobby correspondents. No one doubted Charles was ill – a virulent stomach bug was the official explanation. What everyone wanted to know was whether alcohol had caused it.

The crisis grew worse over the next week because Charles went to the Liberal Democrat spring conference at Southport and sweated profusely during his leader's speech. I remember putting my arm around him at Southport and being shocked by feeling bones under his jacket. He looked awful and was obviously as thin as a rake underneath the padding of his suit. Now the party was engulfed by speculation over Charles's health and his fitness to remain as leader. Patrick Wintour wrote in the *Guardian* about Charles 'facing a further test' when he appeared before the parliamentary party to deliver his leader's report.

'He will have to convince MPs he is fit for the job . . . amid continuing uneasiness, speculation and discussion of whether a Tory-style "coronation" – most probably of his deputy – would be possible.' An unnamed Lib Dem MP spoke in Charles's defence saying his evident illness at the party conference proved his absence on Budget Day was not caused by alcohol: 'The suggestion he was drunk on Wednesday doesn't make sense if he was feverish on Sunday.'

Another spin to deflect attention from alcohol appeared in the *Telegraph*: 'After a dismal week, senior party officials suggested the real reason for Mr Kennedy's curious disappearance from the Budget debate last Wednesday was crippling nerves and a lack of self-confidence, rather than the "violent stomach bug" that the party had reported.'

By a quirk of bad timing I attended a parliamentary lobby lunch at the height of the gossip. I was asked about Charles and my own leadership ambitions. I stuck to the party line over the former but unwisely said too much about the latter. I repeated the phrase about regretting not standing in 1999 for '10 minutes a day until common sense kicks in'. The *Guardian*, in particular, interpreted this as a veiled bid by me to show I was ready to take over from Charles. It was nothing of the kind, just ill-judgement on my part but it set a different hare running. 'Kennedy defiant as deputy raises leadership spectre' was the *Guardian*'s heading.

The story below it said I had 'fuelled speculation by declining to deny recurring leadership ambitions'. It went on: 'Admitting that he regretted not standing against Mr Kennedy in 1999 "for about 10 minutes a day" he told reporters: "One should rule nothing in and nothing out. Who knows?" '

I read the article with growing alarm at my unintended indiscretion and also with worry at Charles's denial of drinking before the Budget. 'Utter rubbish,' he was quoted as saying. 'I was at home having a quiet time, as you would expect, the night before the Budget.'

Charles's office now viewed me with suspicion. Was I about to challenge for the leadership? Nothing was further from my mind. My anxiety was Charles's illness and the impact it was having on him and the party. We were all trying to protect him. During this time of heightened concern – I cannot remember the exact date – a group of us met Charles again. Matthew Taylor, who was chairman of the parliamentary party, Lord (Chris) Rennard, the chief executive, Andrew Stunell, the chief whip, and I went to see him. As he had done in 2003, Charles again undertook to seek treatment. Andrew Stunell was given the job of keeping in touch with Charles and monitoring whether he was as good as his word. We left hoping he would be.

Then, just like the year before, Charles's crisis became Charles's triumph. In the local elections in June, the Lib Dems gained more than 130 seats, won control of Newcastle and pushed Labour into third place, according to the BBC's projection of the vote's national implications. Then, in July, the Liberal Democrats won a by-election in Leicester South from Labour and almost won Birmingham Hodge Hill from Labour with a swing exceeding 27 per cent. Chris Rennard, who masterminded our by-election campaigns, said, 'In real elections we are now overtaking the Conservatives, and in many, many seats we are now the true challengers to Labour.'

We broke for the summer recess with a renewed sense of momentum and gathered again after our holidays for the September 2004 conference in Bournemouth wanting it to be a springboard for our general election campaign the following year. We rode on the flow of optimism and allowed Charles's illness to slip to the back of our minds. Charles's closing conference speech was a triumph. He was coruscating in his attacks on Blair over Iraq and buoyant about the party's summer election results. He concluded by saying, 'There is a fundamental choice before us all at the next general election. The British people have probably not more than 225 days left to choose between two essentially conservative parties – and the real alternative which is the Liberal Democrats. 225 days. Then a stark choice. A serious choice. And we, increasingly, are the winning choice.' It was one of his best conference speeches and the message we all wanted to hear.

The political context could hardly have been more promising for us: a government with its moral reputation in shreds for taking the country to war on a flawed prospectus and with its backbenchers increasingly dismayed by its right-wing policies on education and civil liberties; a Conservative opposition with an unpopular right-wing leader and an unsympathetic tone of voice; and the Liberal Democrats with a buoyancy in the opinion polls and a charismatic, popular leader whose strength was 'man of the people' electioneering. All of us dared to believe in the possibility of an electoral breakthrough. If not now, then when?

I shared the confidence of my colleagues not least because 2004 turned into a year of reward and recognition for me. It started with the knighthood and carried on with awards for my performance as the party's foreign affairs spokesman. I won three awards: the Channel 4 Opposition Politician of the Year, the Hansard Society/House Magazine Opposition Politician of the Year and the Herald/Diageo Best Scot at Westminster award. I put out a statement after receiving the last of these: 'Both my health and my politics seem to have looked up in 2004. It is amazing what an enforced period of absence from the House of Commons does for a politician's reputation!'

Perhaps the best accolade (and the most nerve-racking) was appearing on BBC Radio 4's *Desert Island Discs* with Sue Lawley. We talked about my life and played six of my chosen recordings (the 'Ride of the Valkyries', *Under Milk Wood*, 'Chariots of Fire', 'Mr Tambourine Man', the 'Prisoners' Chorus' from *Fidelio*, 'Dies Irae' from Verdi's *Requiem*) before Lawley pounced. She asked me a question about Charles's health and about a newspaper story that I had been 'asked to act as caretaker leader' after his Budget 'stomach bug'.

'Is that true?' Lawley asked bluntly.

She caught me by surprise. I made a few gurgling noises in my search for the best answer, knowing that radio magnifies any hesitation.

'Twelve months out from elections one covers all contingencies,' I answered, forcing confidence into my voice. 'Charles got this stomach bug at a bad time. It upset him and there were some anxieties but these have all been overtaken—'

Lawley interrupted. 'But the story was that you said if you would be installed and not have to compete in an election then you would accept this. I mean the party was definitely gearing itself up in case something awful happened.'

'Well, the party was anxious and when he appeared to have this health scare then not surprisingly twelve months out from an election people began to think, Well what if something terrible happens and he's not able to go on? And so there were some contingency arrangements . . .' And I added forcefully, 'But we don't need them.'

Lawley came back. 'You are the contingency, the safety net, the safe pair of hands?'

'Let me put it this way,' I said. 'If it was necessary for some reason to take the party through to an election I would most certainly do that. I have no ambition to be the leader of the Liberal Democrats. I have an ambition for the Liberal Democrats, which is we should get many more votes at the next election and many more seats.'

Lawley refused to let it go. 'Well, you say that . . . there are those who believe that's going to happen but it's been said on so many occasions. There have been so many dawns based on the statistics of by-elections. Where would you put it honestly, now?'

'I genuinely think it's the best opportunity we've had in my active political lifetime. As I said elsewhere recently I have been to more dawns than the arch-druid of Wales . . . this is quite the best opportunity.'

I thought Lawley had left behind the leadership question but she tried it again.

Lawley said, 'If this dawn again proves false what happens then to the man who likes to win? Does he give up or does he challenge for the leadership then?'

I replied, 'You with your experience know politicians never answer hypothetical questions.'

She was not to be put off. 'You with your experience as a politician know I must ask it,' she said.

'We will have to agree a truce or a draw on this topic,' I said, trying finally to close it down.

Lawley doggedly continued fluttering her eyelashes at me to encourage disclosure. 'So you might put that icing on the cake . . . ?'

'I think it is so far beyond the bounds of possibility it is not worth considering.'

Lawley tried again. 'But you stopped short of saying highly unlikely.'

'Politicians never say never, but I think on this occasion I can say never with some confidence.'

Lawley gave up having finally got my answer. 'Record number seven?' she asked.

I hoped by ruling out the leadership so emphatically I would kill off any more damaging speculation about rivalry at the top of the Liberal Democrats. None of us needed it going into an election year, least of all me.

My last two records were 'Highland Cathedral', which reminds me always of Murrayfield stadium in Edinburgh and the Scottish rugby team, and Mahler's Fifth , the fourth movement of which features hauntingly in Visconti's film *Death in Venice*.

The general election campaign started officially in April but unofficially on 1 January 2005. It sounds clichéd to say so but we felt our moment had come. Would we ever again have a governing party so riven by its rightward drift and war, and a Conservative opposition so unattractive? Defecting voters from either party only had the Liberal Democrats for refuge.

The run-in to the election campaign through January, February and March passed without any real change to the political landscape or to our optimistic analysis of its consequences for the Liberal Democrats. Wherever we went we found goodwill, Charles especially so since by now his wife Sarah was expecting their first baby. Would the Lib Dems benefit from a baby bounce? A woman even berated Jeremy Paxman for being aggressive with me on *Newsnight* during a discussion about the first Iraqi elections at the end of January 2005. Sir Jeremy Greenstock, the British ambassador to the United Nations in New York in the build-up to war in Iraq and Blair's special representative to Iraq after it, was on the programme too when Paxman suddenly blurted at me: 'If you'd had your way there wouldn't have been any elections at all.' Greenstock said something which prevented me from replying.

Paxman sent me a funny letter relating his subsequent mauling at the hands of one of our supporters.

Dear Menzies,
I was minding my own business ambling through the middle of Oxford last Friday when a little old lady in a dark tweed suit, with white hair and a shopping trolley, approached me.

'Normally,' she said, in a cut-glass accent, 'I like you, and I like your programme. But you've gone too far now.'

'Er,' I groaned, 'what have I done now?'

'You were perfectly beastly to Ming Campbell the other night.'

'But I like him. We all like him,' I cried. 'Why, he even has his own memorial chair.'

'Well, you were horrid to him,' she said.

'I'm sorry you felt that way.'

'Well, you're not to do it again,' she said, and bustled off into the crowds of lunchtime shoppers.

I just thought you ought to know about your fan base.

With every good wish,

Jeremy

When April came and the campaign began in earnest our private polling showed how well we were doing. Coordinating our attacks on the Conservatives with Labour was paying off. Then we had to postpone our manifesto launch because Sarah, Charles's wife, was taken to hospital. Donald James Kennedy was born at 12.14 the following morning. I stood in for Charles while he spent two days with his newborn son. He returned to the campaign shortly before 7.30 a.m. on Thursday, 14 April to launch our delayed manifesto, a twenty-page document called 'The Real Alternative'.

I was sitting on the platform with Charles when he began to explain our income tax proposal to introduce a 50p rate for people earning more than £100,000 a year and to replace council tax with a local income tax. Charles said the local tax would raise 'no more than the total sum that is presently being raised by council tax, full stop', adding, 'but not less and we are not saying less'. The media was quick to spot his error. 'In fact, it would be £2.4bn less. The gap would be subsidised by the 50% top tax rate,' reported the *Guardian* later.

Then he struggled to answer a question about the earnings trigger for paying more under local income tax compared to council tax. He said a double-income couple each earning £20,000 a year would pay more: 'That's what you are talking about, £40,000.' Again the media latched on to his error. For a dual-income household it was slightly higher, in the low £40,000s.

I was in the difficult position of not knowing whether to intervene or let him carry on. I did nothing hoping Charles would collect himself and move on. He could have said, 'Well, Ed Davey is an expert on this so perhaps he can take the question,' and then let Ed, who shadowed John Prescott's Office of Deputy Prime Minister and was sitting with us, answer. Charles attempted later to explain away his performance by saying, 'It may be something to do with the fact I'm a bit short of sleep,' after the birth of his son. It may have worked with some mothers with babies but the whole episode left us, including Charles himself, aghast. The 50p top rate of income tax and the local income tax were two of our flagship policies and among our most controversial. Vince Cable, our shadow Chancellor, was off camera holding his head in his hands.

The *Guardian* reported the following morning: 'His error is particularly galling for the party because it has been at pains to cost all its policies thoroughly, publishing its spending figures in a separate 16-page document to prove it can be trusted to handle power responsibly.'

Charles recovered and did well during the rest of the campaign, working crowds with his usual charm and appeal. An election rally in Cambridge at which we both spoke was crowded out. Hundreds were turned away. All the speakers had to go outside one by one to address the crowds who could not get in. Our opinion poll performance also began to move again as the manifesto launch dimmed in people's memories. We dared to hope once more of a breakthrough, our optimism assisted by the defection to the Lib Dems of left-wing Labour MP Brian Sedgemore, who accused Tony Blair of 'stomach-turning lies'.

We won sixty-two seats, the best Lib Dem performance for eighty years and ten more than at the general election in 2001. I increased my majority in North-East Fife by 2,835 to 12,571. Everyone was saying how marvellously the Liberal Democrats had done but Labour had won its historic third term with a much reduced majority of sixty-six. Charles put the best gloss on it in public in the way that leaders have to do in the aftermath of an election but we all knew it was an opportunity missed. The new intake of MPs, fresh from other careers, arrived on our benches in the House of Commons eager and ready.

13

Kennedy's resignation

As May 2005 proceeded into June we all worried away in private at a gnawing feeling of disappointment. None of us could remember such a favourable conjunction of circumstances for a Liberal Democrat breakthrough. How long would it be before they coincided at election time again? A generation? More? In private conversation we talked increasingly of a missed opportunity. I heard later that Charles had reached a similar conclusion. He was as disappointed by the result as the rest of us. Perhaps it explains why he sought re-election as leader as quickly as he did after the election. When Anna Werrin asked me to sign his nomination form so soon after May I remember feeling surprise. Was he concerned that Simon Hughes was preparing a bid to challenge him? Simon was certainly rushing round the country. In the event, Charles was re-elected unopposed as leader during the summer of 2005.

In the House of Commons I detected the emergence of a different dynamic in the parliamentary party with the influx of our new MPs. They arrived at Westminster full of ambition and excitement only to confront the usual frustrations of joining a new institution, of not having offices, not knowing what they were doing or where they were going in the House of Commons. These were bright young MPs who had left behind good careers and families to make their mark at Westminster. Some of them had substantial overdrafts because of their commitment to the party. They thought they would be joining an organisation like the ones many of them had left: efficient, strategy-driven, well-led and focused. They were impatient for success. The election of David Cameron as Conservative Party leader later in 2005 also brought a new ingredient to the political landscape, and one with immediate and serious implications for the Liberal Democrats. If the Conservative Party revived, how many of our novice MPs would retain their seats at the next general election in five years? They saw looming danger, as did many of the more senior MPs, and they wanted the party to respond with drive and efficiency. Where the conjunction of events favoured the party in May, by the winter it was to change.

In July, we won a by-election but it was a bitter-sweet victory. Patsy Calton had terminal cancer when with great bravery she held Cheadle for the Liberal Democrats in the general election. She came to the Commons to take the oath some time after the rest of us and we could see she was dying. John Barrett, Lib Dem MP for Edinburgh West, pushed her in her wheelchair up to the Mace to take the oath and sign the book. Michael Martin, the Speaker, left his chair to shake her hand and said, 'You've come home, Patsy.' It was a memorable and deeply emotional occasion. We never saw Patsy again. She died at the end of May. We called an early by-election for 14 July to prevent the Conservatives having time to pick themselves up from their own general election disappointment and their leadership uncertainty. (By now Michael Howard had set in motion the process for his departure in December.) Even though the Tories spent a fortune on their campaign, Mark Hunter for the Liberal Democrats held the seat easily with 52 per cent of the vote and once again Charles's popularity proved a powerful electoral asset. The parliamentary party departed for the summer recess with a fine election victory to temper the memory of the general election.

I spent the summer attending constituency events and maintaining the party's high media profile over Iraq. We went fishing with our friends Johnnie and Claire Blair to the River Gruinard in Wester Ross where I broke my left ankle. I fell over stepping from the path beside the river on to a clump of grass which gave way beneath me. I thought I had torn some ligaments and continued to hobble around on it. I had it x-rayed when I returned home. It was broken. Surgeons at the Royal Infirmary in Edinburgh inserted a metal plate and I spent the rest of the summer on crutches and in plaster. People were wary of asking me what had happened because they were nervous of being told my cancer had returned.

This reticence showed itself particularly at Robin Cook's funeral, the third of my Scottish Labour friends to have died. Although familiarity with Robin came much later than it did with Donald Dewar or John Smith, I trusted him and admired his parliamentary skill. We worked together across the party divide on arms to Iraq, proportional representation and the build-up to war in Iraq. Our relationship was the strongest and most constructive of those to spring from the joint cabinet committee when Ashdown and Blair were talking coöperation and coalition. His death on 6 August 2005, from a heart attack when hill-walking in Sutherland, was a terrible shock to everyone. He was only fifty-nine. After it happened my phone rang constantly with media organisations hunting for comments and appreciations.

The funeral service, at St Giles Cathedral in Edinburgh, the High Kirk of Scotland, was a gathering of the Labour Party bidding farewell to the keeper of its conscience over the Iraq war. The contrast with John's and Donald's funerals was subtle but marked. Robin's was a Labour occasion; John's had been a Westminster one albeit in Scotland; Donald's an unofficial Scottish state funeral. Aly Bain and Phil Cunningham again played the Internationale as they had done so memorably at Donald's. The service was notable for three reasons. First, Robin was an atheist although Richard Holloway, the former

Episcopalian Bishop of Edinburgh, described him as a 'devout atheist . . . a Presbyterian atheist'; second, Gordon Brown delivered a eulogy from the pulpit which sounded like his manifesto for leadership; and, third, the extraordinary attack by John McCririck, Channel 4's racing pundit, on Tony Blair's 'petty vindictiveness' for staying away from the funeral. I remember Gordon Brown dominating the event in Blair's (I thought, tactful) absence. The wake afterwards at Edinburgh City Council's headquarters across the road from the cathedral took on the character of a Labour Party social. I found myself talking to Margaret Cook, Robin's ex-wife, when Brown joined us and put his arm round my shoulders. Elspeth told me later she had spoken to John Prescott and Jack Straw, both of whom she liked.

The Lib Dem conference at the Winter Gardens in Blackpool in September 2005 was the start of the new political year. With the benefit of hindsight, I can see its significance in the chronology of events that led to Charles's resignation although I had little sense of its potential at the time. There was background chatter about Charles's leadership but so there had been for the past two autumn conferences and he had always managed to overcome it. What was new? Maybe the new MPs had given it an intolerant edge. Andrew Rawnsley, writing in the *Observer* on the eve of conference, hit on a similar theme.

> Nagging away at ambitious Lib Dem MPs is the fear that this is the best it is ever going to get . . . Some of this restiveness among his colleagues is a product of success. As the party has grown in size at Westminster, a new creature has evolved in the political jungle. This beast is the careerist Lib Dem. These younger MPs have given up well-paid jobs and sacrificed family lives to come to Westminster. They are not prepared, as previous generations were, to settle forever for being third best. They are hungry for progress and impatient that Mr

Kennedy is not leading them towards power more quickly and aggressively. They are anxious that opportunity may not knock again.

Richard Grayson, Charles's former speech writer and adviser, provided a spark that turned the mix combustible. He put into words what so many Liberal Democrats felt but until then had been unable to express so succinctly or tellingly. Grayson said Charles's style was 'more chairman than leader' and he told the BBC 'the party wants to be led rather than necessarily being chaired'. Grayson wrote in the *Independent* on the opening day of conference: 'Mr Kennedy needs to take the policy debate by the scruff of its neck. Mastery of policy would help him to meet his second big challenge – convincing people he can lead the party to greater achievements.

'Ever since Mr Kennedy became leader there have been grumblings about his leadership style. Much of that is just politics. What is different now is that the next election is a long way off, and there is a general sense in the party that greater energy is needed between now and 2009/10.'

A hare had started running. The people around Charles were getting more and more nervous about it. He went on the BBC's *World at One* to try to kill it off but did the opposite when he seemed to agree with Grayson's analysis. 'It is a reflection of what I am feeling myself.' From then on the unofficial theme of the conference became Charles's leadership. It entered every conversation even if it stayed off the conference agenda. Charles tried again to kill it off the following day when he appeared on the *Today* programme and talked about his 'consensual' style but also his ability to show leadership over issues such as opposing war in Iraq.

The pressure built on Charles to deliver a motivational leader's speech. And, as he had done on so many occasions, he rose to the challenge. The first half of the speech was uninspiring but in the second half he spoke passionately about his vision of a fair and tolerant society which tackled poverty, spread opportunity and paid its debt to the elderly, a society fit for his growing child. He attacked his critics as people who 'may have become so full of themselves that they think they are full of better ideas about the leadership'.

I sat beside Sarah, Charles's wife, and applauded genuinely and enthusiastically when he finished speaking. The last part was the best passage of public speaking I'd ever heard from Charles and I told Tim Razzall and Jane Bonham Carter so straight afterwards. We left Blackpool with a spring in our steps. Charles's speech had given us momentum again. How long would it last?

The answer came in mid-November. The first I knew of anything untoward was when two of our new and talented MPs, Tim Farron and Julia Goldsworthy (Tim became my PPS and Julia shadow Chief Secretary to the Treasury), returned from accompanying Charles to the London School of Economics. They listened to his speech with growing alarm. His delivery was rambling and they wondered whether he would be able to finish it. They were so concerned by his performance they mentioned it to colleagues when they returned to the Commons. The worries and concerns that Charles's end-of-conference speech had allayed came rushing back.

The shadow cabinet meeting the following day made it worse. I was not there but I was told later that Charles had taken little part in the proceedings. I sat beside him the next day at Prime Minister's Questions and he was clearly unwell. My dilemma, as before, was what I should do about it, if anything. I had known, liked and admired Charles since he was twenty. My natural instinct was to avoid confronting him although my role as deputy leader was to protect the party and the careers of those who worked so hard for it. I think it was the next day that Charles went to King's Cross Station with a female party employee to travel to Newcastle as part of our local election campaigning for the following May. She rang his office to say she did not think Charles should carry on with the journey. His office agreed. A statement was put out to cover for Charles's absence. The statement had the desired effect. Nobody in the media questioned it, but the incident had a disturbing effect on the party.

It had such damaging potential that it passed in whispers among the MPs. Charles tried to deal with the growing clamour of complaint by demanding the loyalty of his front-bench team. A shadow cabinet meeting was held on the morning of Tuesday, 13 December.

Charles was obviously on the warpath. 'There's too much gossip. It must be stamped out. It's deeply corrosive and damaging to the party. I expect total loyalty from the shadow cabinet. Anyone who can't subscribe to that, see me by this afternoon.'

The inference was clear: speak up and leave or shut up and stay. Sandra Gidley, MP for Romsey and shadow spokesperson for older people, objected. 'Wait a minute. I've got some anxieties I'd rather address to the chief whip.' Mark Oaten, the home affairs spokesman, and Lembit Opik, shadow Welsh and Northern Ireland Secretary, then spoke with passion about loyalty to the leader.

I became concerned at the tenor of the meeting and said, 'Look, it's pretty clear this is a difficult issue for everyone. We've all got affection for each other and we've got personal baggage which is awkward when dealing with these sorts of things. I think it would be entirely sensible if people who have issues they want to raise can go to the chief whip to raise them.' I also suggested we 'go below the line' which was our code for asking everyone at the meeting who was not an MP to leave.

'No, not having that,' said Charles peremptorily. 'The people in my office who deal with these matters should hear what's being said.'

In the discussion that followed a number of shadow cabinet members expressed their concerns about the leadership but in the normal way of politics much of it was coded and hedged. I said nothing. Charles stuck by his deadline but approved my suggestion of letting anyone who wanted to express concerns to do so to the chief whip if they did not feel able to do so to his face.

The story broke in the newspapers the following morning. 'Kennedy crisis as doubters round on leadership' was the headline in the *Guardian*. The story mentioned Simon Hughes and me as leadership contenders 'though both have said they would not stand against the leader'. Westminster was awash with gossip.

I went to see Andrew Stunell, the chief whip, and told him I had reservations about Charles remaining as leader. Stunell, not surprisingly for a chief whip, wanted conciliation not confrontation. Then, the following day, I went to see Charles in his office.

I said, 'I think it's in the interests of yourself, your family and the party that you should now step down. I don't think we can go on as we are. It's not tolerable. There's drift and the parliamentary party is in a state of anxiety.'

I tried to find an elegant way out for him.

I told him: 'You can say you've led the party to its best general election results since the 1920s. You've got new family responsibilities. You've got a wonderful wife and a beautiful son. You want to spend as much time with them as you can. You're leaving the party a legacy of achievement of which you're proud. All of this is true.'

Charles listened intently.

I remember his response clearly. 'Ming, we've always been friends,' he said. 'I value your advice but you'll understand that on an issue like this I'll need to talk to Sarah, as you would to Elspeth. I've listened very carefully to what you've had to say.'

He came out from behind his desk, shook my hand and said, 'Thank you for being so frank. We've had a long friendship. It's survived this long and I hope it'll survive all of this.'

We parted company, each of us knowing the significance of the exchange between us.

I left his office and went out to the committee corridor. If I had turned left and gone down the stairs I could have avoided what became a damaging episode for me.

A group of reporters was waiting in the corridor alerted to the prospect of Liberal Democrat shadow cabinet members emerging from meetings with Charles. Inevitably they asked me about my meeting and I said, 'No comment, no comment, no comment.' Someone asked me whether Charles should continue as leader and I knew I could not respond 'no comment' to that or ignore it altogether without the risk of it being interpreted as an attempt by me to destabilise him.

I said the only thing I could without lying: 'Charles and I have had a long and very profitable relationship.'

I walked on and went to my office thinking I had given nothing away but I was angry with myself for walking past the reporters. I heard rumours of other people going to Charles and to the chief whip saying they too thought he should go but I did not know who they were and did not enquire further.

I went to the weekly parliamentary party meeting later in the afternoon with apprehension. The Charles Kennedy I saw there was the same one who had addressed the shadow cabinet meeting the day before. He demanded an end to the gossip and rumour-mongering and asked for loyalty to the leader. It was as if my conversation with him had never happened. Then MP after MP, including Mark Hunter, the new MP for Cheadle, spoke passionately in support of Charles. Mark Oaten made another impassioned plea for loyalty. The traffic was all one way. I cannot remember anyone speaking against Charles even though I knew half the MPs now opposed him. Certainly no one from the shadow cabinet spoke and neither did I. The only thing I had to say I had already said to him in confidence. Other members of the shadow cabinet felt similarly inhibited.

In hindsight, I should have restated the opinion I expressed privately to Charles, although it would have raised the stakes. If I had told the parliamentary party I thought Charles should go and he declined to do so I would have had to resign as deputy leader. It would have led to an immediate and very public crisis. As I know now, my silence spoke for me. The meeting ended inconclusively and I left it feeling uncomfortable.

I made my way to a pre-arranged Christmas dinner for Scottish Lib Dem MPs and their researchers and when I walked into the restaurant Michael Moore, my number two in foreign affairs and an MP from the Scottish Borders, said to me, 'You've been fingered for failing to give Kennedy support publicly.' He showed me a newsflash text message on his mobile phone. Nick Robinson, the BBC's political editor, had put out a story about my running the gauntlet of the reporters in the committee corridor and his interpretation of it was damaging to me. It made me look as though I was trying to increase the pressure on Charles by being less than loyal to him in public whereas my intention had been the opposite. I was furious at what I regarded as wilful misrepresentation and jumped wrongly to the conclusion that Charles's office had briefed against me.

I rang Jackie Rowley, Charles's press spokeswoman, and said, 'I'm not going to be set up as some kind of patsy. I gave my advice to Charles in private. I haven't discussed it with anyone. When I was asked about it by reporters I said no comment.' I ranted at her but later I had to apologise without qualification when I realised Charles's office had not briefed against me. After the dinner I went to bed troubled about what new dramas the morning would bring. When I woke up I switched on the *Today* programme as usual and to my dismay John Humphrys read out a news headline to the effect that I had withdrawn my support from Charles. That morning's headline in the *Guardian* was: 'Kennedy refuses to sack disloyal deputy'.

I went to my office and called in two colleagues to ask them what I should do. We agreed that I should put out a statement in an attempt to stop the rumour mill running. Because of other commitments I wasn't able to issue the statement until after the lunchtime news bulletins. I knew it might just pour petrol on the flames because I could hardly issue a statement of unequivocal support for Charles. What alternative was there? If I said and did nothing, my silence would damn me since a deputy's role is to ride to the rescue of his leader unless he has very good reasons for not doing so.

My statement was: 'As long as Charles Kennedy remains the leader of the Liberal Democrats, he has my full support.'

It did not, of course, address the question of whether I thought he should remain leader of the Liberal Democrats and so its effect was to increase the speculation about me. I went to Heathrow Airport in the afternoon to fly to Scotland and a BBC TV news crew jumped me when I got off the Paddington Express. I said I had nothing to add and went quickly into the security of the airport departure lounge.

The *Guardian* reported the following day that Charles 'threatened to wield the knife against disloyal Liberal Democrats' and that 'at least six senior MPs have told him privately that he should resign'.

The story was moving so fast that it seemed unstoppable. Would the Christmas recess put a brake on it as MPs and journalists went home to their families? Sometimes it can happen that way. The recess can rob a story of its momentum or it can fuel it because the news agenda dries up and editors and reporters keep doggedly working away at the stories running when the House of Commons closed down. Paul Marsden, the former Labour MP who defected to the Lib Dems and then went back to Labour before the 2005 general election, kept it going the weekend before Christmas by writing in the *Mail on Sunday* that Charles had a 'serious problem' with alcohol. Charles went on Jonathan Dimbleby's Sunday programme to say he would be 'coming back with fresh ideas and fresh impetus for the party in the new year'. If people were concerned about his lifestyle 'they need not be'.

Dimbleby then asked, 'Does that mean you're cutting back?'

Charles replied, 'Yes, I'm actually an extremely moderate and infrequent consumer of alcohol, as a matter of fact.'

After that I began to hear rumours about eleven members of the shadow cabinet signing a letter of no confidence in Charles's leadership. No one approached me to sign it or to discuss it.

Every Christmas party during the recess was the same. All anyone wanted to speak about was Charles's leadership and whether he would survive. Our MPs were in a similar turmoil. Some of them began to contact me to ask obliquely whether I would take over from Charles to stabilise the party. I tried to deflect them by saying, 'It depends on what the doctors say.' I had one of my regular check-ups just before Christmas. The doctors pronounced themselves satisfied with my continuing progress. Otherwise I tried to be as non-committal as I could. Between Christmas and New Year I went on the *Today* programme and made what supportive comments I could about Charles without contradicting my advice to him. I said the Liberal Democrats were at their best when Charles was at his best and I praised the social justice theme of his message for 2006. He paged me to thank me.

The New Year brought no respite in the quickening pace of events. (Lord) Tom McNally, the Lib Dem leader in the Lords, said: 'Is it terminal for Charles? My view is that it is not. Does his leadership need a radical, rapid and sustained change in style and content? The answer is yes.'

Then the dam broke. Susan Kramer, MP for Richmond Park, called for a snap leadership ballot to 'clear the air'. Alistair

Carmichael, the MP for Orkney and Shetland, said Charles should force a vote of confidence among the MPs, and Norman Baker, MP for Lewes and the party's shadow Environment Secretary, said on BBC2's *Newsnight* that Charles should face a ballot of either the party membership or the MPs at Westminster. Jenny Tonge, a Lib Dem peer, said, 'The boil has to be lanced.' I watched it all from the relative calm of my home in Edinburgh with a growing feeling of inevitability about what would happen next. Then Charles pulled a surprise.

The chief whip rang me on Elspeth's birthday, 5 January, to warn me about a statement Charles planned to make. I didn't know what he intended to say. Charles called the TV cameras to the Liberal HQ at Cowley Street in London. He said he had been treated for a drink problem for the past eighteen months and that he had wanted to overcome it privately but had been forced to go public because it was about to be broadcast (ITN apparently had the story of his treatment). He said his drink problem was 'essentially resolved' and he was in good health. He ended it by calling a snap leadership election.

I watched his statement on television with admiration for the quiet dignity with which he admitted his problem with alcohol, although I doubted it was 'essentially resolved'. It had not been as recently as mid-November. The snap leadership election also concerned me. I had no intention of standing against Charles as I said immediately after his statement. My worry was more about the parliamentary party and the consequences of Charles's attempt to reach over the MPs by appealing for support from the membership. I doubted whether it would work. Too many people now knew too much about Charles's problem for it not to be exposed in detail. Charles was still popular among the party's 70,000 members, but would he continue to be if his drinking and its consequences on the running of the party were splashed all over the newspapers? Chris Davies, leader of the Lib Dems in the European parliament, said Charles was 'a dead man walking', a comment that caused considerable upset at the time and still rankles in the Kennedy camp. My phone rang constantly and Elspeth became agitated about her birthday party at the theatre and dinner afterwards. She worried that we would no longer be able to go, so frequently was the phone ringing with people in the party wanting to discuss Charles's statement and journalists looking for a comment from me.

'Let's go,' I said and opened the door on January blackness. Elspeth and I walked down the path to our front gate when suddenly television news crews turned on their lights and newspaper photographers flashed their cameras. The effect was blinding and, for Elspeth, disconcerting. She was not used to such media attention.

As we passed them I said, 'It's my wife's birthday and I'm going to the theatre.' We went to see *My Fair Lady*, with Christopher Cazenove starring as Professor Higgins. When we walked out at the end to cross the road to have dinner in an Italian restaurant another camera crew was waiting for me. The camerawoman was the daughter of Margo MacDonald, now an Independent member of the Scottish parliament. Scotland is a small place. Elspeth was behind me talking to our friends. We strode resolutely towards the camera (after I asked Elspeth to hide her cigarette). The die was cast. If Charles carried out his threat to stand as leader I would not stand against him but I had decided not to continue serving under him as deputy leader and foreign affairs spokesman.

The next day, Friday, brought a flurry of meetings in London and an ultimatum from twenty-five MPs, more than a third of the parliamentary party, who threatened to resign their portfolios if Charles had not resigned by the following Monday. I knew little of the ultimatum to Charles because the MPs understood that compromising me would jeopardise my caretaker role if Charles did as they demanded. On Saturday, 7 January, I received a phone call to warn me that Charles was about to ring.

So I was prepared for what I had come to regard as inevitable. Charles phoned to tell me he was about to resign. We had a calm, civilised and amicable conversation. I said I was sorry it had come to this. It was sincere. When I told Elspeth Charles was resigning, she burst into tears. She had been one of the first people Charles rang when he announced his engagement to Sarah.

I had conflicting emotions: sadness for Charles personally, relief the crisis was finally over and apprehension about taking over as acting leader. I didn't think, 'This is my big chance to be leader.' I thought, 'I'm taking on a big responsibility and there's got to be a sense of purpose and clarity about what we do. I've got to get the party back on an even keel.'

Charles's resignation statement for the media was dignified, good-humoured and free from rancour of any kind. It had been forced on him but he did it with grace and elegance. After such a display of dignity, my declaration as a candidate seemed precipitate. I did it quickly to fill the vacuum. MPs were asking me to declare or else it might look as though nobody wanted to lead the party.

'We'll have a vacancy and no bloody candidates,' one said to me.

I talked it over with Elspeth. She thought I should stand and so did I. I opened my front door and walked towards the reporters gathered outside. I paid tribute to Charles's dignity and courage. 'The party will forever be in his debt,' I said.

'As deputy leader I will be assuming his responsibilities with immediate effect and over the next forty-eight hours will obviously be consulting colleagues. But I can confirm today that I intend to be a candidate in the leadership contest which is to follow.'

14

Leadership contest

The phone rang incessantly. Reporters. Political editors. MPs. Party officials. Friends. Relatives. Saturday passed in a blur of telephone conversations. I spent most of the day telephone in one hand and legal papers in the other. By an unfortunate quirk of timing I was due to appear for a client in Dunoon Sheriff Court on Monday morning. Every time I settled down to read the case papers the phone rang or my pager went off. I wondered whether I should still be doing the case since I was now acting leader of the Liberal Democrats and the only declared candidate to succeed Charles. I had so much else to do, and I had a niggling concern about the impression it could give. I worried too about letting my client down at such short notice. I rang Archy Kirkwood to ask his advice. 'Do it,' he said. 'It doesn't matter. Just go. If you're in London by Monday night it's fine.'

So, on Sunday evening, I packed my court clothes, set off in the car and left behind the headlines and media talk about 'Ming the Merciless' and 'plots' by my supporters when the truth was that the parliamentary party had reached breaking point. I turned off my mobile phone, switched on Classic FM and left Edinburgh to drive west to Argyll with a feeling of escape and isolation. I do not ever remember enjoying the journey to Dunoon quite so much. I spent the night in a comfortable hotel and arrived in court before 10 a.m. slightly apprehensive about running into TV cameras or photographers. There were none.

Who would have expected the newest, albeit acting, party leader in Britain to spend the first Monday morning in a sheriff court in the west of Scotland? It was comical, if inconvenient. My case was one of a number scheduled for that morning including a child custody case which by convention took precedence over the others. The parties involved in my case decided to seek another date for the hearing. By 11 a.m. I was on the ferry crossing the Firth of Clyde to Gourock. I drove past Greenock and Port Glasgow, where my political journey had begun more than thirty years before, through Glasgow, my birthplace, and along the M8 to Edinburgh Airport from where I flew to London and my new responsibilities of acting leader of a party bruised and battered by the recent events.

I wondered who else would stand for the leadership. Mark Oaten? I thought not. Simon Hughes? Probably. Like me, he said he would never stand against Charles but there was a vacancy now. The twenty-five MPs who delivered the ultimatum to Charles before the weekend had agreed to support me, or so I thought. On my first day back in London, the party's elder statesmen and former leaders, Ashdown and Steel, declared for me. Paddy said I had 'weight and substance and seriousness' and David referred to my 'unimpeachable integrity'. The federal party executive met that night to decide the timetable for an election contest ending just before the party's spring conference at Harrogate in March 2006. My concern at the timetable was a practical one: how was I going to attend hustings all over the country as well as run the party at Westminster at such a crucial time? The local council elections in England and Wales were in less than four months. There was talk of a 'coronation' because it would have allowed the party to concentrate on council election campaigning but the mere mention of the word caused anger among the membership who wanted a contest. Mark Oaten, one of Charles's most vocal supporters and the home affairs spokesman, declared his candidacy the next day. All talk of a coronation died.

Now there was to be a contest Archy Kirkwood gave me some early advice after reading a story in the *Independent* about my Jaguar, a metallic red, seventeen-year-old 5.3 litre XJS with a V12 engine which I kept in London and drove infrequently. The *Independent* thought it doubtful I would be keeping the party's 'smokeless flame burning and embracing green causes'. With a pang of regret I asked my stepson, James, if he would drive it north for me. (I donated it later to the Myreton Motor Museum at Aberlady in East Lothian.) Also I remember thinking, I must drink less and sleep more. I realised health, stamina and mental alertness would be important in the leadership campaign and beyond. I didn't want to risk them by having even one glass of wine too many late at night. It was a throwback to my years as an athlete: I knew I had a better chance of winning by doing whatever was necessary to be most competitive.

The party was suffering badly in the polls: a Populus poll in *The Times* put the Lib Dems down three points at sixteen points, the lowest rating since the 2001 general election. Nearly three-fifths of Lib Dem voters thought Charles should have remained leader. The party's sense of crisis was hardly lessened by my first appearance as acting leader at Prime Minister's Questions. I stood up to a lot of catcalling and asked a question about public services.

'The National Audit Office today reports that one million people are being failed by our schools,' I said. 'The Health Committee has described the latest proposals for health service reforms as ill judged. The police are up in arms about the Prime Minister's costly proposals for centralisation. Why are the Government making such a mess of public service reform?'

Blair responded by cherry-picking the positives from the Audit Office report: the number of failing schools halved; the number of secondary schools getting less than 30 per cent of five good GCSEs down from 900 in 1997 to 340 in 2005 and so on. I had another prepared question to ask him but I persevered with schools because the subject was so important.

'While the Prime Minister is anxious to achieve some balance in the argument,' I said, 'perhaps he would like to explain why one in five schools do not have a permanent head teacher.'

A Labour MP to my left immediately shouted, 'What about a permanent leader?' and the chamber erupted with laughter.

The Speaker asked for order and I continued: 'I just knew it was going to be one of those days, Mr Speaker. When the Prime Minister entered No 10 Downing Street, he rightly abandoned socialism, but has not Blairism become a byword for centralisation and a failure to deliver?'

Blair added to the merriment by saying to me, 'As the right hon. and learned gentleman knows, it can be difficult to find the head of an organisation when the post is vacant, particularly if it is a failing organisation.'

I was astonished at Blair's reply and the reactions of MPs. Had Blair intended to brand 20 per cent of schools 'failing' as he seemed to have done to the great amusement of all? I was angry with myself for having taken too little time to think about any bear traps in my questions.

The sketch writers had a field day. 'Ming falls victim to merciless ambush' and 'Ming the Merciless rebranded Ming the Massacred', filled the next morning's papers. I received a forest of letters afterwards. They all followed a similar theme: 'My child's at a school without a head teacher. Why didn't the Prime Minister answer the question?' I felt vindicated.

Simon Hughes, the party president, declared his candidacy the day after PMQs and Chris Huhne, a former Euro MP who entered the Commons in 2005 as MP for Eastleigh, the next day. Chris's candidacy was a surprise. He had been one of the twenty-five MPs who had delivered the ultimatum to Charles and who were bound by a collective agreement not to stand against me. Chris came to see me in my office in Portcullis House and asked if I would free him from the undertaking which, he said, had been made at a meeting he had not attended. I said I would but I took the opportunity to set out the reasons why he should back me instead of standing himself. After more than an hour's discussion we shook hands, with Chris saying he would support me.

I rang Archy. 'I've squared Huhne,' I said. 'He's not going to stand.'

Chris appeared back in my office three-quarters of an hour later and said he had to discuss it with his wife and was sure I would understand if he changed his mind. We didn't shake hands when he departed for a second time.

Simon Hughes's campaign team began sounding out my advisers. They had a proposal. If I undertook to make Simon deputy leader, he would withdraw from the contest and declare his support for me. Most of my people were opposed to a deal. They thought he would be too much of a maverick. I shared their reservations about him as deputy leader. The negotiations ended in failure.

Nine days after declaring his candidacy Mark Oaten suddenly withdrew. As my campaign team thought, he had minimal support in the parliamentary party. Only Lembit Opik backed him. In popular mythology his withdrawal has become conflated with the newspaper revelations about him three days later which prompted Mark's resignation as home affairs spokesman. But he had retired from the contest before these became known. The lurid headlines were helped along by Simon Hughes admitting to both gay and heterosexual relationships after previously denying homosexuality. I sympathised with Simon's predicament: his denials of homosexuality started many years earlier when the political climate was hostile to gays in parliament. There is never a good time for a politician to change a story. Was the leadership election about to be picked apart by a frenzy of journalists raking through all of our lives to find the next story?

Then a former Liberal Democrat party employee working in public relations rang to alert my team to a damaging e-mail. It accused me of taking money from defence manufacturers in return for asking questions in the House of Commons. If true, which it most certainly was not, it could have led to my expulsion. I was furious about its potential to damage my reputation and to destroy my leadership campaign if any newspaper published it. We had lawyers standing by every Saturday night in case one of the Sunday papers decided to run with it. The e-mail trail led back to a press officer in the Conservative Party. We suspected a political smear. Ben Stoneham, the Lib Dem head of human resources, complained to the Tories who apologised immediately. A letter arrived from Henry Macrory, head of the party's press department.

'I am writing,' he said, 'to offer my sincere apologies for a serious error of judgement last Friday when a Conservative press officer e-mailed three university friends in a private capacity with comments about you which we fully accept were defamatory. Her e-mail was sent without the knowledge of anyone else at Conservative Campaign Headquarters, and she bitterly regrets her action.'

Macrory detailed how the press officer had been back in touch with her friends to tell them her e-mail was 'unfounded gossip' and 'untrue'.

'I apologise once again for her actions,' he concluded, 'and would like to take this opportunity to thank you for your party's helpful and understanding attitude towards this very regrettable incident.'

Another far greater and private worry was Elspeth's health. She discovered a lump which unnerved and frightened us both. Elspeth was stoical about it. Her view was that we should say and do nothing until she had the results of a biopsy. For ten days Elspeth didn't know whether she had cancer and I didn't know whether I could carry on my leadership campaign. If the lump had been malignant I would have felt the same obligation to her as she had shown to me when I had been ill with non-Hodgkin lymphoma. I would have withdrawn from the contest to be with her. We sighed with relief when the biopsy detected no malignancy. Elspeth's consultant said he was 99.5 per cent certain the lump was benign. (She had it removed after I became leader.)

In the middle of worrying about Elspeth I was criss-crossing the country for leadership hustings. It was exhausting, especially so since I was suffering with a chest infection. I was taking antibiotics for the duration of the campaign. Though Simon, Chris and I were rivals we tried to be good-natured to each other. A newspaper poll of party members attending a hustings at Cardiff University gave me a shock. Almost a third said they would support Chris, a quarter me and less than a fifth Simon. The bookies' odds also began to move Chris's way. Did he have enough momentum to overtake me? I thought he might but the odds were moving so strangely I couldn't tell what was happening. When the three of us appeared on BBC TV's *Question Time*, my campaign team thought I had done well and so did the bookies because the odds went back in my favour. Then someone placed a £5,000 bet on me to lose and my odds lengthened again. Was someone trying to manipulate the odds to make it look as though I was doing worse than I was? We never did find out but we had our suspicions.

Even the sensational Lib Dem victory on 9 February at the Dunfermline and West Fife by-election in Gordon Brown's back yard didn't seem to help my campaign. I thought it would give my candidacy an immediate boost because it demonstrated the party winning a safe Labour seat, overturning a majority of 11,562 with a swing of 16 per cent, with me as acting leader and next door to my own constituency. The final hustings was at the Friends Meeting House in Euston Road, London, organised by the *Independent* newspaper. There must have been 1,000 people there. I put aside the speech prepared for me and spoke with passion about my vision as party leader.

'I have never been more proud,' I remember saying, 'than when every single Liberal Democrat MP went through the lobby together to vote against the war in Iraq.'

The last question of the evening was: 'What have you learned from each other?' Simon answered first and went into a long account of why he should be leader and how he would be a vote-winner for the party. I spoke next. 'From Simon I've learned modesty and humility. And how not to answer the bloody question.' The audience roared with laughter.

After that hustings, the mood changed. The momentum started to swing back towards me. Even so my calmness on the eve of the result was unusual. My composure stemmed, I think, from a private decision I'd made. Simon, Chris and I had said we'd work with each other whoever won but I'd come to realise it was a commitment I couldn't keep. If I lost I would resign as deputy leader and foreign affairs spokesman. Elspeth and I had talked about it. I would return to the back benches, spend more time with my legal career and look for membership of a select committee such as defence or foreign affairs. My letter of resignation to the new leader was composed in my head.

Dear Chris/Simon,
Since the announcement of the leadership election result on Thursday morning I have been giving careful consideration to my future. The new leader of the party should have a blank sheet to work with and should be free to choose his own team to serve in the shadow cabinet. Consequently, I have decided to step down as deputy leader and to return to the back benches. I think this is the best course of action for you, for me and for the party etc, etc.

On the morning of 2 March, the day of the election result, I went calmly to my office to await Archy's phone call with the result of the vote. Elspeth flew down from Scotland and joined me before lunchtime. Archy rang at about 1.15. 'We've done it,' he said. I turned to Michael Moore and the two aides in my office, Carrie Henderson and Emily Walch, and said, 'We've won.' They shrieked so loudly that MPs in the offices around mine must have known I had won. Michael said, 'Shush.' Elspeth returned from the loo and when I told her everyone shrieked again. 'Shush,' said Michael more emphatically.

We walked to the Local Government Association headquarters in Smith Square, where the result was to be announced. Cameras followed us all the way so we had to pretend we did not already know the result. When we arrived I was taken into a room to see the detailed figures. I had polled 29,697 votes to Chris's 21,628 after the second preferences among Simon's supporters had been redistributed. I remember all three of us being called on stage and holding Simon's and Chris's arms aloft when the result was announced. 'Today is not a victory for me; it is a victory for all Liberal Democrats,' I said in my acceptance speech, deliberately avoiding any note of triumphalism.

I praised Simon and Chris. To Simon, I said, 'I never cease to admire your tireless efforts to promote the cause of liberal democracy. I look forward to continuing that work with you as a valued friend and campaigning president of our party.' To Chris, I said, 'You are a formidable asset for our party and will be a big part of our future. I look forward to working with you and the others of the brightest and best generation in politics to develop and strengthen our party.' Both of them said generous things about me in return. I also made mention of the 'remarkable legacy' of Charles Kennedy.

I knew Charles would be sitting in the first row of seats in front of me. I had been forewarned. I admired him for his courage. By prior arrangement Charles had agreed to shake my hand after the result was announced. I walked off stage to where he was sitting. He said, 'Congratulations,' and I replied, 'Thank you very much.' We exchanged brief platitudes. What else could we do with so many flashbulbs bursting around us? It was the picture all the photographers wanted.

It made me acutely aware of the fragility of leadership. Would Charles still have been leader if he had taken a week off after the birth of his baby instead of two days? Sometimes I think so because he wouldn't have made the council tax gaffe, he wouldn't have blamed himself afterwards, he wouldn't have gone into the September conference in a weakened position and he wouldn't have felt so under pressure in November.

Elspeth and I led a phalanx of MPs and camera crews out of the LGA building into Lord North Street and to the party's Cowley Street headquarters. The staff crowded round the banisters above and below me in the stairwell as I addressed them for the first time as the party's new leader. I felt emotional doing it, and a terrible sense of responsibility to these people who depended on me for the party's success.

My victory was unlike any other in my career, whether on the athletics track, in the courtroom or in the County Buildings, Cupar, waiting for the returning officer to announce North-East Fife general election results. Winning this time was not the end of the process but the beginning. My thoughts turned to Harrogate and the spring conference the following day and the local elections in May. I had two speeches to write and a party to galvanise.

Kirsty Wark interviewed me for BBC *Newsnight* and concluded by asking me four general knowledge questions. Where did the Arctic Monkeys come from? What was the minimum wage? Who won *Celebrity Big Brother*? Who was the Chief Inspector of Schools? I knew the minimum wage and the only thing I knew about the Arctic Monkeys was that their first album had outsold the Beatles. Tomorrow's commentators would probably say how out of touch I was with contemporary music and TV culture, but I didn't mind. I felt profound satisfaction at my election (as did Elspeth; she put an early bet of £50 on me and won £1,000). I was leading the party of Grimond, Steel and Ashdown, all of whom I had known and admired; and of Herbert Asquith, who represented the same part of Fife as me.

15

Leader and firefighter

'You'll never be as popular or as powerful as you are now,' one of my supporters confided to me on the day of my election as leader. I resisted its implied pessimism. Whoever I spoke to, wherever I went, I found enthusiasm for my election and the party's prospects. It was written on the faces of delegates at Harrogate and in the hundreds of congratulatory letters I received from party members. There was overwhelming relief that a damaging and fractious episode was behind us. Most people wanted the wounds healed as soon as possible. I shared their desire.

What the party desperately needed now was strong leadership after its long period of introspection. The Harrogate conference gave me an immediate opportunity to provide it. I supported a controversial proposal to part-privatise the Post Office (which was wrongly interpreted as a drift to the right), backed green taxes on air travel and signalled my opposition to the 50p top rate of income tax which had been Liberal Democrat policy at the 2005 general election. My first big speech as leader was well received with a standing ovation. Archy Kirkwood, now my principal political adviser, and I were driven to York Station to catch a train to London. We heaved a sigh of relief at a job (so far) well done. The train was late and a wind was blowing along the platform. I remember thinking I'd better get used to wind-blown platforms.

Part of my inheritance was a threadbare campaign plan for the 2006 local elections two months after I became leader. I was horrified to discover the party had done little if any preparatory campaign work, just a few random visits by the leader pencilled into a diary. There was also the controversy over the party's largest ever donation of £2.4 million. I had known nothing about it when it was made but now as leader I had to deal with it. The money had come from a Scots-born millionaire called Michael Brown, and was for the 2005 general election campaign (it was spent on advertising). Seven weeks after I became leader Mr Brown appeared in court in Madrid on charges including forgery, perjury and perverting the course of justice. He was later extradited to Britain. As a result the party was threatened with legal claims for the return of the money. I stuck to the line that it had been accepted in 'good faith', spent for the purposes for which it had been given and no preferment had been sought or offered. Inevitably, my attacks on the government over the 'cash for honours' furore had to be restrained. Whenever I tried to raise the issue, Tony Blair would hit back by referring to my party's own difficulty with Mr Brown's £2.4 million.

My first task was the new shadow cabinet. I was determined to conduct the reshuffle quickly but what should I do with my two recent rivals for the leadership? My closest advisers were wary of Chris Huhne, who was shadow Chief Secretary to the Treasury in Charles's front-bench team. They wondered whether he could be trusted after he had undertaken not to stand against me. Although I shared some of their reservations, I came to the conclusion that the new front-bench team must engage all our best talents. Chris Huhne's abilities were beyond dispute. I made him environment spokesman, a key role which he wanted, as the party moved towards green taxes. The headline writers made much of me appointing my rival. I didn't regret it.

My instinct with Simon Hughes was different. I thought he should concentrate on being party president and not have a front-bench role. He made strong representations against my view and I gave way. I made him constitutional affairs spokesman. The other appointments were easier: Nick Clegg as home affairs spokesman, Michael Moore as foreign affairs spokesman – he had been my deputy in the role and had stood in for me during my illness with cancer – and Julia Goldsworthy as shadow Chief Secretary to the Treasury and deputy to Vince Cable, who continued as Treasury spokesman. At twenty-eight, Julia became the youngest front-bencher in the House of Commons. Steve Webb, who supported Simon Hughes for the leadership, remained at health.

I announced my shadow cabinet, including four women, the following day and all the other front-bench appointments within forty-eight hours. I said, 'We have the brightest political generation in our ranks and I'm relishing the opportunity to lead them.'

The only position left undecided was not mine to award: chief whip. It's one of those Liberal Democrat curiosities that the person in the front-bench team who works closest with the leader is not chosen by him but elected by the parliamentary party. I thought it would be difficult for Andrew Stunell, the chief whip under Charles, to carry on and I asked him to move to a role shadowing John Prescott and his Office of the Deputy Prime Minister for which he was outstandingly qualified. My candidate for chief whip was Paul Burstow, MP for Sutton and Cheam and a stalwart of my leadership campaign. I knew I could work closely with him. A rival candidate, Richard Younger-Ross, MP for Teignbridge, offered himself. When the election was held Burstow won by thirty-eight votes to Younger-Ross's eighteen. One MP told me: 'You may be leader but don't think you've got unlimited authority. It's not good for you to have everything your own way.' The experience irritated me but hardly surprised me. Lib Dems have always had an anarchic tendency.

The chief whip's election coincided with Budget Day, my first big set-piece parliamentary occasion as leader. After David Cameron's predictable sound-bite attack on Gordon Brown's 'old-fashioned tax and spend' politics, I questioned the detail of the Chancellor's statement. I pointed out his failure to help pensioners with council tax ('Why was it they deserved help immediately before the general election and didn't deserve help a year later?') and Labour's omission to increase environmental taxation 'to encourage people to change the way they live'. Anatole Kaletsky in *The Times* commented: 'Where the Chancellor is vulnerable is where Sir Menzies Campbell, the new Liberal Democrat leader, quite rightly focused his attack.' A few days later the *Guardian* ran a leader comment on my first month in charge. 'A capable if low-key opening spell from Sir Menzies Campbell has put a smile back on the faces of the party's MPs.'

Even my critics acknowledged I was providing a sense of direction whether it was in policy-making or in organisation. To sharpen our political focus, I set up a leader's group which met every Monday at 5 p.m. and every Tuesday, Wednesday and Thursday at 9 a.m. The membership was Archy Kirkwood, Norman Lamb, MP for North Norfolk and my chief of staff, Mark Littlewood, head of press, and Lord (Chris) Rennard, the party's chief executive. Vince Cable, who was elected deputy leader at the end of March, joined the group later. A forward planning grid was produced for every meeting to enable us to prepare coherent media and parliamentary responses to the running political agenda. Staffing my office took longer to arrange: Alison Suttie, my new head of office, and Puja Darbari, my press secretary, had to work out their notices at their existing jobs before moving into my Commons office. But gradually it was all coming together.

One weekend in April, during the English local election campaign, I was able to escape briefly from politics to be installed as Chancellor of St Andrews University in my

North-East Fife constituency. It was a memorable and happy occasion. First I received an honorary degree of Doctor of Laws. Then, having been installed as Chancellor, wearing a newly made gown of gold and black, I conferred honorary degrees on three deserving friends: Anna Ford, the broadcaster; Dame Jennifer Jenkins, the widow of Roy Jenkins and a champion of consumer and conservation issues; and Lord (Brian) Gill, the second most senior judge in Scotland and one of my oldest legal friends. (My one great sadness at becoming Lib Dem leader was giving up my legal work and becoming a non-practising member of the Faculty of Advocates. My wooden box for receiving legal papers, which had been in the corridor of the Court of Session in Parliament House in Edinburgh for thirty-eight years, was unceremoniously removed.)

The local election results were a mixed bag. The Lib Dems polled 27 per cent, pushing Labour into third place on 26 per cent. But we gained only two seats, far short of the 100 or so psephologists were predicting on a bad day for the government. I talked publicly of 'consolidation' and said the election had not been a test of my leadership but a test of the party after the 'difficulties' earlier in the year. 'I think we have come through this test,' I said confidently but I was very disappointed. We had made the mistake of mismanaging expectations. We should have countered the optimism of the predictions. That failure allowed the media to report the results as a missed opportunity for the party.

By now I had set myself three tasks. First, I had to put the party back on an even keel after the traumas of Charles's resignation and the leadership election; second, I had to make the party more professional in its outlook; and, third, to ensure we would be ready for a general election whenever it might come.

To begin with I found Prime Minister's Questions difficult. What counts at PMQs is the quality of performance, not the quality of argument. It's theatre, not debate. I'm uncomfortable with that type of politics, and it showed. David Steel, Paddy Ashdown and Charles Kennedy, all good Commons performers on their day, found it tough in their time. I remember having lunch with Paddy and discussing my difficulties. He told me of one occasion where the baying cries from the massed government and opposition benches were so loud his voice could not be picked up by the microphones. Unlike the Prime Minister or the leader of the Opposition, the Lib Dem leader stands without a despatch box on which to rest any papers or notes. The leader of the Opposition asks six questions and chooses the big issues of the day. The Lib Dem leader follows and has only two questions. I set to work to improve my performances. I knew it would never be my strength.

At one PMQs in May 2006, I stumbled over my words on a question about farm policy, hospital closures and the Home Office. At the parliamentary party meeting that evening I decided to talk candidly about my difficulties and to reassure my backbenchers I was working hard to improve my performances. Much to my fury, my comments were leaked to the *Daily Telegraph* under the heading: 'I'm sorry for my poor showing, says Sir Menzies'. It went on to report: 'The failures at Prime Minister's Questions . . . have bemused friends and foes alike given his background as a barrister and QC.

'At Wednesday night's private weekly meeting of the Lib Dem parliamentary party, he surprised MPs by confessing that his court experience was no preparation for the cut-and-thrust of Prime Minister's Questions.

'According to one person present, Sir Menzies lamented: "Juries don't normally answer back." ' It was an attempt at humour on my part which was deliberately misrepresented.

At the parliamentary party meeting the following week, I rounded on the MPs. 'Look, if you want me to be frank with you at these meetings,' I said, 'I can only be so on the basis that what

I say within these four walls is confidential. If you do talk about it outside then the obvious consequence is that I can't talk in the open way I would want to.' Paul Holmes, the chairman of the parliamentary party, weighed in on my behalf to the same effect.

Simon Hughes, my erstwhile rival for the leadership, then went on GMTV and said my expertise was in foreign affairs, implying I was weak on domestic policy. He added: 'I think we need to judge him when it comes to the autumn conference.' The media interpretation was inevitable: party president gives Campbell four months to prove himself. At one of my regular meetings with Simon as party president, I told him how angry I was at his intervention. As Simon usually did when he said something that rebounded on me, he apologised. Then I went on BBC Radio 5 Live and announced I'd had 'a frank exchange of views' with Simon. My intention was to deter anyone else in the party raising doubts about me. I said, 'I'm not setting any time limits for my leadership and I don't expect anyone else to do so – and that includes Simon Hughes.' What I did not say was that I was having secret coaching to help me with PMQs.

The Liberal Democrat peer, Lord Watson, has advised UK and international companies on their communications strategies. I was his next project. A studio in his office in London was turned into a miniature House of Commons. Archy and Alan Watson pretended to be hecklers to mimic the Labour and Tory MPs who shouted at me whenever I rose to speak. The mock PMQs was filmed by a fixed camera set at exactly the same angle as the one that covered me in the Commons chamber. After asking my 'questions', Alan Watson, Archy and I would watch the film and try to work out what to change. The problems were my glasses, my hands and the length of the questions. I had four sessions in the studio (for which we paid) before we were happy with our new approach to PMQs. In future, I would memorise the questions making it unnecessary for me to hold any papers. It would mean shorter, punchier questions which would have the benefit of reducing the heckling. Also, I would hold my glasses in my right hand. This would have two advantages: wearing glasses played to the media caricature of me; and holding them would give me something to do with my hands.

My confidence at PMQs grew and, gradually, over a number of months, my performances fell out of the headlines. Another unwelcome factor played a part. Week after week Tony Blair began PMQs by paying tribute to the latest British soldiers killed in action in Iraq and Afghanistan. The leader of the Opposition did the same when he stood up, and so too did I. Instead of a growing crescendo of heckling, my opening words were greeted with respectful silence. The sombreness of the mood continued while I asked my first question. It was a better atmosphere for serious political discussion. As an opponent of the war in Iraq, I would rather have suffered the heckling than listen to the PM's weekly litany of wasted British lives. He, Cameron and I repeated the almost identical words week after week. I wondered what the families and friends of the dead would make of this ritual. How would the families of the injured regard it? Once or twice I extended my expression of condolences to the wounded. I resented how the toll of dead and wounded in Iraq had been reduced to routine in the Commons.

My continued criticisms over the Iraq war led to a cooling in my relationship with Blair. Although we used to see each other by chance at various public occasions and, of course, across the floor of the House of Commons, we met only once formally as party leaders. It was in Downing Street. Archy accompanied me. Blair had three advisers with him, including Jonathan Powell, his chief of staff. We had no written agenda and no one took minutes. I had asked for the meeting out of courtesy – to talk to him as Liberal Democrat leader.

The conversation was polite and businesslike. I raised a practical issue about rewarding MPs for long service. What was the procedure now that the rules had been changed? As examples I raised the possibility of a Privy Council appointment for one colleague and a knighthood for another. It provoked an amusing exchange between Powell and Blair, who didn't seem to realise he had given up his powers of patronage.

When Blair heard the names he said, 'Well, of course that's something I would support.'

Powell interrupted, 'But you cannot support him. You've relinquished it.'

Blair said, 'Oh, yes I can.'

Powell replied, 'Oh, no you can't.'

Then we discussed the unequal treatment by the public purse of the two principal opposition parties. By way of illustration I mentioned the anomaly of the leader of the Liberal Democrats only receiving the basic salary of an MP, unlike the leader of the Opposition, who received the equivalent of a minister of state's salary plus a car and a driver. Blair looked taken aback as if he were ignorant of this anomaly. 'Is that true?' he said, sounding surprised. I had cause to regret mentioning it.

Six months later, Elspeth was talking to Cherie, Blair's wife, who piped up, 'The only thing Ming's asked Tony for is an increased salary for himself.'

Elspeth stood her ground and replied, 'I don't think he was looking for a pay rise for himself. It was for the leader of the third party.'

Before leaving 10 Downing Street, I had a private conversation with Blair. We talked about our families. Then I said to him, 'Look, I'm sorry the way this Iraq business has turned out. It has meant you and I have been at daggers drawn.'

He shrugged and said, 'Well, that's just politics.' His increasingly defensive reactions in the Commons told a different story.

When our meeting ended I asked him what he was going to do next.

'I'm going upstairs to read Leo [his young son] a story,' he said.

We parted on good terms.

My 100 days relaunch, as the media liked to call it, came soon after. It was at the Atrium, a short walk away from the House of Commons and chosen deliberately for its modern, glitzy setting. The media was there in force, as were MPs and party workers. Elspeth flew down from Edinburgh for the day. Paddy was impressed by the arrangements and the venue. 'In my day,' he said, 'the party might just about have afforded a few balloons.' It was an opportunity to say what I believed. My speech portrayed the party as modern, innovative, forward-looking and serious in its ambition to make Britain a better, fairer country. I revealed more of our tax plans, which were being developed for presentation at the September conference. 'My aim,' I said, 'is to cut the burden of direct taxes on the low paid and Middle Britain and pay for it by raising taxes on those who pollute the environment and on the very wealthy.' We would cut 2p off the income tax rate and remove 2 million low-paid workers and 1 million pensioners out of income tax altogether. As a warning of my intent to those in my party wedded to a 50p top rate of income tax, I had this to say: 'We are the one major party which believes in redistribution: the very wealthy should pay more; but not in the form of 50p marginal rates on high incomes.' The speech was well received in the party and in the media. For once, they had portrayed me as I am: a reforming liberal. I felt more and more comfortable in the job. My leader's office was working well. My relations with the federal executive and the Policy Committee were constructive.

On 15 June 2006 Elspeth and I attended the celebrations for the Queen's eightieth birthday. At the service in St Paul's Cathedral we sat with David Cameron and across the aisle from Tony Blair, who greeted us warmly. Cameron too was friendly. We walked with him afterwards to the bus which took us to the Mansion House for lunch. At the reception before lunch I was ushered up to the Queen. I said, 'Dare I wish you a happy birthday, Ma'am?' and she replied sternly, 'Only if you want me to hit you.' I was probably the hundredth person to wish her a happy birthday in the previous hour. Elspeth talked briefly to Blair. He gave her the impression he was looking forward to leaving Downing Street. He said, 'I can't wait.' Elspeth felt he meant it.

After the success of my Atrium speech at the beginning of June, the Bromley and Chislehurst by-election gave me another boost at the end of it. The Tory majority was slashed from 13,342 to 633 by the Lib Dems under the skilful near wizardry of Chris Rennard. Labour came in fourth, behind the UK Independence Party. For about an hour we thought we had won. I described it as a 'stupendous result' in 'one of the safest Conservative seats in the country'.

By now I was also putting in better performances at PMQs: the coaching was working. A few days after the by-election, I tackled Blair at PMQs about the impending extradition to the United States of three bankers – the so-called NatWest 3 – who were accused of a fraud related to Enron, the collapsed American company. I thought it was a disgrace that these men should be extradited under a treaty that was not reciprocal and which America itself had not ratified. I asked Blair simply, 'Does he still believe the extradition arrangements are fair?' Blair blustered on about the arrangements with the US being brought into line with Australia and other countries. 'What about the principle of reciprocity?' I asked to loud cheers from my own benches and, unusually, from the Tory ones. I rang Elspeth afterwards and she congratulated me. She told me Andrew Neil had said, 'Didn't Ming Campbell do well,' on his lunchtime political programme.

Before the recess at the end of July an ICM poll in the *Guardian* had the Lib Dems on 17 per cent, the lowest poll rating for four years, although a few weeks before the party conference we were back up to 22 per cent. 'Conservative revival is bad news for Lib Dems', said the *Guardian*'s headline. The *Telegraph* followed it with a YouGov poll showing the Lib Dems flat-lining on 18 per cent. Then the *Observer* ran a story about Charles Kennedy's plan to present a Channel 4 documentary and to make a 'major speech' at the party conference in September. The headline was: 'Kennedy revival rattles Campbell'. A month earlier he had appeared on BBC *Question Time* and was asked whether, one day, he might lead the party again 'Who knows?' he said. 'I don't want a headline saying "Kennedy suggests this or implies that" . . . [But] the one thing we can all be sure about in politics is you are as well to expect the unexpected.'

I went on holiday to the Hebridean island of Tiree and then to Lake Como in Italy knowing the conference would be the biggest test so far of my leadership. I had to carry the party in abandoning the 50p tax rate and my speech had to be of the highest class. How would I be judged by the conference, as Simon Hughes had said I would be? The other concern was a biography of Charles which was due to be published before the conference. It was written by Greg Hurst, a political correspondent with *The Times*. He had such good contacts within the Lib Dems I used to think he was in the shadow cabinet.

The serialisation of the book began in *The Times* at the end of August. It brought back those difficult days where I was caught in a dilemma between my duty to the party as deputy leader and my instinct that Charles should be allowed privacy and sufficient time to deal with his illness. My reluctance to intervene was criticised as I knew it would be, but I was exonerated on the more damaging charge of conspiring to bring Charles down. Hurst did criticise me for 'allowing a conflict of interest' to arise between my duty as deputy leader and my position 'as a potential candidate when the final crisis in Kennedy's leadership arose'. Was I merciless or was I too merciful was the question posed by Magnus Linklater in his column in *The Times*: 'After being dubbed Ming the Merciless for joining the faction that forced Mr Kennedy from office . . . he now stands charged with being Ming the Merciful – over-protective towards a colleague and failing to give the party and the public the true facts. Politics is an unforgiving business.' I was content with that judgement.

I travelled to the Brighton conference knowing my leadership was at risk if I lost the vote on abandoning the 50p tax rate for people earning more than £100,000 a year. Archy had already warned me, during the summer, that I would become a caretaker leader if the party went against me on such an important policy. I agreed with him. The stakes were as high as they could be. I wasn't prepared to equivocate or back off. One commentator said my leadership would be 'political toast' if I lost the vote.

The tax debate and Charles's speech were scheduled for the same day. It was to be a day of drama. My advisers worried about distancing me from the tax vote if it went against me. Should I even be sitting on the platform during the debate? I didn't speak because there was no expectation I would do so but I sat on the platform to show my support for Vince Cable who was proposing the tax changes. Just in case the vote went against me there were elaborate arrangements for hurrying me back to my hotel suite out of the gaze of the watching television cameras. After the first two or three speeches I began to relax. The applause in favour of the reform proposals was the louder. Paddy picked up the same signs as me and passed me a note. It said: 'I've sat in your position many times dreading the outcome of a conference vote but I know you're going to win this one.' He was right: the tax proposals were carried by a bigger margin than I expected after a passionate debate which revealed the party at its combative best. Commentators said we were the only one of the three parties that could have held such a well-informed and passionate debate.

I had spoken by telephone to Charles before the conference to find out what choreography he wanted for his valedictory address. He said he wanted it kept very low key – 'no hand-shakes or anything like that'. I sat in the front row as the party welcomed him back with affection. His speech was typically Charles: informal and engaging. He spoke for much longer than scheduled and concluded: 'Let the message go out . . . from each and every one of us, as British Liberal Democrats, the best is yet to come.' I made sure I was first to my feet to give him a standing ovation. The party rose behind me. After the clapping ended, the critical comments began.

My speech on the closing day was the final hurdle. It was preceded by thumping music and a series of photographs of me, tracing my career from Olympic runner to lawyer and then to politician. When I arrived on stage the applause was thunderous. I started by making a reference to the tax vote two days before. 'This has been my first autumn conference as Liberal Democrat leader, and I have enjoyed it, particularly since Tuesday lunch-time.' I complimented the delegates for debating the important issues. 'This week we have shown what politics ought to be about.' I was enjoying it, partly because I was using an autocue for the first time which freed me up.

I ran through the tax policy, attacked Gordon Brown for his stealth taxes, criticised the government for its threats to civil liberties and for Iraq. Then I talked about my parents: how they had worked hard to provide me with the opportunities they had never had; how my father had wanted to be a doctor but couldn't afford to go to university.

'Opportunity,' I said, 'should not be an accident of birth. It must be open to everyone in Britain.'

Also, I tackled criticisms about my age: 'Some mourn for what is past, but not me. I hunger for what is to come.' I finished by looking forward to a Britain that was 'free, fair and green'. The conference erupted. Elspeth joined me on stage for the ovation which lasted five minutes. I left the conference with an overwhelming sense of relief. I had survived it. The press coverage the next day was generally favourable but not eulogistic. I had no complaints.

Three days later I was flying to America with Michael Moore, our foreign affairs spokesman, Lorely Burt, spokesperson for small business, women and equality, and Puja Darbari, my press secretary. We were staying at the British Embassy in Washington for a series of appointments at the State Department, the Pentagon, the National Security Council, the Senate and then at the United Nations. I was also going to meet Hillary Clinton. As we flew over the Atlantic for an evening touchdown at Washington Dulles Airport I felt an enormous sense of release. We were making good progress.

16

At last, I've cracked it

A change came over the political landscape in the autumn of 2006. It was largely due to the abortive coup mounted by some of Gordon Brown's supporters against the Prime Minister. Inside Westminster the talk was of one era ending and another beginning. Wherever MPs met the questions they asked were: when would Blair go; would he be forced out; and would Brown call a snap general election when he took over? Even if he didn't, there were important local elections and elections to the Scottish parliament and Welsh assembly in May to prepare for. I put the party on general election alert and took the shadow cabinet for a two-day election strategy meeting to the Henley Management Centre. 'Lib Dems preparing for snap general election,' the *Guardian* reported accurately but incompletely. Our spinning had worked. I wanted also to talk to my closest colleagues in secrecy about our post-election strategy. What would we do if there was a hung parliament? What were our terms, if any, for coalition? After a long discussion, we reached an agreement. It boiled down to this. We would tell Labour or Conservative suitors: 'Don't bother to lift the phone unless proportional representation is on the agenda.'

There were signs everywhere of the political pace quickening. At the reception after the wreath-laying at the Cenotaph on Remembrance Sunday, 12 November 2006, John Major said to Elspeth, 'I hope David Cameron is talking to Ming. We'd give our eye teeth for some of your people.'

Elspeth replied, 'As a matter of fact he isn't.'

Major said, 'Well, I suppose it's PR that's the obstacle.'

As Blair, Cameron and I were lined up near the Cenotaph to place our wreaths one of us mentioned it was like waiting for PMQs. All three of us agreed how nerve-racking PMQs was and how drained we felt after it. I was consoled they felt the same as me.

The Queen's Speech three days later made Brown's succession even more certain. Blair effectively endorsed him as his successor by saying the party would be led at the next election by a heavyweight whose 'big clunking fist' would knock out Cameron and the Conservatives. I called the Queen's Speech 'a miserable swansong from a lame duck'. I felt confident as I laid into Labour and the Tories, swatting away interventions like flies. My experience in the House of Commons was beginning to tell. My press team got a DVD of my speech and presented it to me with a great flourish.

At the beginning of December our working group's report into the Trident nuclear missile system was published. It said Britain's Trident warhead capacity should be cut in half and the decision to replace Trident should be postponed until it was necessary in 2014. We scored a pre-emptive strike on Labour. Three days later Blair announced his backing for renewing Trident. Cameron supported him. I questioned the rush to make a decision. Did it owe more to Blair's legacy than to Britain's national interest? I asked. Tory MPs and (fewer) Labour MPs jeered me loudly. I knew there was also dissent among unilateralists in my own party. Would I be able to win them over by our spring 2007 conference in Harrogate where the issue was to be debated? I reshuffled my front-bench team just before Christmas, moving Norman Lamb, my chief of staff, to health to give him time for fresh thinking on the delivery of public services before we were pitched into a general election campaign. He replaced Steve Webb who was put in charge of preparing and writing the election manifesto. Ed Davey became my chief of staff. His trade and industry portfolio was taken over by Susan Kramer. We broke up for Christmas confident we were ready for whatever 2007 would throw at us.

The day after the recess a new bout of speculation about my leadership started. An ICM poll published in the *Guardian* showed the Conservatives on 40 per cent – eight points ahead of Labour – and the Lib Dems falling four points to 18 per cent, the lowest rating since the summer. I had to begin the New Year defending my leadership. 'I'm not setting any time limits for myself and nor should anyone else,' I told Radio 4's *Today* programme in an echo of the comment I made after Simon Hughes's unwelcome intervention the previous May. It was a nuisance to start 2007 in this way. In optimistic moments, which were frequent, I thought my work-rate (sometimes eighteen hours a day) and my success in professionalising the party would eventually change the media commentary about me. I used to say to Elspeth: 'I can trade my way out of this.' The *Guardian*'s first ICM poll of 2007 gave me some encouragement. It put the Lib Dems on 23 per cent, a rise of five points from our pre-Christmas rating. The year began with volatile polls and continued with them throughout.

At PMQs the next day I attacked Blair over Iraq. He began by sending condolences to the family and friends of Private Michael Tench of A Company, 2nd Battalion the Light Infantry, who had been killed in Iraq the previous weekend. 'He was only a very young man, but his country should be very proud of him and the work that he and his colleagues have been doing in Iraq in the service of our country,' Blair said.

I was angry that Blair intended to absent himself from the debate on Iraq which I was to open after PMQs. I expressed my sympathies for the fallen soldier and added, 'On this occasion can we also remember those who have been wounded, some grievously, and whose lives have been deeply affected by that as a result of their service in Iraq.'

I continued: 'Later today, in the debate on Iraq, we will set out our proposals to bring the troops home by October. Should not the Prime Minister set out his proposals in that debate as well?'

Blair looked angry with me. He said, 'for us to set an arbitrary timetable . . . would send the most disastrous signal to the people whom we are fighting in Iraq. It is a policy that, whatever its superficial attractions may be, is deeply irresponsible – which is probably why it is Liberal Democrat policy.'

I retorted equally angrily, 'If the Prime Minister feels that strongly, he should come and debate the issues this afternoon. What can possibly be more important than that the Prime Minister should be here to debate the issue of Iraq at a time when the lives of British forces are at risk every day? Is not that the kind of leadership to which we are entitled?'

Blair replied, 'I am debating the issue with the right hon. and learned gentleman now.'

Blair left the Commons ten minutes before the debate began.

When I spoke in the debate I said, 'Today British soldiers and their families deserved to hear all the party leaders – the Prime Minister owed that to them.'

For once the sketch writers and commentators were universally favourable.

My first anniversary as leader was approaching and the spring conference once more at Harrogate. The pre-conference press coverage focused again on leadership: 'Campbell tells critics to put up or shut up', in the *Telegraph*; 'One year in, and Sir Ming still has to face the doubters', in the *Guardian*. But there was also commentary on the prize that could be ours in little more than six months if Gordon Brown called a snap election. 'Take note. The Lib Dems may hold the key to Number 10', was the heading on Andrew Rawnsley's column in the *Observer*; 'Dependable Ming must play a long game', on Peter Riddell's political briefing in *The Times*. First I had to win the Trident vote which my advisers were telling me was too close to call. Archy warned, as he had done over the 50p tax rate vote six months before at Brighton, 'If we lose, you'll be a caretaker leader.'

Nick Harvey, MP for Devon North and the defence spokesman, addressed a fringe meeting to drum up support for the leadership line the evening before the crucial debate. To our dismay, the Parliamentary Candidates' Association, which is usually supportive of the leadership, arranged a rival meeting and asked Bruce Kent, the high priest of unilateralism and former general secretary of CND, to speak. Alison Suttie, my head of office, went to take the temperature of the rival meeting. She came back looking concerned. 'The wind's blowing strongly their way,' she said. My advisers were telling me: 'The people we've relied on in the past to support the leadership are flakey. The unilateralists and CND supporters are pulling in more support.' The discussion took on a defeatist tone. My supporters were beginning to talk about contingencies for spiriting me quickly from the conference hall if the vote was lost. Should I sit on the platform as I had done for the tax debate at Brighton? Nobody thought I should. Instead I would sit in the front row readying myself to be rushed out of a side door by a protective phalanx of my supporters and taken to my hotel room. Should I speak? Everyone advised me against it. Even Elspeth insisted it would be a mistake. 'Too high wire,' she warned me. Everyone told me my leadership depended on distancing me from defeat tomorrow.

I went to bed unable to reconcile the advice I was being given with my instinct to fight. After a sleepless night my mind was made up. I had decided to speak. How could I possibly stay silent when defence was one of my specialist subjects and when I had persuaded the party to back multilateralism seventeen years earlier, my first Brighton conference success? If I couldn't carry the party on this how could I continue as leader?

Early that morning I summoned my closest advisers and friends. Again they warned me off speaking. They were saying: 'You're putting your leadership on the line if it goes the wrong way.' I said something about hating 'the pressure this job is putting on my family' and Carrie Henderson was so alarmed when she heard this she went outside and rang Ian Wright, one of my trusted advisers. She asked him to hurry along to the meeting in case his steadying counsel was needed. Then Mark Littlewood, the head of media, said exactly what I had been thinking: 'If you speak and the vote goes against you it'll be very damaging. But if the vote goes against you and you don't speak it'll be less damaging but you'll always think, What if I'd spoken . . . ?' I asked Carrie to warn Elspeth of my intentions before she joined me in the conference hall for the debate while I jotted down some speaking notes.

As I took my seat in the front row of the hall the delegates sensed the unfolding drama though none of them knew Archy was informing Duncan Brack, who was chairing the debate, about my intention to speak. He handed him my speaker's card and Duncan looked at him aghast: 'Are you sure this is right? Will you double-check he really wants to do this?'

Tim Garden, a former air marshal and our defence spokesman in the Lords, opened the debate with his usual calm authority. (Tragically, he died suddenly five months later after being diagnosed with cancer.) Other speakers followed him to the microphone and then Duncan Brack sent an emissary to check with Archy once more whether I was certain I wanted to speak. When Duncan called my name to stand by to speak a whooshing sound like a gust of wind went through the hall as the delegates gasped in astonishment. They realised I was staking my leadership on the vote.

The conference rules gave me no concessions. Like any other speaker I had four minutes to win over the conference. I spoke logically but passionately in favour of reducing the number of warheads and postponing a decision on replacing Trident until 2014. I urged the conference not to hand Labour a propaganda gift by reverting to unilateralism in what might turn out to be an election year. I could tell by the applause that I had made an impression. Nick Harvey closed the debate with a well-judged speech. Would we win? Everyone said it was still too close to call. When the vote on the unilateralist amendment – making the decision there and then to scrap Trident when it became obsolete – was announced, we had won by 454 votes to 414. I tried not to look too jubilant because it was an issue that split the party. But I felt an overwhelming sense of triumph. I had carried the party against the odds. I had won. I had done it. It was my victory. It was an extraordinary feeling.

Phil Willis, MP for Harrogate and Knaresborough, who had argued for scrapping Trident, told reporters: 'He swung it. I take my hat off to him. It was a speech of passion and anger.'

I said, 'I know only one way to lead this party and that is from the front.'

In my leader's speech to the conference I set out five tests for Gordon Brown when he became Prime Minister. They were: ending Labour's authoritarian attack on civil liberties by scrapping ID cards; grasping the challenge posed by climate change; breaking open the poverty trap; trusting the people by devolving more power locally; setting Britain's foreign policy in London not Washington. I asked, 'The question is – can Gordon Brown meet that challenge? Does he have the courage to take Britain in a new direction?'

My view was Brown would fail the five tests (an intentional reference to Brown's own five tests for joining the euro which he said Britain had failed). But the media interpreted the speech as my terms for joining a coalition with Labour. More damaging still was a briefing by Mark Littlewood that proportional representation was no longer a coalition 'deal-breaker' for the Lib Dems although I had mentioned it three times in my speech. Ed Davey had to contradict him in public saying, 'PR remains critically important to us. In any future government which Liberal Democrats would be part of, it would be a critical and key issue for us.' But the damage had been done. We had managed to confuse one of our key policies. Mark's authority as the party's spokesman had been destroyed, as he recognised. He stood aside four days later. The following weekend I used my speech at the Welsh Lib Dem conference to emphasise the importance of electoral reform to the party. 'Be in no doubt of my commitment to proportional representation,' I told them.

Soon after, Elspeth and I went to a state banquet at Buckingham Palace for the Ghanaian President. Elspeth had a long conversation with Tony Blair about the pressures of leadership.

Blair said, 'Ming's doing a fantastic job.'

She said, 'But he's going through hell.'

Elspeth remembers Blair's reply: 'If you become a party leader that's what happens. You become a commodity. How do you think I get up every morning? You have to just stick at it.'

The political tempo was rising. Local elections in England and Scotland and the elections to the Scottish parliament and Welsh assembly were less than two months away. Our internal analysis painted a grim picture of our potential losses to the Tory revival in England: as many as 600 seats. The forecasts in Wales and Scotland (where we were in coalition with Labour) were more encouraging. We expected to make gains in Scotland, giving the party a stronger hand in any new negotiations with Labour or with the Scottish National Party (but only if it dropped its commitment to a referendum on independence). The SNP was riding high on an anti-Labour tide as was Plaid Cymru in Wales where we expected to hold steady. The Budget, Brown's swansong as Chancellor, was the last big political event before campaigning began. We wondered what he would announce to help his party in May's elections and also to give him, as Prime Minister, the option of calling a general election in

October. His last-minute rabbit-out-of-the-hat 2p cut in the basic rate of income tax caught everyone by surprise.

By custom the leader of the Opposition replies to the Chancellor. David Cameron flannelled. 'He is conceding what we have said all along: you can increase spending and you can cut taxes. Yes, you can share the proceeds of growth.'

The Brown trick had caught him unawares. By the time I rose to speak I had the figures that revealed what I called Brown's 'sleight of hand'. Steve Webb and David Laws had calculated that Brown's tax cut and the simultaneous abolition of the 10 per cent tax band would leave many lower paid workers worse off. 'This,' I said, 'is an income tax cut for the wealthy dressed up as a tax cut for the poor.'

Our analysis, gratifyingly, was the one that was picked up in the media. I may have outwitted Cameron in parliament but I was still fearful of the havoc the Tory revival under Cameron was about to wreak on our councillors in the south of England at the elections on 3 May.

A different election was on Gordon Brown's mind when he rang my home unexpectedly on Easter Sunday. He wanted to meet the following day in Edinburgh. We settled on 11.30 but I had to postpone it by half an hour when a photocall at Edinburgh City Chambers overran. Elspeth rang Brown's home in North Queensferry. The phone was not receiving incoming calls. Then she rang the Treasury pretending she needed to speak to Brown on an urgent constituency matter. Brown's invitation to a rival party leader was best kept secret. Brown rang back twenty minutes later and agreed to a noon meeting.

Elspeth said to him, 'Very cloak and dagger.'

Brown replied, 'Not too many daggers I hope.'

Brown arrived at the discreet meeting place we had agreed with his security men in tow (not very discreet). Like me he was anxious about the possibility of the SNP governing in Scotland, our back yard. Was there common ground between Labour and the Lib Dems to tackle the SNP together? He made a number of suggestions. I told him I would have to discuss them with Nicol Stephen, the Scottish Lib Dem leader. He then raised the possibilities for a new coalition agreement between the Lib Dems and Labour on the assumption that the two parties had enough seats jointly to form a government. This was all difficult territory for me, partly because these matters were Nicol's responsibility under the party's federal constitution. As I told the PM-in-waiting: 'We practise institutional and constitutional devolution in our party.' In addition, there was a mood among some Lib Dems against going into a new coalition with Labour. The coalition had worked well when Donald Dewar and Jim Wallace were respective party leaders in Scotland but less well thereafter. The meeting lasted a little over an hour before we went our separate ways. Elspeth and I drove to the Lake District for a three-day Easter break. We discussed Brown's approach to me on the journey. 'Riveting stuff,' Elspeth wrote in her diary.

No sooner had parliament returned from the Easter recess than it was David Cameron's turn to put out feelers. I was travelling on a train with Alison Suttie when she was paged by her opposite number in Cameron's office. He told her Cameron wanted to talk to me about the elections for London Mayor in May 2008. We agreed to meet him after PMQs the following day.

As Ed Davey and I were leaving my office to go to the shadow cabinet room Andrew Neil said at the end of *The Daily Politics* programme on BBC2 that rumours were circulating Westminster about Greg Dyke, former BBC director-general, standing for the Conservatives in the mayoral election. Cameron was apologetic about the leak (which the Tories later tried to blame on us). He explained his proposal to field Dyke as a joint candidate.

I saw an immediate objection. 'It won't work because you can't be a candidate for the Lib Dems unless you are a member of the party. Isn't that the case for you?'

Cameron, who was wearing a T-shirt, jeans and trainers after a photocall about cleaning up London, replied, 'Yes, but we can get round it.'

I said, 'Well, we can't.'

The conversation was amicable but brief. It wasn't exactly the approach John Major had in mind when he talked to Elspeth on Remembrance Sunday the previous November. I spent the next two weeks criss-crossing the country electioneering.

An agonised debate was going on inside the party. We knew the Cameron bounce was going to hurt us harder in the English local elections than the commentators were forecasting. Should we try to dampen down media expectations or else risk adverse headlines when the results came in? Jonny Oates, our new director of communications, said we should condition expectations. Chris Rennard, the party's chief executive, took the other view. 'If we let people think we're not going to do very well we'll discourage people coming out for us,' he argued. I sided with Rennard. It proved to be a mistake.

Gordon Brown's people had been in touch again. Could we talk again, in Edinburgh, on election day? We met at the same discreet meeting place as before. Throughout the campaign the polls had put the SNP ahead of Labour. Was there scope for an arrangement between our two parties? What would be the consequences for Scotland and our parties if the SNP used the £30 billion Scottish Executive budget to build support for independence over the next few years?

By the following day I had another, more pressing problem. The party lost 246 seats in the English local council elections, much better than we had feared privately. The national share of the vote at 26 per cent, only one point lower than the previous year and more or less neck and neck with Labour, didn't stop a new bout of speculation about leadership. We lost control of four councils overall, including Torbay, but we won Eastbourne. *The Times* reported: 'The Liberal Democrats' vulnerability to a Tory revival was laid bare yesterday as a string of poor results forced Sir Menzies Campbell to insist he would not quit before the next general election.'

The elections in Scotland were marred by a farce over the high numbers of spoiled ballot papers. When all the results were declared, we emerged with one fewer seat in the Scottish parliament. We had expected to make gains. Alex Salmond, the Nationalist leader, had snatched the north-east constituency of Gordon from us. The SNP had one seat more than Labour. No party had a majority. Should we go into coalition with Labour to spoil the SNP's party? Archy and his wife Ro were coming to dinner with us the evening after election day. As he was travelling up from his home in the Borders, he rang to say Nicol Stephen wanted to speak to me. I told Archy to bring him along for a drink before dinner. The drink turned into a summit in our dining room. Nicol came with his wife Caris and his special adviser Sam Ghibaldan. Tavish Scott, the Scottish Lib Dem deputy leader, and his girlfriend Kirsten Campbell came too. Instead of a quiet dinner with Archy and his wife there were nine of us in the dining room. We sent out for pizzas and talked post-election tactics. Nicol and Tavish were feeling bruised: not only was the election disappointing but our MSPs faced being in opposition for the first time since the Scottish parliament opened in 1999. After two hours we packed away our pizza boxes and any possibility of a coalition with the SNP. (Like me, Tavish was clear about 'no deal with the SNP'. None of us could see a Lib Dem/SNP coalition working in practice.) Coalition with Labour was still a possibility when Elspeth and I said goodnight to Nicol and Tavish. After we shut the door Elspeth said, 'They're not prepared for any of this, are they?'

Brown telephoned me the following morning. Neither Nicol nor Tavish knew I was speaking privately to him but I am fairly certain they must have worked it out. I had to be circumspect. One of the reasons was confidentiality: the fewer people who knew about our sensitive talks the better. The other was the federal nature of the Lib Dems. I had no right to muscle into the negotiations between Nicol and the other parties in Scotland. I would be portrayed as the heavy hand of Westminster telling the Scottish parliamentarians what to do.

The next day, Sunday, Tavish went on *The Politics Show* on BBC Scotland and ruled out a coalition with the SNP and then ruled out one with Labour too. Although exploratory talks continued, the mood for a coalition with either party moved from cool to cold. Nicol rang me one day and asked my view if the SNP acceded to his demand and dropped its independence referendum commitment. The feeling in the party was strongly against a coalition with the SNP and the mood in the country was against a deal to keep Labour in power when it had lost the election. Soon after, the SNP formed a minority administration.

I had a different crisis to attend to in England. My leadership, my age, my ability to galvanise the party in time for the next general election were filling newspapers and blogs. Matthew Parris in *The Times* wrote: 'To run out of steam, mid-term when the ruling party is plumbing near record depths of unpopularity must be deeply worrying for Sir Menzies Campbell.' The intensity of the personal attacks on me made it more so, even though I had grown a much thicker skin in the year since I became leader.

Suddenly, the political landscape changed again. A week after the elections Blair announced he would be leaving Downing Street on 27 June. Brown was finally to become Prime Minister after wanting it so badly for so long. We wondered whether it would put us under more pressure. Would Labour voters who had defected to us in protest at Blair's war in Iraq abandon us when Brown took over? A Populus poll in *The Times* increased the pressure on me. Under the headline, 'Weakened Campbell in trouble as most Lib Dem voters want him out', it said 54 per cent of Lib Dem voters wanted me to go and 39 per cent wanted me to stay. 'This means that Lib Dem voters are more hostile than the public generally who favour his departure by a 45 to 33% margin.' The sample of Lib Dems voters was tiny but that did not stop the inferences being drawn.

Elspeth recorded a conversation between us in her diary: 'He's not sure he can take two more years of this. His argument is if he can't take the party forward he should stand down and let someone else have a go.' Elspeth expressed sympathy for me. 'The trouble is we're in a classic squeeze between the two big parties. Gordon Brown (not yet crowned but taking over in six weeks) is crawling all over our territory – constitutional reform, troops out of Iraq etc. It's a hellish situation but Ming and I will discuss things over Whitsun. His well-being and health come first.'

We never did have the discussion in the sense Elspeth meant. It was a continuing conversation between us. There would be difficult headlines, I would react, and we would discuss whether I should go on. Then something would happen – for example, an initiative of mine being well received – and the headlines would fade and my resolve to carry on and to shrug off temporary setbacks would be reinforced. Elspeth always supported me. Her attitude was if I wanted to carry on I should. I convinced myself hard work, a professional organisation and sound policies would succeed in the end. By the early summer there were signs that David Cameron's honeymoon might be over. The Conservative Party was tearing itself to pieces over its policy on grammar schools. The next Populus poll in *The Times* carried the heading: 'Cameron's image as leader damaged by Tory schools dispute'. The Lib Dem poll rating was unchanged at 17 per cent, but my personal rating had improved: 34 per cent saw me as strong, a rise of five points since the previous autumn; and 38 per cent said I stuck to what I believed in, up eight points.

I had tried to take the political initiative on constitutional reform from Brown before he became Prime Minister. I wrote him a letter proposing a cross-party convention on the constitution, similar to the Scottish Constitutional Convention which met from 1989 to draw up devolution proposals and on which both of us had sat. I decided also to fight back against the insidious and persistent criticism that I was too old to be Lib Dem leader. My line of attack was to talk up the advantages of age, how it provided experience and judgement, how it would have kept Britain out of Iraq. I tested it out at a private conference for Lib Dem MPs, candidates and agents at Wyboston in Bedfordshire. They liked it. I returned to London persuaded it was a line of attack I should use again at a meeting of party officials and workers the day before Blair bowed out.

The next day, Sunday, 17 June, an intermediary rang Elspeth at home in Edinburgh. She was told Brown wanted to talk to me by phone that evening. My preference was to meet him face to face. A meeting was arranged for Monday lunchtime in his office in the House of Commons. I presumed he wanted to speak to me about my letter on the constitution. I arrived at his office first after taking the back stairs to lessen the risk of being spotted. A secretary was waiting for me and made me a cup of tea. While I waited I looked with envy at the grandeur of the Chancellor's office compared to the Commons accommodation of the Lib Dems. What made the contrast so stark to me was that this was an office that Brown hardly even used because he worked out of the Treasury.

When Brown came in looking and sounding friendly the secretary left us to talk privately. Brown said he had three propositions to put to me. 'Will the Lib Dems,' he said, 'oppose things simply for opposition's sake?'

I said, 'Of course not.' I mentioned my letter on the constitution as an example of our cooperative approach. 'If we think you're doing the right thing we'll support you. We'll look at it on a case-by-case basis,' I said, or words to that effect.

Brown seemed satisfied with my answer. Then he asked what my attitude would be if he appointed Lib Dems as advisers. By way of illustration he mentioned three names, all Liberal Democrat peers – Julia Neuberger, Shirley Williams and Anthony Lester.

I told him I had no objection to capable and well-qualified Lib Dems advising the government though I set out three conditions. These were: the appointments weren't tokenism; the peers involved retained total independence; and there was a reasonable chance of any proposals they made being taken up by government. This last condition was a barbed reference to Roy Jenkins's electoral commission. It reported to much fanfare in 1998 and proposed a reformed election system for the House of Commons generally described as AV plus as a first step towards a proportional system. Blair had ignored it.

Brown readily agreed to the three conditions. His last proposition was a novel one.

'What,' he asked, 'would your reaction be to the idea of Lib Dems becoming ministers?' He told me the Lib Dems had some very talented and clever people. He talked about his desire to reach out and utilise talent wherever it was for the good of Britain. Paddy Ashdown's name was mentioned, again by way of illustration. Brown clearly had him in mind for Northern Ireland Secretary, a cabinet post. This was ground-breaking stuff.

I told him I'd give him a reply quickly after I had considered the implications, and we ended the meeting as amicably as we had begun it. I returned by the back stairs and summoned Archy and Ed Davey, my chief of staff, into my office. We talked over Brown's proposal for less than half an hour. None of us could see it working. How could a Lib Dem, a former leader of the party, join the cabinet while we were still at loggerheads with the government over Iraq? What would happen if there was a vote on university tuition fees in the Lords? Would Paddy be expected to vote with the government according to the convention of cabinet collective agreement? Archy and Ed confirmed my instinct that it could never work. I told them I would convey that to Brown. However I had a string of diary commitments that prevented me from speaking to Brown immediately. Another meeting was arranged for the next day but had to be postponed until the following day, Wednesday, after Brown discovered another engagement in his diary.

Paddy came to see me on Monday afternoon. He'd been asked to see Brown. 'Do you know what about?' Paddy asked.

'I think he may offer you Northern Ireland,' I said, feeling surprised that Brown had made his approach to Ashdown before hearing my response to his proposal. I told Paddy, 'It won't work.'

Paddy agreed with me. He said, 'Well, I think I ought to go and see him anyway.'

I had no objection. For all I knew Brown might also want to talk to Paddy about him doing a similar job in Afghanistan to the one he had just completed in Bosnia-Herzegovina (where he had been the UN's High Representative). Rumours of a new posting in Kabul for Paddy were doing the rounds of the Westminster gossip mill.

On Tuesday evening – the day before Paddy and I were due to meet Brown separately – Michael White of the *Guardian* rang my office and asked mysteriously if he could speak to me about 'government'. Archy rang him instead. At the end of their conversation, White asked Archy whether Brown had offered Lib Dems ministerial positions. Archy tried to put him off the scent though White seemed to know more than he was letting on. White said, 'I do not regard that as a denial.' The *Guardian* published the story the next day.

It was the beginning of a very uncomfortable media storm. I was criticised for not rejecting Brown's proposal there and then.

Members of my own party criticised me for even meeting Brown. I went on Radio 5 Live on Wednesday morning and said 'there was no question of any Liberal Democrats joining the government'. Brown had got his answer. Our meeting never took place. I wondered who had leaked the story and why; very few people knew about it. I asked Archy to make some enquiries but we never found out.

My immediate concern was how to survive PMQs that day without being howled down by Labour and Conservative MPs. My first question was short and to the point: 'Does the Prime Minister believe it right for private equity executives to pay tax at a lower rate than those who clean their offices?' Blair said it was because of this concern that a review had been set up. I continued on the same theme: 'While this review is taking place, we are giving a tax break of £6 billion per annum to some of the wealthiest people in the United Kingdom. Would it not be much fairer to give tax cuts to lower and middle income families, who have suffered most under this government? Would that not be an illustration of governing for the many, and not the few?' Blair did not refer to the *Guardian*'s story and I left the Commons chamber feeling I had got off lightly.

That afternoon Paddy went to see Brown who offered him Northern Ireland. Paddy turned it down. He said to Brown, 'I'm a good soldier. I do what my commanding officer tells me.'

I missed the Lib Dem parliamentary party meeting that evening because I was presiding over graduation ceremonies at St Andrews University for the following two days. I was told the MPs were in a fractious mood. The headlines were not kind to me in my absence. 'How Chancellor's leaked offer of co-operation has left Lib Dem leader dazed and confused', was one. I was neither – I had simply thought I should think about Brown's proposal before responding to it.

The next time I spoke to Brown was the day he became Prime Minister. He rang me out of courtesy as he did David Cameron and others including Nelson Mandela and Bill Clinton. After he told me he wanted to govern for all the people I made a reference to the leak about Lib Dem ministers. 'Gordon,' I said, 'what I've learned in the last week is that you are the only person I can trust on your side and I think I'm the only one you can trust on my side.'

He agreed.

Two days later Brown announced Neuberger, Williams and Lester as government advisers. As long as my three conditions were met I had no objections. The parliamentary party took it in its stride.

The Lib Dem membership was torn about these events. Half of those who wrote in were favourable to the idea of Lib Dem MPs being ministers. They were saying in effect: 'This was an opportunity you should have taken. Ashdown in the cabinet would have given us credibility.' The parliamentary party was less benign in its reaction.

Tony Blair's final PMQs on the day of his resignation posed two dilemmas for me. The first was the tone of my questions in the Commons. Should they be critical or congratulatory? We agonised about misjudging the mood of the Commons on such a day. Blair had started by sending condolences to the families of three soldiers who had died in the past week. He went on to pay tribute to the dedication, courage and commitment of the armed forces. 'They are the bravest and the best,' he said.

I took up a similar theme but one that had become one of our complaints about the government during the hostilities. 'Is he satisfied,' I asked, 'that proper provision has been made for those servicemen and women who suffer both physical and psychological injury as a result of their service in Iraq and Afghanistan? What assurances can he give them and their families that they will not be forgotten?'

My second question was really a farewell. 'As the Prime Minister knows, he and I have had a number of disagreements, not least on Iraq. In our personal dealings, however, he has been unfailingly courteous, and I should like to express my gratitude to him for that. As he leaves office, may I, on behalf of my colleagues, extend our very best wishes to him and his family?'

He repaid the compliment by saying, 'Whatever differences we have had politically, I do not think anybody in the House would think that he is a person other than one of generosity of spirit and courtesy.' I thought about sending him a personal letter as I would have done in the past. What could I write that wasn't artificial? The truth was Iraq had distorted our relationship however friendly and respectful our last Commons exchanges sounded. I didn't send him a letter.

The bigger worry of Blair's departure was Brown's popularity. No sooner had Cameron's bounce come to an end than Brown's began. It posed different political problems but it was still a third party squeeze.

My leadership was again being questioned. The results of two by-elections, Ealing Southall and Sedgefield, on 19 July, were crucially important to me if I was to stifle my critics over the summer. And I had a personal and painful dilemma to resolve. For the previous eight months I had been having physiotherapy every Tuesday afternoon in London. I'd made no secret of it. I told people: 'The hip where I had cancer is giving me a bit of trouble. It gets a bit stiff.' It was true as far as it went. Only those closest to me knew the whole story. I needed a hip replacement operation. The hip was deteriorating and an NHS operation was already booked, for 25 and 26 July, in Edinburgh Royal Infirmary. Elspeth and I discussed whether I could take the political risk of going ahead with it. If the by-elections went badly for the Lib Dems my leadership and my age would be back in the headlines. How would it look if I disappeared from the political fray for possibly six weeks only to return walking with a stick? It was politically impossible. Alternatively, if the Lib Dems did well in the by-elections I needed to be available to capitalise on them. I cancelled the operation even though I knew I had to have it sooner or later. When could I have it without giving ammunition to my critics? I kept my misgivings private and threw myself into the by-election campaigns, visiting Ealing Southall nine times in all.

A fortnight before the by-elections I reshuffled my front-bench team to reflect Brown's restructuring of government departments, including splitting the education department in two and scrapping the Department of Trade and Industry. The key change for me was moving David Laws, the MP for Yeovil, from work and pensions to the important policy area of children, schools and families. His brief, like Norman Lamb's in health, was to introduce new thinking to our general election manifesto. The week before the by-elections I launched our new tax policy: a 4p cut in the basic rate of income tax paid for by green taxes and cutting tax relief for the very rich. 'Only the Liberal Democrats have produced a costed plan to create a tax system that is fair, simple and green,' I boasted. It was a good pitch for the by-elections.

An unhelpful intervention by Tim Razzall, the party's election campaign manager under Charles Kennedy, brought questions about my leadership back into the headlines. He said on BBC Radio 4's *World at One*: 'There are clearly some people in the party who are complaining about Ming as leader and I think a lot of them are using the Ealing by-election as a sort of catalyst to bring things to a head.'

When the results were announced, it was Cameron's leadership that was making the news. The Lib Dems pushed the Conservatives into third place in both seats. Labour retained them. Peter Riddell, analysing the results in *The Times*, wrote: 'Sir Menzies looks more secure, although his party enemies will no doubt stir doubts at the Lib Dem conference in two months. Mr Cameron is likely to have the roughest summer, under pressure from the party Right and activists.' Cameron's summer was about to get worse. At the peak of the July floods in England he went to Rwanda. The criticism of him was intense.

On 24 July, five days after the by-elections, I had dinner in the House of Commons with a group of Lib Dem peers. The dinner had been suggested by Lord McNally, the leader of the Lib Dem group in the House of Lords, to assist communication between the party in the Lords and the Commons. Tom McNally came with David Shutt, the Lib Dem chief whip in the Lords, Martin Thomas, Shirley Williams, William Wallace, Navnit Dholakia and Bob Maclennan, who led the SDP into merger with the Liberals in 1988. I brought along Archy and Ed Davey. The dinner, in a private room, began with McNally welcoming us. I gave my assessment of the political challenges for the party and then Tom asked the peers to speak in turn round the table. One after the other Maclennan, Williams and Dholakia tackled me about my performance as leader. Maclennan said to me, 'There are so many other ways you could contribute.' Shirley said something along the lines of, 'What a great man you are but . . .' Dholakia said, 'Why is it that everywhere I go people ask about the leadership?' They made it quite clear they thought I should resign.

I felt I had been ambushed. The three of them had clearly prepared their attack. McNally and the other peers were looking as surprised as I felt. Thomas was wide-eyed in astonishment throughout. I fended off the criticisms. I said, 'Look, I've had to pick up what was left behind by Charles's resignation and some of the people in this room could have done a hell of a lot more to help.' The conversation became so difficult and so sensitive we had to ask the waiters to stay outside while we talked.

Ed Davey and David Shutt weighed in behind me. Archy stayed quiet because – he told me later – he was so angry he thought he would lose his temper with his fellow peers. The temperature cooled when it was the turn of Lords Wallace and

Thomas to speak. They raised issues about foreign policy and twenty-eight-day detention for terror suspects. McNally later apologised through Archy and said he'd known nothing about the 'ambush'.

The next day in a Commons statement Brown outlined plans to increase the period for detaining terror suspects without charge from twenty-eight to fifty-six days. I attacked him for it (he complimented me on my response as later did Jenny Tonge, who had been in the peers' gallery of the Commons during Brown's statement). Afterwards I went to the weekly meeting of Lib Dem peers. It was another pugnacious encounter but this time I landed the blows. My comments at a meeting with them a few weeks before had been leaked to the media. I told them I expected better behaviour. 'You shouldn't imagine,' I added, 'that journalists are entirely discreet about their sources.'

These brushes with the peers were a bad way to start my summer holidays. We went to the island of Tiree for a week to stay with friends Raymond and Sarah Johnstone. On our last day there *The Times* published one of its Populus polls. The Lib Dems were on 15 per cent, down three points, Labour on 39 per cent, up two, and the Tories on 33 per cent, down one. Would I ever be able to escape the media's negative commentary?

Elspeth and I went away for a last-minute week in the south of France – we had booked nothing in advance because of my expected hip operation – and when we returned the media had moved on.

After the floods of July, there was foot and mouth disease in Surrey in August. The political story of the summer silly season was capability Brown. The leader who was under pressure was David Cameron. Was Cameron's long honeymoon over for good? Would Brown call a general election if Labour's lead in the opinion polls extended into the autumn? The Lib Dems were ready for it. I had appointed Chris Rennard to run our campaign nearly a year before. Our candidates were being chosen, our manifesto was work in progress.

My priority when I returned from France was to prepare for the September conference, to make it as strong an election launch pad as possible. My speech was almost complete: it had been started in July. I lamented to Paddy Ashdown that we were on the seventh or eighth draft. He was dismissive. 'I used to do at least twenty,' he claimed. I added to the speech in August after making a number of private visits around England. I met a twenty-year-old woman called Anne who was in prison for drugs offences and who was studying to take GCSEs and wanted to enrol in the Open University. At a hostel for the homeless I met a former heroin addict called Jane who was hoping to regain custody of her four young children after beating her addiction. I went to Birmingham, to the hospital that treats wounded soldiers from Iraq and Afghanistan. Michael, a twenty-nine-year-old soldier, who had suffered dreadful injuries in a mortar attack, told me he was determined to rejoin his unit when he recovered. He'd been lucky, he said. One of his best friends had been killed by a small piece of shrapnel two days before he was injured. All these encounters made a strong impression on me. They were why I was a liberal, why I was in politics, but it was all so far removed from the media commentary in London. I wrote them into my speech, which I knew would have to be good. I was confident it would be.

At the end of August, I sent a letter to Gordon Brown urging him to announce an exit strategy from Iraq. He used it as an opportunity to set out his thoughts on Iraq and to reassure America that Britain wasn't about to cut and run from its international obligations. The letter had done what I intended: to keep the Liberal Democrat profile on Iraq high as the political tempo changed with the approaching conference season, election speculation turning into election fever, and the long-talked-about credit crunch claiming its first victim, Northern Rock.

We prepared to travel to Brighton to the extraordinary television pictures of the first run on a British bank for more than a century. Would it dent Brown's lead?

In the weeks before the conference there had been endless discussion among my advisers about how I should travel, how I should be dressed when I arrived, even how Elspeth should be dressed. It was a symptom of the pressure on us all. We knew the conference had to be choreographed to perfection. Elspeth resolved the question of my dress. During the Edinburgh Festival in August we had gone to the premiere of the film *Hallam Foe*. I had worn a suit and an open-neck shirt. Elspeth said, 'That's what you should wear at the conference.' Our travel arrangements were more complicated. We went to Brighton by train where we were picked up by a borrowed Saab which ran on bio-ethanol. My press team were determined to prevent any media stories questioning the party's green credentials. I told the *Observer* in a pre-conference interview that I would lead the party into the next election and beyond.

I spoke at the conference rally on the first night about personal freedoms and human rights. The next day Sandi Toksvig interviewed me in an informal question and answer session in the conference hall. It was good-humoured and well received by the delegates. I touched on a number of themes that were to be in my end-of-conference speech. Toksvig asked if I was sick of being asked about my age.

I replied with good humour: 'It's not about age, it's about values. I promise not to take advantage of the youth and inexperience of my opponents.'

My press team calculated that I did about sixty interviews during the Brighton conference, including thirteen with various regional ITV news programmes. Without exception they all contained questions on leadership and age. The next day the leadership issue became headlines again. Nick Clegg, the home affairs spokesman and my favourite to succeed me, made the mistake of admitting to leadership ambitions at a fringe meeting.

He said, 'If you are asking me would I stand against Ming, the answer is no. If you are asking me would I throw my hat in the ring if there was a vacancy in the future, I probably would – but my crystal ball is no clearer than yours.'

Nothing he said was surprising or newsy. What's wrong with a rising star in the party having an ambition to be leader some time in the future? But it became an argument when Chris Huhne said, 'There is no vacancy and it would be premature to even talk about the position of there being a vacancy.'

The media loved it. It was what they were waiting for. I tried to defuse it by saying I was relaxed about the party having ambitious young Turks, and I was. But I was cross with Nick because he should have known the potential of his comment to cause difficulties in the media.

Elspeth reflected my feelings when we bumped into Nick later. 'I don't know if you're being helpful or not,' she said.

'I'm trying to be,' Nick said, looking uncomfortable.

I saw a television camera recording the exchange and quickly said, 'He's being very helpful.'

The camera then caught Elspeth saying, 'It's so tough.'

The clip ran on every news bulletin for twenty-four hours. Elspeth's stock rose.

For once an opinion poll came to my aid at the right time. The day before my big speech the *Guardian* reported ICM's latest findings. Cameron and the Conservatives were in trouble on 32 per cent, an eight-point gap behind resurgent Labour. The Lib Dems, on 20 per cent, were up two points. Cameron's approval ratings had fallen behind mine. I was more popular than he was. Even so I knew my speech would have to be the best of my political career. Charles Kennedy generously sent me a 'good luck' letter.

On the conference's closing morning I had to pack up our hotel suite as well as make final amendments to my speech. After a much rehearsed entrance I walked out on to the stage calm and confident. What I had not prepared for was one of the autocue screens failing. The skill of using autocues is to read your speech across all three screens, moving seamlessly from left, to centre to right and back again. The right-hand screen was blank. Fortunately, I knew the words well enough. I set out my liberal beliefs, the party's radical policy programme, including a Bill of Rights to create a legally enforceable right to clean water, pure air and unpolluted land. I laid into Labour and the Conservatives, attacking their cosy consensus. I'd been told delegates were becoming annoyed at the journalists trying to find negative stories at the conference so I included this line: 'You might have noticed this week that we have one or two critics in the media. Well, I'm happy to say that I answer to you and not to the media. Thank goodness.' It got a roar of approval.

There was also a humorous passage following Margaret Thatcher's visit to Gordon Brown in Downing Street. 'Gordon wants to be like Maggie. But he doesn't want to be like Tony. Tony also wanted to be like Maggie. But Maggie only wanted to be like Ronnie. Now Dave, he wants to be like Tony. But he doesn't want to be like William, or Iain, or Michael. And certainly not like Maggie either. Confused? You must be. But you can be clear on this: I don't want to be like any of them.' The hall burst out in applause. I tackled the age issue again. 'Now when it comes to the next general election, I believe there is some speculation that age will be a factor. You bet it will, because I'll make it one. With age comes experience and with experience comes judgement. When you are deciding whether to send our young men and women to war, it pays to have that experience and it pays to have that judgement.'

The speech was as successful as I hoped it would be. I was interrupted by applause thirty-five times. I was even enjoying it by the end. The headlines were universally favourable: 'Ming rallies the troops with the speech of his life'; 'Defiant Campbell fights on radical agenda'. Paddy complimented me on a classic Liberal speech. The atmosphere at the after-speech champagne party was extraordinary with everyone expressing enthusiasm. I thought, I've cracked it. I've laid the leadership questions to rest. I left Brighton relieved and secure. What I didn't know then was that Paddy had advised Elspeth during a shared cigarette break: 'The only thing I beg of you is to let Ming go when he wants to. Don't let them force him out.'

The momentum towards an October general election seemed unstoppable by the end of the Labour conference a few days after ours. I called a Saturday meeting of the shadow cabinet followed by a meeting of the Federal Policy Committee to finalise our manifesto. I was in the chair for eight hours until we signed it off. I felt fully in command of the party. By the end of the Conservative conference at the beginning of October the polls were beginning to swing away from Labour. Brown's gaffe in going to Iraq to announce (exaggerated) troop withdrawals and the Conservative pledge to raise the inheritance tax threshold to £1 million had turned it round for the Tories. I appeared on BBC *Question Time* the Thursday of the Tory conference. The audience, with a lot of young people, was very receptive to me. Another member of the panel sent a text message to a friend of mine saying I had been brilliant. It was a good period for me. I was doing interview after interview telling Brown to 'put up or shut up' about a general election. Then a slew of post-conference-season polls revealed the Tories closing fast on Labour. Brown's comfort zone had gone. But was the momentum to an election now unstoppable?

I was at a Lib Dem conference in Glasgow on Saturday, 6 October when rumours began to reach me that Brown had given an interview to Andrew Marr for broadcast the following day. Was he calling it off? Our people in London didn't know. I started to drive back to Edinburgh. Elspeth and Euan Roddin, my speech writer, were in the car. The radio news bulletins were full of speculation about Brown abandoning the election. Half-way along the M8 the phone rang. It was Puja Darbari, my press secretary. She said, 'We're hearing Brown's going to call it off.' So were we. It was on the radio news.

17

Can I trade my way out of this?

Elspeth said from the back seat of the car, 'Ming, can you take it for another two years?'

I said, 'Shush,' to stop her saying any more.

I drove straight to the BBC studio beside the Scottish parliament to beat David Cameron to be first to comment on Brown's decision. I was interviewed so much over the next twenty-four hours there was hardly any time to think of anything else. Then I flew to London on the evening of Sunday, 7 October to prepare for my response to Brown's House of Commons statement on Iraq the following day. Had I asked myself the same question as Elspeth? I was beginning to. If the general election was postponed until 2009, perhaps 2010, I would be sixty-eight or sixty-nine. Could I take the constant references to my age for another two years, maybe longer? Could the party? What frustrated me most was how the media's obsession with my age obscured the party's radical policy agenda and the progress it had made under my leadership.

When I arrived in my office on Monday morning I sent e-mails to my front-bench team asking them urgently to make appointments with me. Now that the election was delayed I wanted them to prepare a series of policy initiatives to give us political momentum over the next year or two. I went to the chamber for Brown's statement at 3.30 p.m. feeling more confident about the future. Among a number of announcements, he said of British troops in southern Iraq would be cut to 2,500 by the following spring. I replied: 'The harsh truth is that Britain's involvement in Iraq has been a catastrophe. We have paid dearly in lives, resources and reputation. Is it not time to acknowledge that the presence of British troops in Iraq no longer serves any realistic military or political purpose?' My use of 'catastrophe' was widely picked up in the media.

On Tuesday Alistair Darling presented his first pre-Budget report and caused uproar by mimicking the Tories on inheritance tax – the threshold for couples was raised to £600,000 – and stealing from the Lib Dems by proposing taxes on flights. At PMQs the next day Cameron and Brown locked horns as the Conservative leader attacked Brown's credibility for calling off the election and accused him of stealing Conservative policies in the pre-Budget report. They bellowed at each other like two demented bulls. In contrast I probed Brown on what I thought was the big issue for most voters.

'Was not the most glaring omission in yesterday's pre-Budget report the absence of any proposals for reform of the unfair council tax?' I asked. 'Council tax is set to rise by twice the rate of inflation. How fair is that for low- and middle-income families?' Brown avoided answering by attacking me for what he described as 'an £18 billion black hole' in Lib Dem proposals.

The following evening Archy and I had dinner in the Reform Club with the three people who had helped me most in my leadership campaign in 2006. They were Ian Wright, an expert in corporate communications, Neil Sherlock, public affairs partner at one of the big accountancy firms, and Andrew Gifford, the businessman from whose offices my leadership campaign was run. What should the party do now the election's been postponed? I asked them. Our conversation concluded with Ian Wright agreeing to write a 'Going Forward' plan over the weekend.

But by now I was beginning to wonder whether I could ever stop the media commentary about me. The latest opinion polls were the most damaging yet. One notoriously unreliable poll gave the Lib Dems 11 per cent. Anonymous briefings by MPs, peers and party members helped to fuel the growing speculation about a leadership challenge to me. I left London early on Friday for the dedication service attended by the Queen at the National Memorial at Lichfield, Staffordshire. I was made very welcome by the British Legion, the organisers, since I was the senior opposition MP present. It was the beginning of an extraordinary weekend. Wherever I went my welcome and the reactions of the people I met were so at odds with the media view of me. From Staffordshire I went to a dinner for 150 in Rochdale Town Hall. Early on Saturday morning I travelled to Mildenhall, Suffolk, for the Eastern Counties Lib Dem conference. My speech received a standing ovation inside the conference hall. Outside it, reporters only wanted to ask me questions about my leadership and my age.

Simon Hughes made my growing difficulties suddenly more acute. In an interview for GMTV to be broadcast on Sunday he said I had to do better. The interview had been trailed in the Saturday papers. Simon insisted he was only trying to be supportive but considering the media appetite for knocking stories about me his intervention was bound to be unhelpful – and he should have known it. He said I had 'improved considerably' since taking over as leader eighteen months before but I had further to go. 'We live in a presidential system, and therefore the leader has to continually do well and better.'

He was asked if that meant I had to do better and he replied, 'Well, of course.'

The weekend papers were full of it. I flew back to Edinburgh for a day at home with Elspeth on Sunday. I was furious with Simon. I felt his remarks to the media had undermined me, which was unforgivable. Elspeth told me Archy had rung while I was away. He had told her: 'Something's got to be done. Either Ming should consider whether to carry on or he's got to get tough with the people who are briefing against him. He's got to start sacking people.' Elspeth tried to hide from me how upset she had been at the conversation. She had cancelled lunch with her sister Judy because of it.

Elspeth and I discussed the gathering storm over my leadership. 'Can I trade my way out of this?' I asked her. In the past I used to say confidently to her, 'I can trade my way out of this.' Now it had become a question. Elspeth was supportive and encouraging as always. I was due to attend the federal executive in London the following evening. Would there be more criticism of me there? Simon would be chairing it. What could I possibly say to him?

I caught the 9.05 British Airways flight to Heathrow on Monday, 15 October. It never occurred to me I would fly back later that day having resigned as party leader.

I sat as usual towards the front of the plane in an aisle seat. Sandy Crombie, the group chief executive of Standard Life, was two rows in front of me. We chatted briefly and I read the newspaper stories about me. They were universally and depressingly negative. Again I was struck by the contrast between them and my overwhelmingly positive reception by Lib Dem members at the weekend. What more could I do to change the media view of me? I caught the Heathrow Express to Paddington and queued for a taxi with Crombie who said he was going to have lunch with Willie Walsh, chief executive of British Airways. 'Tell him from me how fed up I am with the quality of BA services,' I said. We parted and I took a cab to the Commons. Archy was sitting at his desk in my outer office. I'd asked him to make representations to Tom McNally about a Lib Dem peer who was constantly briefing against me. I wanted it stopped.

'How did you get on with Tom?' I asked Archy.

Archy looked uncomfortable and said, 'I told Tom he'd better come and tell you face to face what he told me.'

I asked Archy to come into my office. I went to my desk and Archy sat on the sofa. Then he told me about his conversation with McNally. As president of the St Albans Liberal Democrats, McNally had attended their AGM the previous week. He reported to Archy that a thirty-to-forty-minute discussion had turned into a complaint about me. Not a single voice was raised in my support. I asked Archy to see if McNally could meet me that afternoon.

Then Archy said, 'David [Steel] and Paddy want to come and see you this week.'

I said, 'To what purpose?'

He said, 'I think they're going to ask you whether you think you can put up with this for eighteen months or perhaps two years because if the economy goes upside down and Brown's forced to wait until 2010 you'll be sixty-nine.'

Suddenly there was a queue of senior party figures at my door. If they wanted simply to encourage me they could pick up a telephone. What was noticeable was the absence of anyone saying to me, 'Sit it out. This is politics. It'll blow over.'

I said to Archy, 'Let me think about this.'

I closed the door and rang Elspeth. She was in her office at the Scottish Liberal Democrat headquarters in Edinburgh.

'I think I'm going to resign,' I said.

'Are you sure?' she said, sounding very concerned.

'I've had enough of this,' I said.

'Do you mean you'll go at Christmas?' she asked.

'No, I mean today. I'm going to come straight home.'

There was a pause before Elspeth replied. 'There's nothing in the fridge,' she said, practical as ever. 'Please don't go until you've taken someone else's advice,' she pleaded.

I rang off and Elspeth e-mailed Neil Sherlock asking him to contact her urgently. When he did, she gave him my private office number.

Neil rang me and I said, 'Can I trade my way out of this?'

'I don't think you can,' he replied. 'You can try to until Christmas or Easter but I don't think it's going to go away.'

I called Archy in and told him, 'I'm going to write a letter.' I had decided to resign immediately. I drafted my resignation by hand and rang Elspeth to read it to her. She told me she had just heard 'some horrible things' on the lunchtime news. Vince Cable had said on BBC Radio 4's *World at One* that my position was 'under discussion'. Dick Taverne, a Lib Dem peer, had told the programme: 'They want a change in leadership. There's absolutely no doubt the overwhelming number of peers want a change.' After hearing that, Elspeth's mood changed from worry I was acting precipitately to acceptance. She told me later that Paddy's advice to her 'to let Ming go when he wants to' weighed heavily with her.

I knew I had to act quickly. Carrie Henderson, my wonderful PA, returned from her lunch break while Archy was typing up the draft of my resignation letter. I went to the outer office and asked Archy, 'Is it ready yet?'

He said, 'I'm not making much progress because people keep on looking over my shoulder.'

When Archy brought it to me, I made a few minor corrections and asked Carrie to come into my office. She sat on the sofa and I stood. I said in a matter-of-fact tone, 'I've decided to resign.'

Carrie burst into tears and was clearly shocked by my decision. All she could say was, 'Are you sure, are you sure?'

I said, 'Yes,' and gave her a hug. I asked her to book me a flight and to type up my resignation letter on Lib Dem headed paper to Simon Hughes as party president. Then I discussed with Archy, Puja Darbari, my press secretary, and Jonny Oates, the party's head of communications, the arrangements for my departure. I told them I didn't want a humiliating press conference like Charles Kennedy's.

'I want to go home, batten down the hatches and do interviews tomorrow.' Now that I had made the decision I wanted to leave the office as quickly as possible. I was told later that Jonny had gone to the outer office, and slumped in a chair, looking ashen-faced with shock.

Carrie booked me on a late afternoon flight. I rang Elspeth to tell her when I would be arriving. I asked Archy to release my resignation letter only after I'd arrived in Scotland.

He said, 'As soon as you're off the plane ring me. When you're halfway home from the airport we'll release it.' It would give me enough time to close my front door before the media storm erupted.

I put on my coat, picked up my briefcase and walked out of my office and down the stairs as though it was any other day. Archy drove me to Paddington for the return journey on the Heathrow Express. We talked about some of the mundane consequences of my decision like when I would clear my office.

As I reached the airport Carrie rang. 'Please don't do this,' she said. 'Think again. It's all too quick.' Carrie had rung Elspeth to commiserate after I left the office. Elspeth had said to her, 'One of the things Ming said to me was that he had told you, Puja and Jonny about his resignation and not one of you said, "Don't do it." ' Carrie, by now recovered from her shock, was so stricken she rang me immediately to dissuade me.

I told her, 'I've thought about this for some time. It's the right thing to do. I can't go on.' I thanked her for ringing.

Unknown to me, while I was in the air flying to Scotland, Archy had gone to see Chris Rennard, the party's chief executive, to prepare a leadership election timetable for that evening's federal executive. My deal with Archy to keep the news of my resignation private led to a comical scene at the executive. It met at 5.30 with executive members grumbling about the party's opinion poll ratings and my leadership. Just after 6 p.m. Rennard stood up and told them about my resignation. Suddenly their tune changed: apparently they complimented me on my statesmanlike qualities and for being such a good servant of the party. My resignation was followed by canonisation.

I arrived home in time to see Simon Hughes and Vince Cable on television announcing my resignation. They were standing outside party headquarters in Cowley Street. Simon said, 'Every Liberal Democrat owes Ming a huge debt of gratitude.' Vince, now acting leader, said, 'During his time as leader, Ming has earned the respect, affection and gratitude of the party.'

My resignation letter was made public.

> When I was elected leader of the party in March 2006 I had three objectives. First, to restore stability and purpose in the party following my predecessor's resignation and the leadership campaign itself; second to make the internal operations of the party more professional; and third to prepare the party for a general election.
>
> With the help of others, I believe I have fulfilled these objectives, although I am convinced that the internal structures of the party need radical revision if we are to compete effectively against Labour and the Conservatives. But it has become clear that following the prime minister's decision not to hold an election, questions about leadership are getting in the way of further progress by the party.
>
> Accordingly I now submit my resignation as leader with immediate effect. I do not intend to hold a press conference or to make any further comment.

I had no sense of regret as Elspeth and I talked over the events of a momentous day for us, nor did I feel relief. My principal emotions were frustration and irritation. The three tasks I had set myself when I became leader had all been achieved but the postponement of the election had robbed me of the chance to show just how far I had taken the party. I also felt a sense of perspective: I had run in an Olympic final, pleaded a case as a QC in the House of Lords, become an MP after an eleven-year campaign, overcome cancer, been knighted for services to parliament, and led the party of Asquith and Lloyd George. It was indeed a long way from 19 Park Road, Glasgow.

Our conversation was constantly interrupted by phone calls from well-wishers and by journalists ringing the doorbell. Jonny Oates rang. 'There needs to be a media plan,' he said.

I said facetiously, 'Well, tell Nick Robinson [BBC political editor] to come to Edinburgh.' We went to bed with a media encampment outside.

Puja Darbari texted me the following morning at 7.10 to say she was on her way north to manage the media. Nick Robinson, Adam Boulton, Sky News political editor, Tom Bradby, ITV's political editor, and Gary Gibbon, Channel 4's political editor, were all travelling north too. Mary Jewell, our daily help, came to the back door to avoid the cameras outside. Throughout the day cards and flowers arrived. There were so many flowers I protested, 'This is like a Chapel of Rest.' One friend sent a case of Bollinger. A former governor of the Bank of Scotland brought round a bottle of Krug.

I spoke to the TV political editors – Robinson, Boulton, Bradby and Gibbon – one after the other in the dining room. I told them I was irritated by the media's concentration on trivia and frustrated that I would not be leading the party in a general election. Such was the fixation on age, I said, the party was unable to communicate its policies and values. Gordon Brown rang to commiserate while I was doing the interviews. So did Alistair Darling. John Major rang: 'When things settle what about dinner at Mosimann's with Norma and Elspeth?' Iain Duncan Smith wrote saying: 'That some should have briefed against you on the basis of age is appalling and should sadden us all.' Charles Kennedy wrote a kind and sympathetic letter. So did Neil Sherlock, whose advice I valued so highly. In his card, he said: 'You were badly let down by a weak party structure, an ageist media and a small number of the most disloyal "colleagues".' Helena Kennedy's letter said: 'No-one held the Executive to account over the Iraq war more effectively than you. Your moral voice was inspirational and remains so.'

The headlines in the morning newspapers had never been more favourable or more complimentary to me. I went shopping with Elspeth in Waitrose two days after my resignation. Strangers kept on coming up to me, shaking my hand and saying, 'We're really sorry you felt you had to resign.'

So was I.

Postscript

The contest to succeed me as leader of the Liberal Democrats was fought out between two MPs who had only been in the House of Commons for two and a half years, Nick Clegg and Chris Huhne. Both were experienced politicians, former members of the European parliament, and talented. The similarities did not end there: both had been to Westminster School and to Oxford; both had been journalists and had equally talented wives.

There was one material difference between them. Chris Huhne had stood against me for the leadership after Charles Kennedy stood down. His decision to do so still rankled with some of his parliamentary colleagues who believed he had broken an agreement with them not to do so.

The contest seemed interminable just as it did to me in January and February 2006. The candidates had to criss-cross the country to speak at specially arranged hustings. Between them they probably spent about £100,000. Lib Dem MPs were visibly distracted. The profile of the party was not assisted by this elongated process. Vince Cable, the party's deputy leader who became acting leader, conducted himself with distinction, wit and sure-footedness.

The contest itself was tetchy and made the news only when the candidates were engaged in a clash of personalities rather than an exchange of ideas. Paddy Ashdown and David Steel declared for Clegg and Huhne respectively. Charles Kennedy and I stayed silent. Clegg had a clear majority of the parliamentary party behind him. Huhne attracted the support of a number of prominent former Kennedy supporters.

On 18 December, in a crowded, sweaty room in the St Martin's Hotel, London, Vince Cable announced the result – Clegg won by a few hundred votes. It was much closer than anyone had anticipated.

Throughout the contest I had maintained a Trappist silence. I had also made sure that Elspeth did not accept any of the many requests for interviews. She and Cherie Blair have a similar capacity for directness.

The declaration was less of an ordeal than I had expected. I did a series of radio and TV interviews in which I repeated the well-worn clichés of the torch passing to a new generation and it being a day to look forward not back (Donald Dewar would have felt vindicated). I made my escape as soon as decently I could. Later I put in an appearance at the party headquarters celebration in the City Inn and went back to Scotland the next day for Christmas and the New Year. I did at last begin to feel a sense of relief. I could now get on with the rest of my life.

I knew from the Clegg camp that he would not ask me to join the shadow cabinet. This chimed with my own view. The last thing he needed was his predecessor getting in his way. Oblique references by me and others to William Hague's return to the Tory front bench left open the possibility that I might be asked to rejoin the shadow cabinet on some future occasion. I was asked if I was prepared to be nominated to the Commons select committee on foreign affairs. I said yes.

Christmas and New Year were remarkably relaxed. I did not listen to the *Today* programme once. There was time for friends, family and sleep.

I accepted an invitation to join the board of an Edinburgh investment trust, drew up a programme of intense constituency activity, and continued in my efforts to persuade an American university to make me a visiting professor. There was plenty to do.

My resignation featured in many of the end-of-year newspaper reviews, but already they seemed to be referring to another person and another time.

A friend who had been close to me during my leadership wrote to say that this was no time for modesty. I had, he said, rescued the party from a potentially fatal position of self-destruction and made it ready to fight an election. I alone had the capacity to do that. If the Prime Minister's nerve had held and there had been an election my judgement and stewardship would have been vindicated. The party might even by now have achieved its long-term goal of proportional representation. It was a generous analysis.

Picture Acknowledgements

Plate section pages 1–8:

Beaverbrook Newspapers, Glasgow: 3 above. Getty Images: 5 above. Glasgow University Union: 6 above. Stan Hunter: 4. PA Photos: 8. Scotsman Publications Ltd: 7. Solo Syndication: 3 below, 5 below.

Plate section pages 8–16:

Camera Press: 8 above. Alex Folkes: 7. PA Photos: 4 below, 8 below. Reuters: 4 above Rex Features: 1 below. Scotsman Publications Ltd: 3 below.

The rest of the photographs come from the author's own collection.

Every reasonable effort has been made to contact the copyright holders, but if there are any errors or omissions, Hodder & Stoughton will be pleased to insert the appropriate acknowledgement in any subsequent printing of this publication.

Index